IMAGES
of America

NUNLEY'S AMUSEMENT PARK

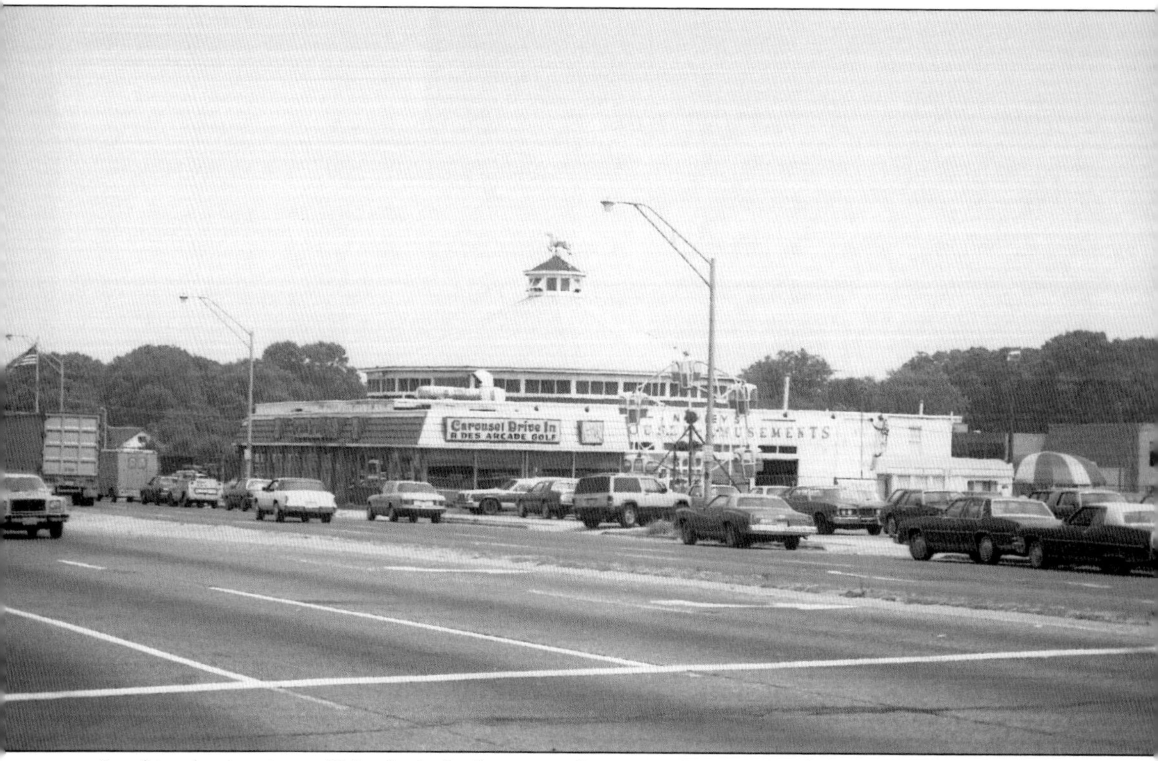

In this classic view of Nunley's, looking southeast on Sunrise Highway in Baldwin, the most prominent aspects of the park from the street are seen: the carousel building, restaurant, and Ferris wheel. This is the view visitors saw from their cars as they excitedly approached the park. (Courtesy of Gary Monti.)

On the Cover: Taken in April 1963, this photograph provides a glimpse of a vibrant family amusement park back when women wore skirts and men always wore hats whenever they went about town. Two of the park's most recognized rides are visible: the Ferris wheel and the boat ride. (Courtesy of Larry Estrin.)

IMAGES
of America

NUNLEY'S AMUSEMENT PARK

Marisa L. Berman

ARCADIA
PUBLISHING

ISBN 978-0-7385-9822-2

Published by Arcadia Publishing
Charleston, South Carolina

Printed in the United States of America

Library of Congress Control Number: 2012945564

For all general information, please contact Arcadia Publishing:
Telephone 843-853-2070
Fax 843-853-0044
E-mail sales@arcadiapublishing.com
For customer service and orders:
Toll-Free 1-888-313-2665

Visit us on the Internet at www.arcadiapublishing.com

To friends and family who we have lost—you keep us young in our memories and remind us of the magic of childhood.

Contents

Acknowledgments

This publication came to be because of the interest and involvement of the public who experienced and loved Nunley's. A special thank-you goes out to each and every person who submitted a photograph, story, memory, or piece of memorabilia towards this project.

I would also like to thank Gary Monti, director of museum and theater operations at Cradle of Aviation Museum/Nunley's Carousel, for his wisdom and insight into the history of Nunley's. All images of the carousel from pages 64 to 85 were provided by Monti in collaboration with the museum. Thanks also go to Dennis Ciccone Jr. for his insane amount of well organized data on Nunley's, and to Steven Lercari, descendant of the Nunley family, for use of his vast collection of photographs documenting the family business.

Thank you Judith Todman, John Hyslop, and all the staff at the Archives at Queens Library and George Fischer and Iris Levin at the Long Island Photo Archive. Amazing additional historical resources included the Queens Historical Society, Long Island Studies Institute, the Baldwin Public Library, the Long Island Memories Project, the Freeport Memorial Library, the Freeport Historical Society (especially Cynthia Krieg and Regina Feeney), the Roller Coaster Database, and the National Carousel Association.

A special thank-you goes to my editors at Arcadia Publishing—Rebekah Collinsworth and Erin Rocha—for all of their expert guidance and support. Also thank you to Jim Kempert and everyone else at Arcadia who played a role in bringing this story to life.

And, of course, thank you to all my family and friends who supported and helped me promote this project. I am especially thankful to the Berman family—my parents, Ed and Carrie, and my brother Steven—as well as the Price family, the Williams family, and the Hollywood family, and especially, my great love, Matt.

INTRODUCTION

Nunley's Amusement Park was not just a small family amusement park on Sunrise Highway in Baldwin, New York; it was a magical place full of wonder. However, one can only understand this seemingly simple description if they have actually experienced the park as a child. If by some miracle Nunley's was still open today, and an adult wandered in to check it out, they would merely find a few rides like the teacups, a tiny Ferris wheel, a small roller coaster, and a beautiful, traditional carousel. It might be difficult to imagine how this small park could have given priceless memories to families throughout Long Island for over five decades. Ask anyone who grew up in the surrounding area between 1939 and 1995 if they had ever been to Nunley's, and they will answer with a bright-eyed smile. Visions of childhood joy will dance through their minds as they recount memories like the first time they were finally tall enough to reach for the brass ring or when they were brave enough to ride the roller coaster. They will recall how the park seemed to grow with them as they matured and soon was the place where they developed what would become life-long friendships and stole their first kisses. A tear may fall as they remember beloved grandparents, aunts and uncles, or maybe even parents and siblings who are now gone. These Long Islanders might pull out dusty scrapbooks and photo albums to share creased photographs of smiling mini-versions of themselves posing proudly on various rides, eating pizza with a party hat on, or making silly faces in a photo-booth printout. One thing will be certain—no matter what they share, their memories will be happy.

When William Nunley established the park in 1939, he understood the power of the amusement park for the American family. A third-generation amusement park entrepreneur, he had already operated parks in two areas of Queens before moving further into Long Island. He clearly understood the potential for success that came from this blossoming market of amusements. New York had long been a hub for the amusement park, and many believe that the American amusement park industry first developed in Coney Island. Operations at Coney Island date back to the early 1800s, where it first began inspiring entrepreneurs across the world. As immigrants were quickly congregating in large cities like New York, the demand for inexpensive open-air amusements soon fell to the seaside areas of the outer boroughs. Open spaces provided a reprieve from the heat and congestion of the crowded city and boasted swimming, restaurants, hotels, and many exciting activities for the crowds. When a railroad line to Coney Island was completed in 1875, visitation numbers swelled, and there was an influx of new booths, games, and rides that were developed by entrepreneurs looking to cash in.

The Chicago World's Fair of 1893 had a profound impact on the development of the amusement park in America. It was where the Ferris wheel, built by George Ferris, was introduced to the public. This original model was 264 feet tall, and each of the 36 cars could hold up to 60 people. The tallest attraction at the fair, it was built to rival the highlight of the 1889 Paris Exposition, the Eiffel Tower. The fair was also where the term *midway* was first used, indicating the area of a fair where the sideshows were located. This came from the Midway Plaisance, which was the center of the amusements at the 1893 fair. When Luna Park opened in Coney Island in 1903, it took a great deal of inspiration from the Chicago World's Fair and strove to lure crowds with its flashy displays and elaborate buildings. It was a new short-lived category of parks called "exposition parks," which were expensive to run with their constant demand for new and lavish displays. By 1904, Coney Island boasted three huge parks: Steeplechase (1897), Luna Park (1903), and Dreamland (1904), all working to create what would be an amusement park boom in America. Unfortunately, these parks were not destined to last. Dreamland burned down in 1911. Luna Park also succumbed to fire in 1944 (after going bankrupt), and Steeplechase closed in 1964. However, the impact the parks made on the rest of country was already established.

The Stock Market crash of 1929, followed by the Great Depression, caused hundreds of amusement parks to close. By the late 1930s the industry was beginning to thrive again, old parks were being updated, and new parks were opening, including Nunley's Amusement Park, which opened in 1939. After World War II ended, the amusement park industry finally seemed secure again. Veterans moved to the suburbs and started families, and a new type of park began to develop to capitalize on this change: the "kiddieland." First developed by C.C. Macdonald when he opened Kiddie Park in San Antonio, Texas, in 1925, these parks were built specifically for children and flourished until the 1960s. When the baby boom came to an end in the mid-1960s, the kiddieland trend began to die out as well. Many of these parks either closed or were modified to attract an aging clientele.

Looking back on the development of amusement parks in America, it is clear how William Nunley was able to create a successful children's park in the suburbs of New York. The thing that is truly amazing is how long Nunley's lasted beyond the demise of other similar parks. This endurance is a testament to the passion of the family that ran Nunley's long past its profitability. Their devotion to their community and desire to keep their cherished family business alive was the visitors' good fortune.

This book illustrates the history of this beloved family-run amusement park. It moves from the story of William Nunley and the amusement parks he developed to a glimpse into childhood memories of Long Islanders through a collection of photographs, stories, memorabilia, and other materials contributed by the public towards this project. Unfortunately, Nunley's Amusement Park now joins the list of lost parks throughout the country. But one way New York has remained unique compared to other areas is the number of family-run parks. These parks not only served to delight the public, but they also tell the story of New York families and unique childhoods.

One

William Nunley and the Family Amusement Park

The American amusement park had its heyday from the late 1800s until the end of World War I, when over 1,500 parks were built. While not every carousel was a part of an amusement park, as some sat in public parks or near beachfronts, it would be rare to find a park that did not boast a carousel as one of its main attractions. William Nunley was born in September 1888 to Thomas and Annie Nunley. The family lived in the South Beach area of Staten Island, a popular resort area at the time. It was also the last stop on the Staten Island Railroad, which brought swarms of regular visitors to the area. It was here that Nunley began a partnership with Timothy Murphy operating carousels. It was this partnership that ultimately led to the future creation of multiple small family parks. Nunley dedicated his life to the entertainment of New Yorkers; it is even believed that he met his wife, Miriam, on the Big Wheel in Seaside. From Staten Island to Queens, to Nassau, Nunley journeyed east across Long Island, establishing amusement parks and entertaining the masses.

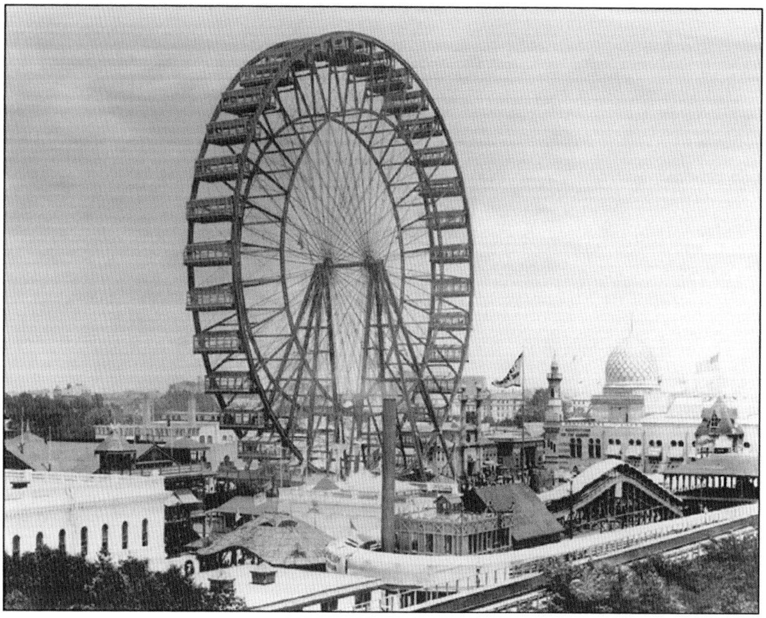

The Chicago World's Fair of 1893 had a significant impact on the development of amusement parks in America. In this photograph from the fair, George Ferris's new ride, on display for the first time, was the tallest attraction. This ride, known as the Ferris wheel, eventually became an amusement park staple. (Public domain.)

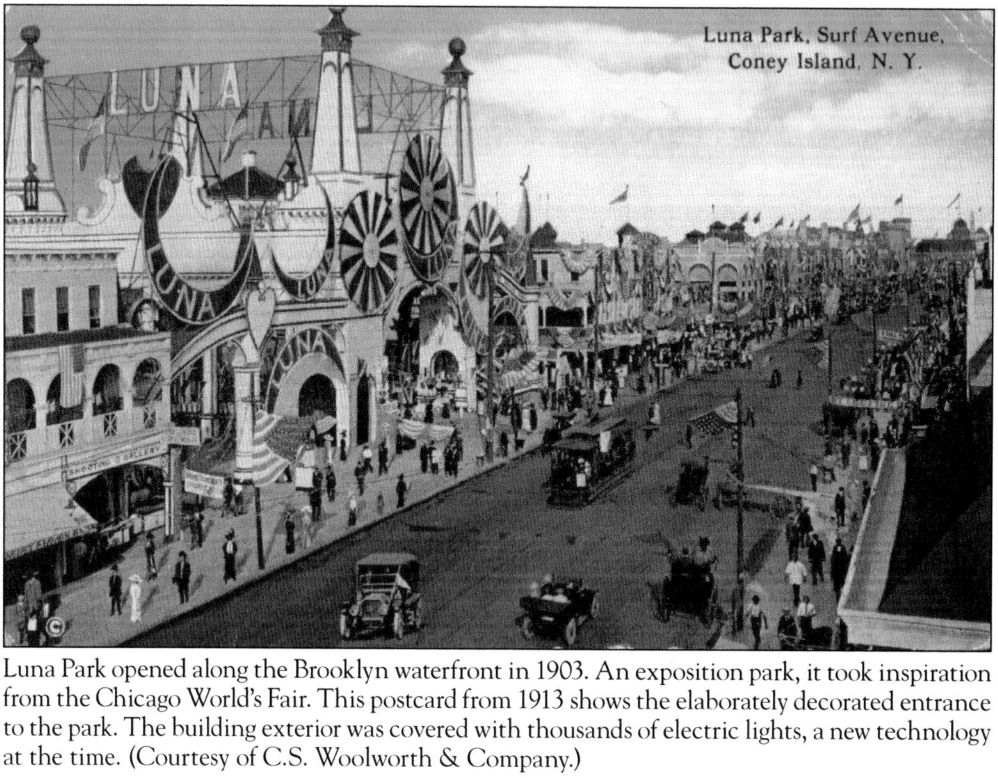

Luna Park opened along the Brooklyn waterfront in 1903. An exposition park, it took inspiration from the Chicago World's Fair. This postcard from 1913 shows the elaborately decorated entrance to the park. The building exterior was covered with thousands of electric lights, a new technology at the time. (Courtesy of C.S. Woolworth & Company.)

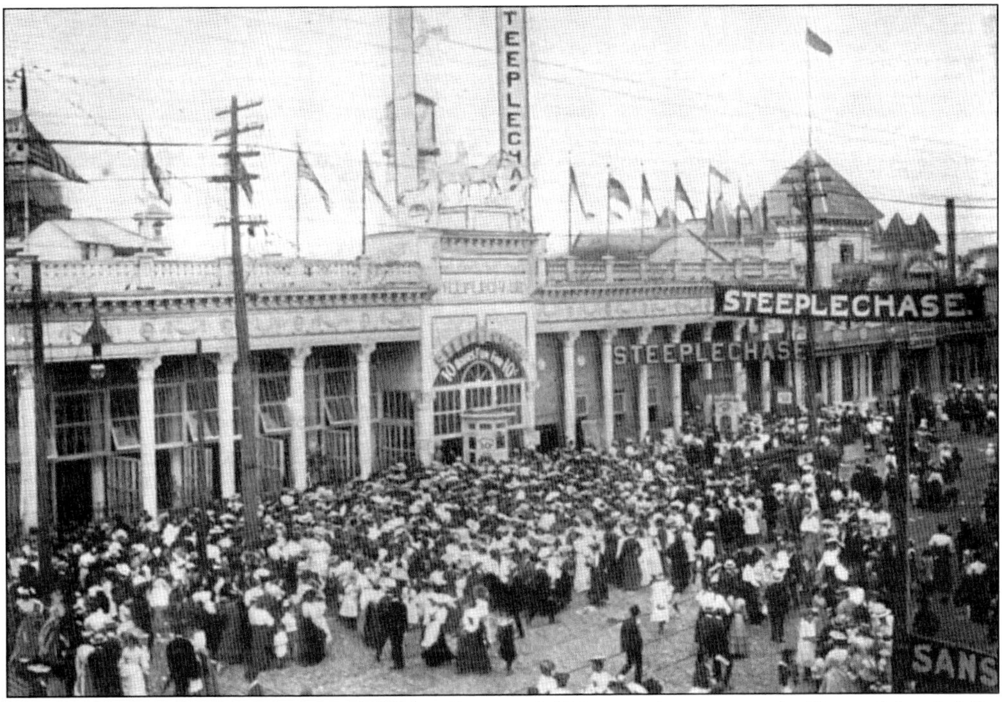

Steeplechase Park was opened in 1897 by George C. Tilyou, who grew up in Coney Island. Like so many amusements parks of the time, it closed in 1964 due to fire. The only piece of the park that still remains is the Parachute Drop ride, which was built for the 1939 New York World's Fair at Flushing Meadows Corona Park. Too expensive to break down, it was eventually declared a New York City Landmark in 1989. (Courtesy of Historic American Buildings Survey.)

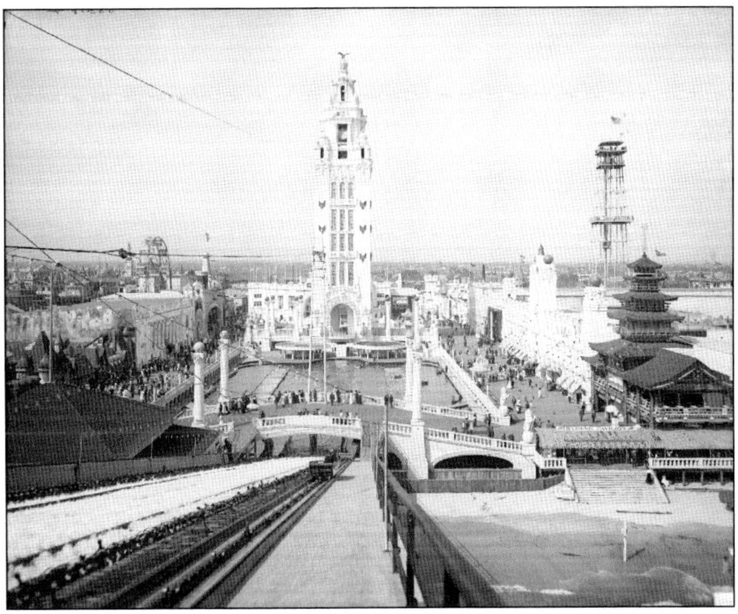

While Luna Park was dazzling, Dreamland Amusement Park and its refined architecture was opulent. Here is Dreamland's Beacon Tower in 1905. It was 370 feet tall and outshone Luna Park's Kaleidoscope Tower. Dreamland was designed to rival any and all existing parks. (Courtesy of Library of Congress, Prints & Photographs Division, Detroit Publishing Company Collection.)

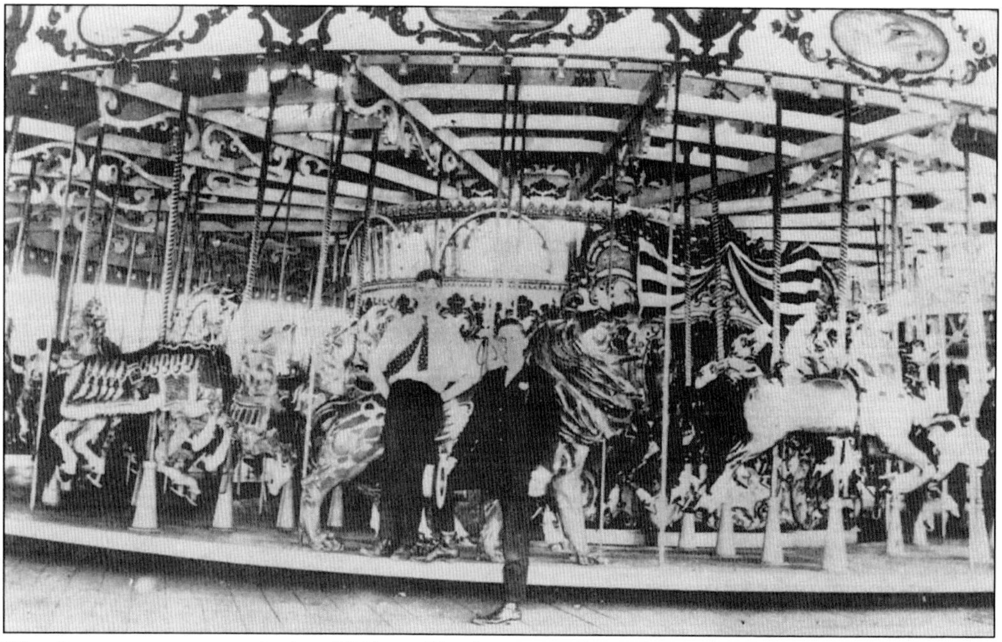

The first amusement park that William Nunley opened was Happyland in Staten Island. This image shows Ed Farrell and William Nunley in front of the carousel in the South Beach area. Nunley worked with Timothy Murphy operating the ride beginning in the 1910s. Their carousel was referred to at the time as "Murphy's Carousel." (Courtesy of Old Staten Island.)

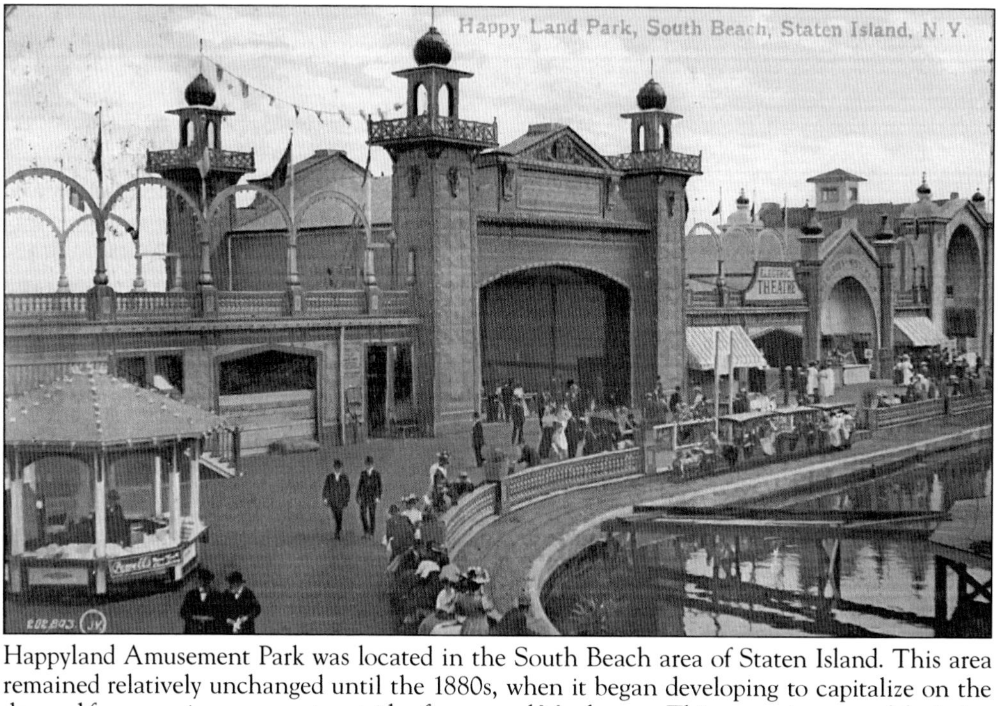

Happyland Amusement Park was located in the South Beach area of Staten Island. This area remained relatively unchanged until the 1880s, when it began developing to capitalize on the demand for open-air amusements outside of congested Manhattan. This souvenir postcard depicting the park, postmarked in 1908, shows the various amusements along the waterfront. (Courtesy of Valentine & Sons Publishing Co.)

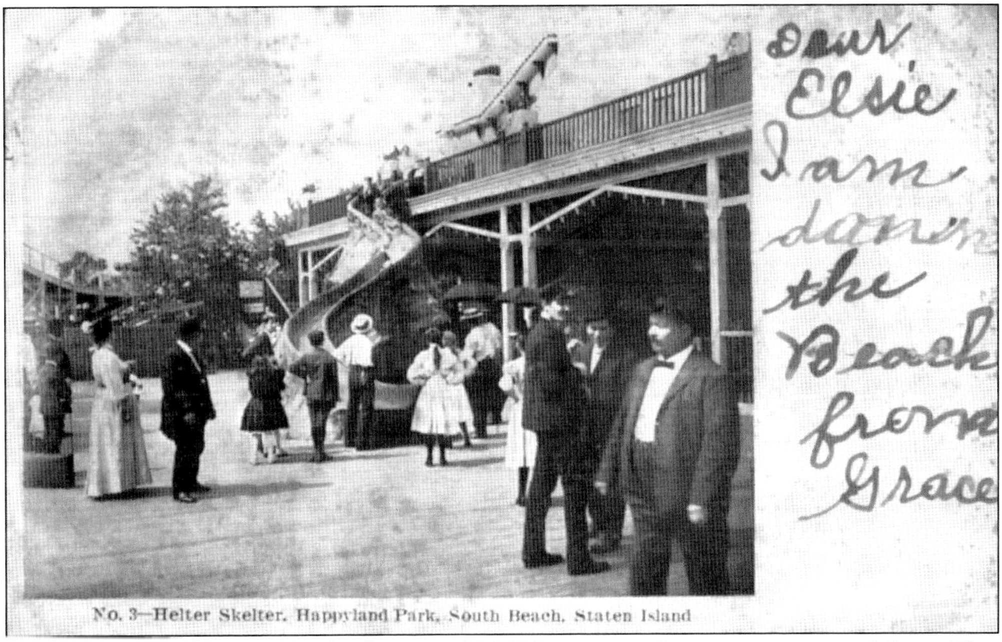

On opening day in 1906, Happyland attracted 30,000 visitors with its amusements and shows. This beachfront resort area thrived until the Great Depression, when it suffered from fire, pollution, and a lack of visitors. The park operated until 1935, when the city took over the land and it became a Works Progress Administration project. All amusements were cleared out for a two-and-a-half-mile boardwalk. The current site is now occupied by South Beach–Franklin Delano Roosevelt Boardwalk, a New York City park. (Public domain.)

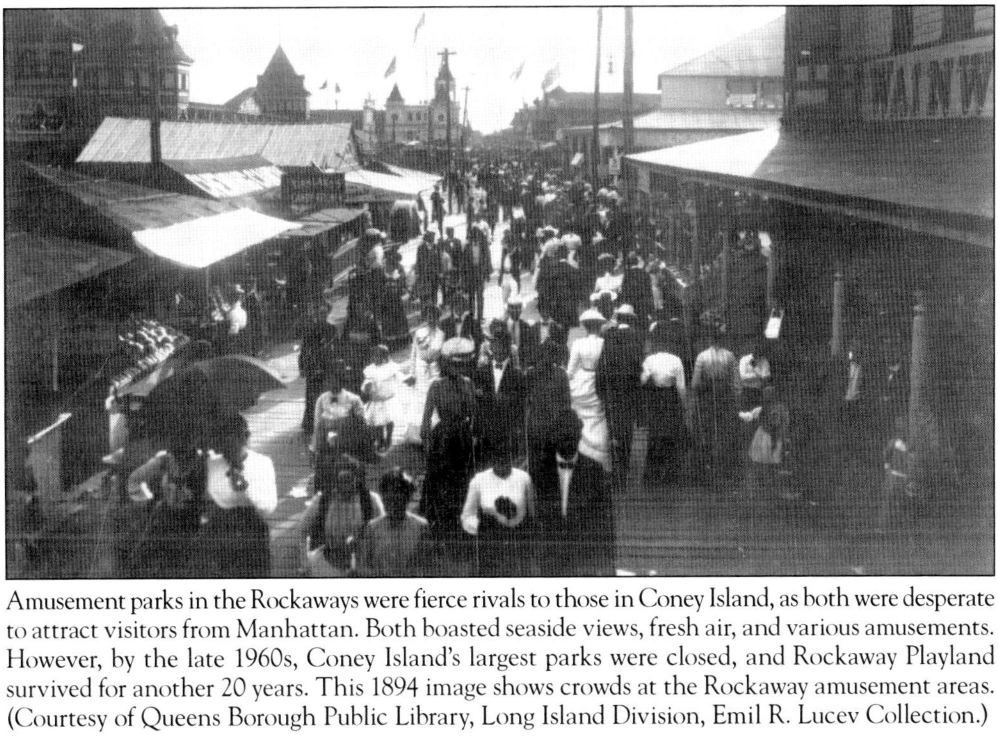

Amusement parks in the Rockaways were fierce rivals to those in Coney Island, as both were desperate to attract visitors from Manhattan. Both boasted seaside views, fresh air, and various amusements. However, by the late 1960s, Coney Island's largest parks were closed, and Rockaway Playland survived for another 20 years. This 1894 image shows crowds at the Rockaway amusement areas. (Courtesy of Queens Borough Public Library, Long Island Division, Emil R. Lucev Collection.)

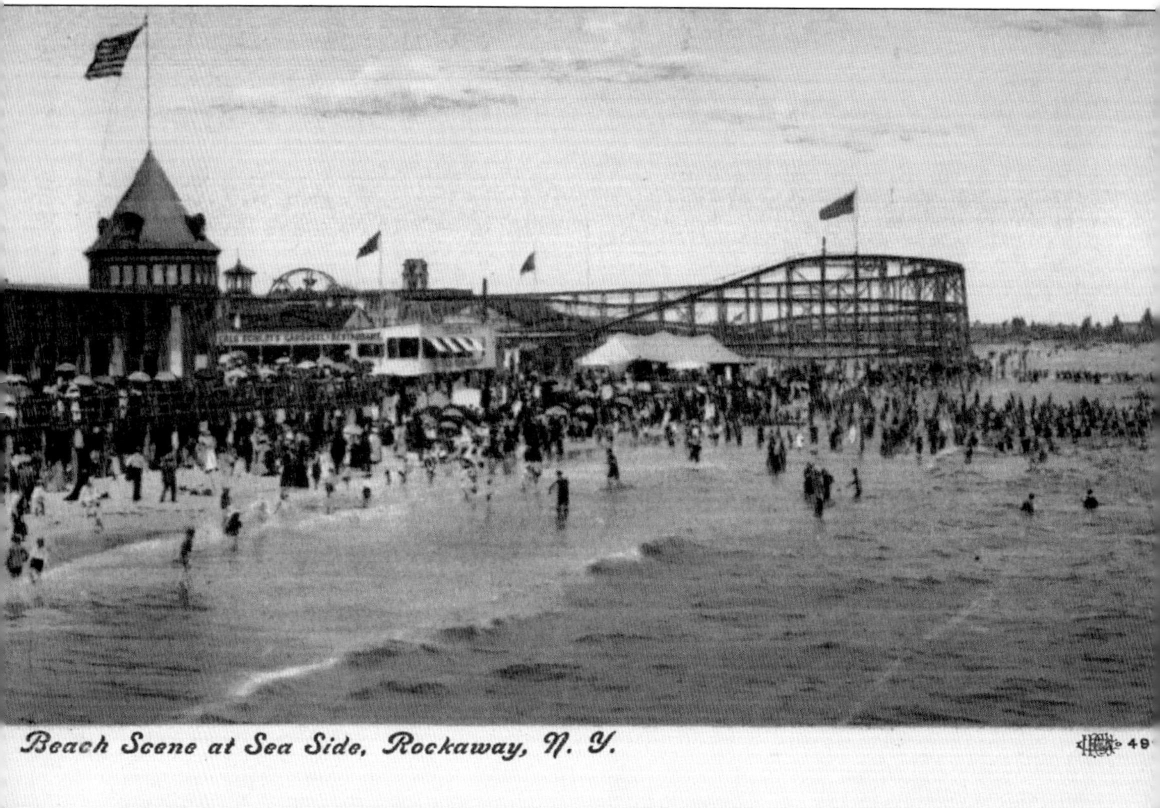

William Nunley operated numerous carousels other than the one in Nunley's Baldwin Park. He ran a carousel in the Seaside area of the Rockaways in 1914 that was near the Rockaway Playland. At the northwest corner of Seaside Avenue and Ocean Avenue, it was previously the site of Hurdlers Pavilion, which housed its own carousel and served various nonalcoholic beverages. It was destroyed by fire in 1911. (Courtesy of HCN Publishing.)

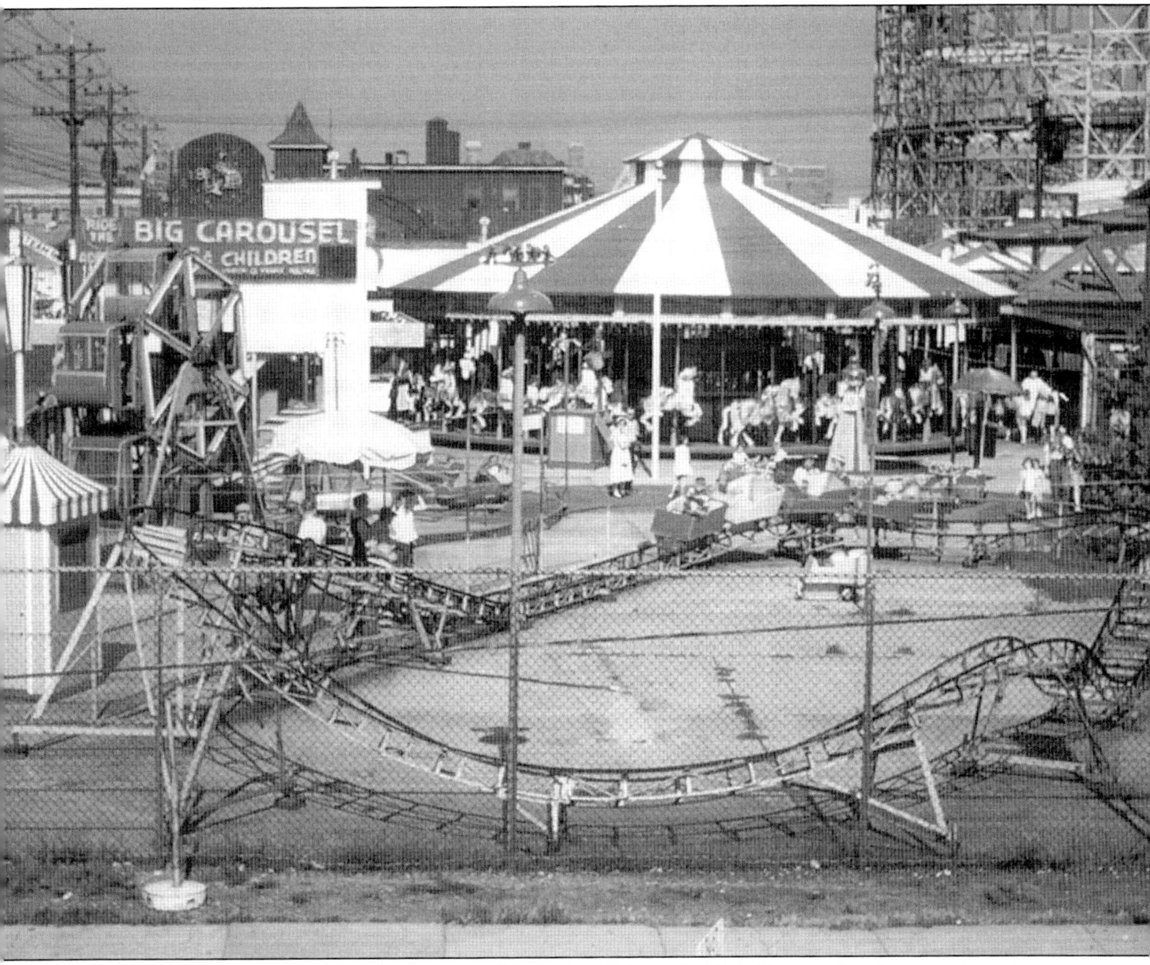

The carousel eventually moved to its new home at 171 Beach 98th Street. At this new location, a kiddie park was added with additional rides and amusements geared for children. This park was known as Nunley's Rockaway Beach. This new park was in close proximity to Rockaway Playland. Since Nunley's Park was geared more towards young children, they were not competitors. Here, the roller coaster at Playland is visible to the right of the carousel. Nunley's Rockaway Beach had a similar fighter plane, Ferris wheel, and roller coaster to those found at Nunley's in Baldwin. The park remained open until William's death in 1950, and the rides and carousel were later auctioned off. The park had a one-of-a-kind A. Ruth & Sohn organ from Germany that dated to 1910. The organ was eventually moved to Nunley's Happyland in Bethpage. (Courtesy of Dennis Ciccone Jr.)

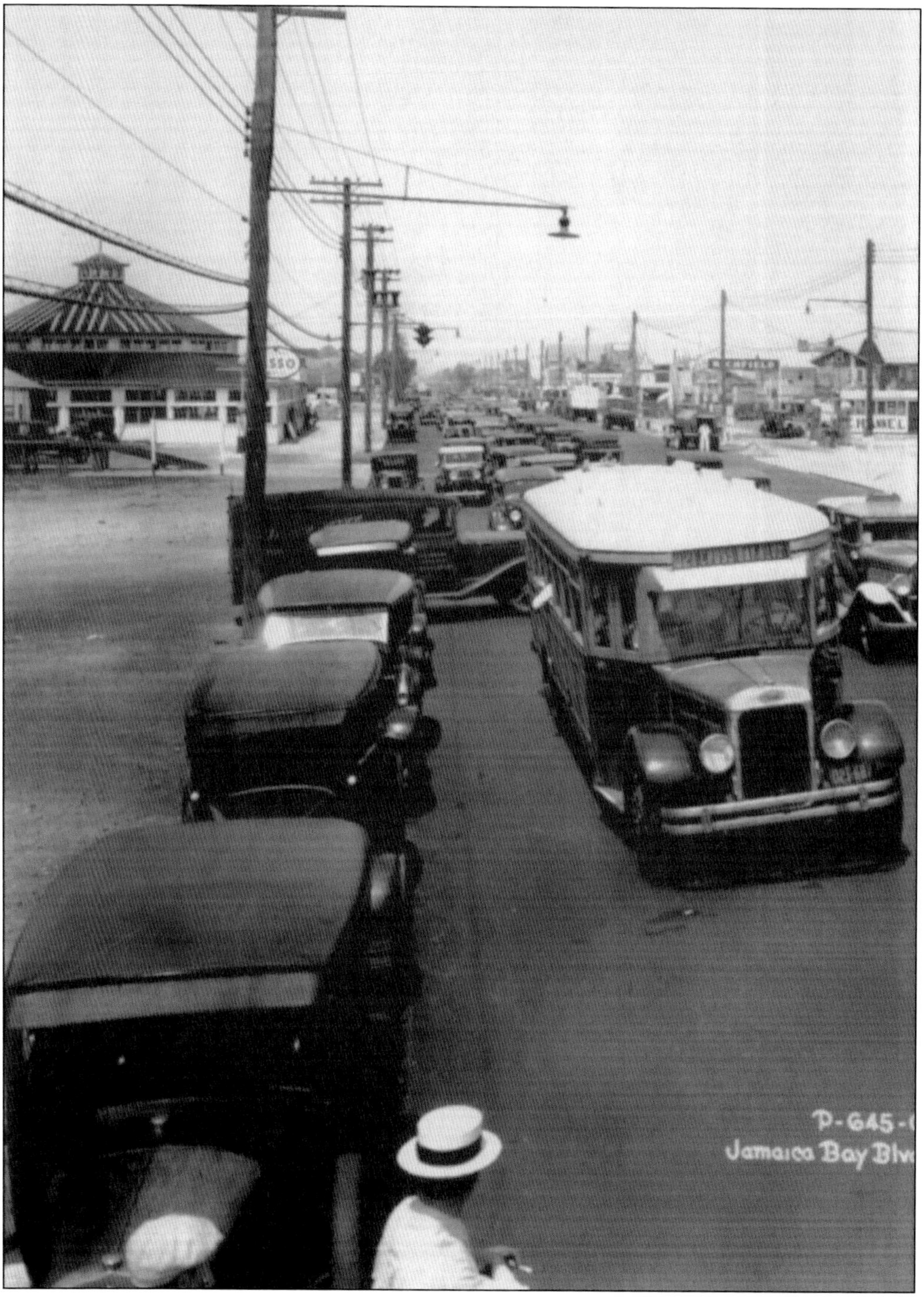

Nunley operated a carousel in Broad Channel, a neighborhood in the borough of Queens, on Cross Bay Boulevard. It is believed that it was located within a park called Broad Channel Amusements. It operated from the 1930s through the 1950s. The carousel was situated on a heavily traveled road that was, at the time, called Jamaica Bay Boulevard. Drivers used this route to get to Rockaway Beach. (Courtesy of MTA Bridges and Tunnels Special Archives.)

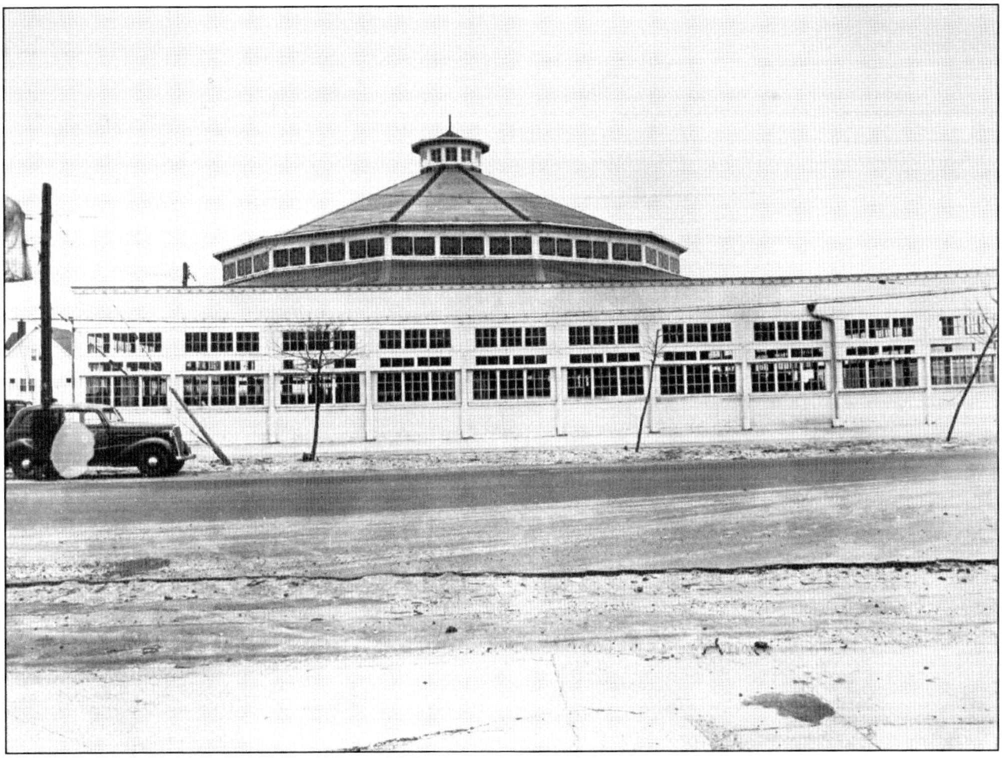

Broad Channel Amusement Park and the Rockaway Park were only a few blocks away from each other. This park may look familiar because the carousel building at Broad Channel was reminiscent of carousel pavilions at Coney Island. (Courtesy of Nassau County Department of Parks, Recreation & Museums, Photo Archives Center.)

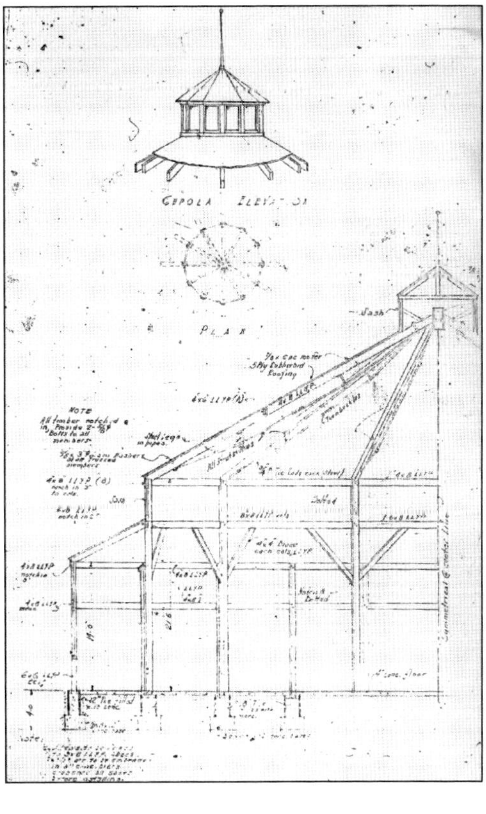

Pictured here are the design plans for the Broad Channel carousel pavilion. When the Broad Channel Park closed, the carousel was moved to Willowbrook Developmental Center, a facility for mentally disabled children located in the Willowbrook area of Staten Island. The carousel was eventually shut down, and there is no record of what became of it. (Courtesy of Dennis Ciccone Jr.)

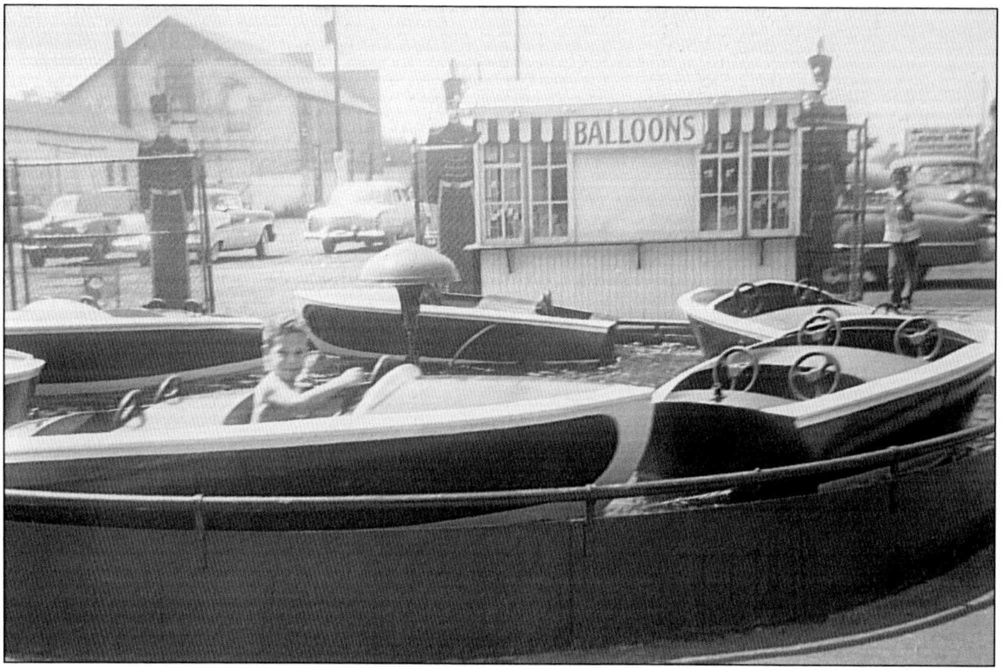

The next amusement park to open, Nunley's Happyland—also known as Smiley's Happyland and sometimes as Jolly Roger's, due to the restaurant on the property with that name—opened in 1951. It was located in Bethpage in Long Island at the intersection of Hempstead Turnpike and Hicksville Road. (Courtesy of Jay Golden.)

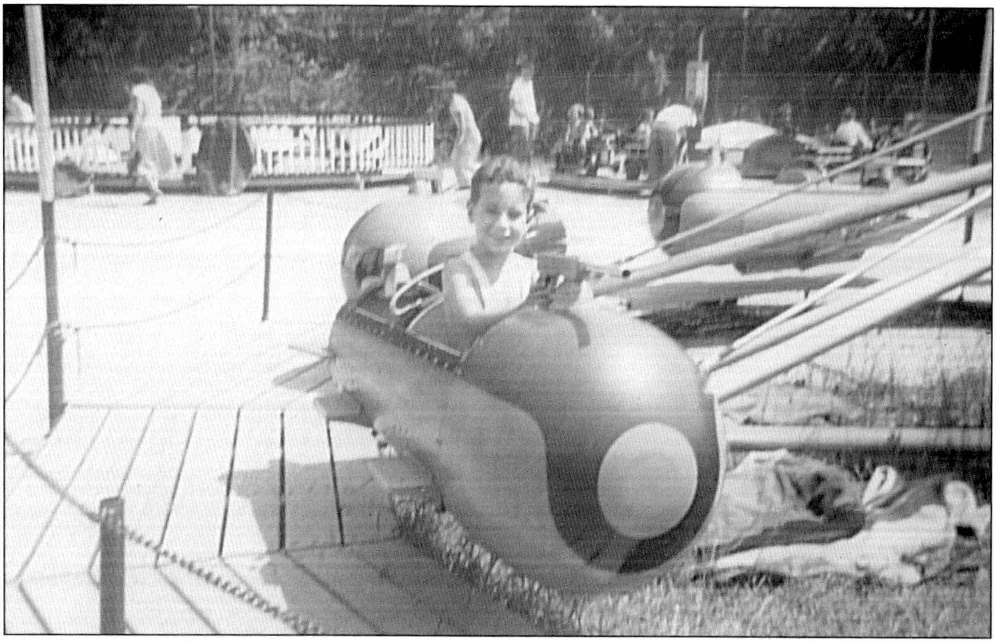

Nunley designed this site to be larger than his previous parks; it was more than six-and-a-half acres and intended for year-round operation. The glass doors of the carousel building were from the 1939 New York World's Fair French Pavilion. These panels could be removed in warm weather. (Courtesy of Jay Golden.)

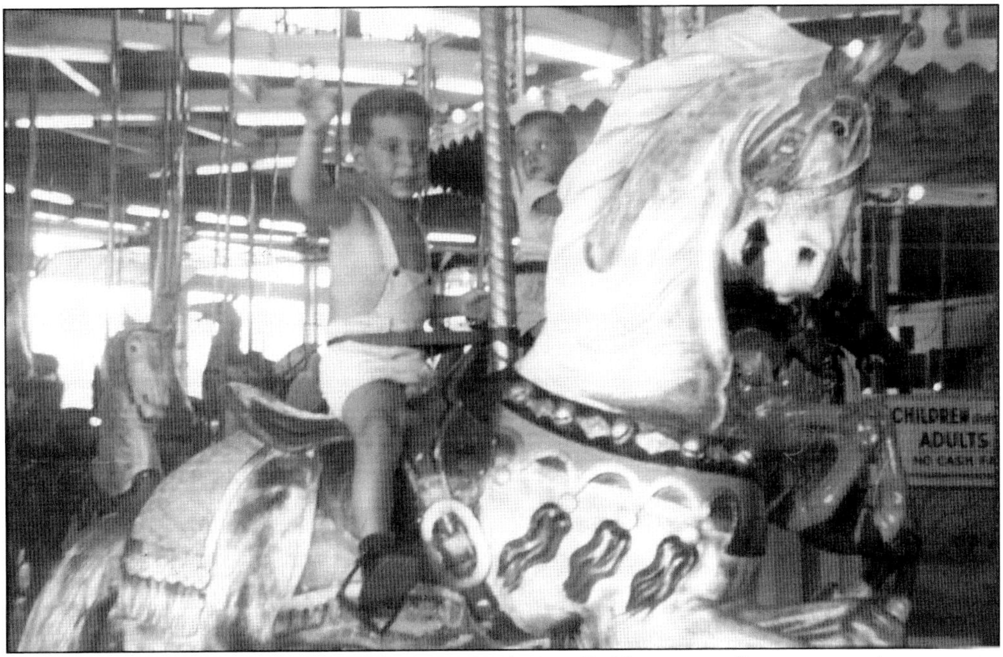

The park had many similar rides to those at Nunley's in Baldwin, as well as a carousel as its main attraction. This carousel, a three-row Dentzel, was made up of various brightly-painted animals. At one point, it was previously located at Rockaway Playland in Rockaway Beach. (Courtesy of Jay Golden.)

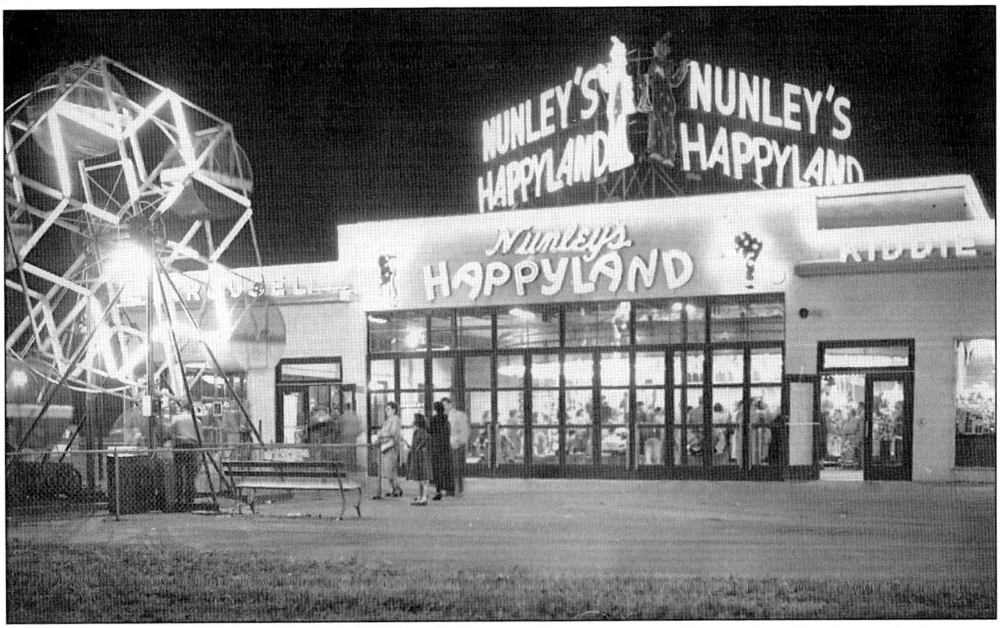

William Nunley received negative feedback from colleagues about Happyland's relatively desolate location and its distance from a railroad line. Nunley, however, was expecting that his park would attract more suburban visitors who owned automobiles. Unfortunately, Nunley passed away six months before Happyland opened, so he was unable to enjoy the great success that the park experienced in its early years. (Courtesy of Dennis Ciccone Jr.)

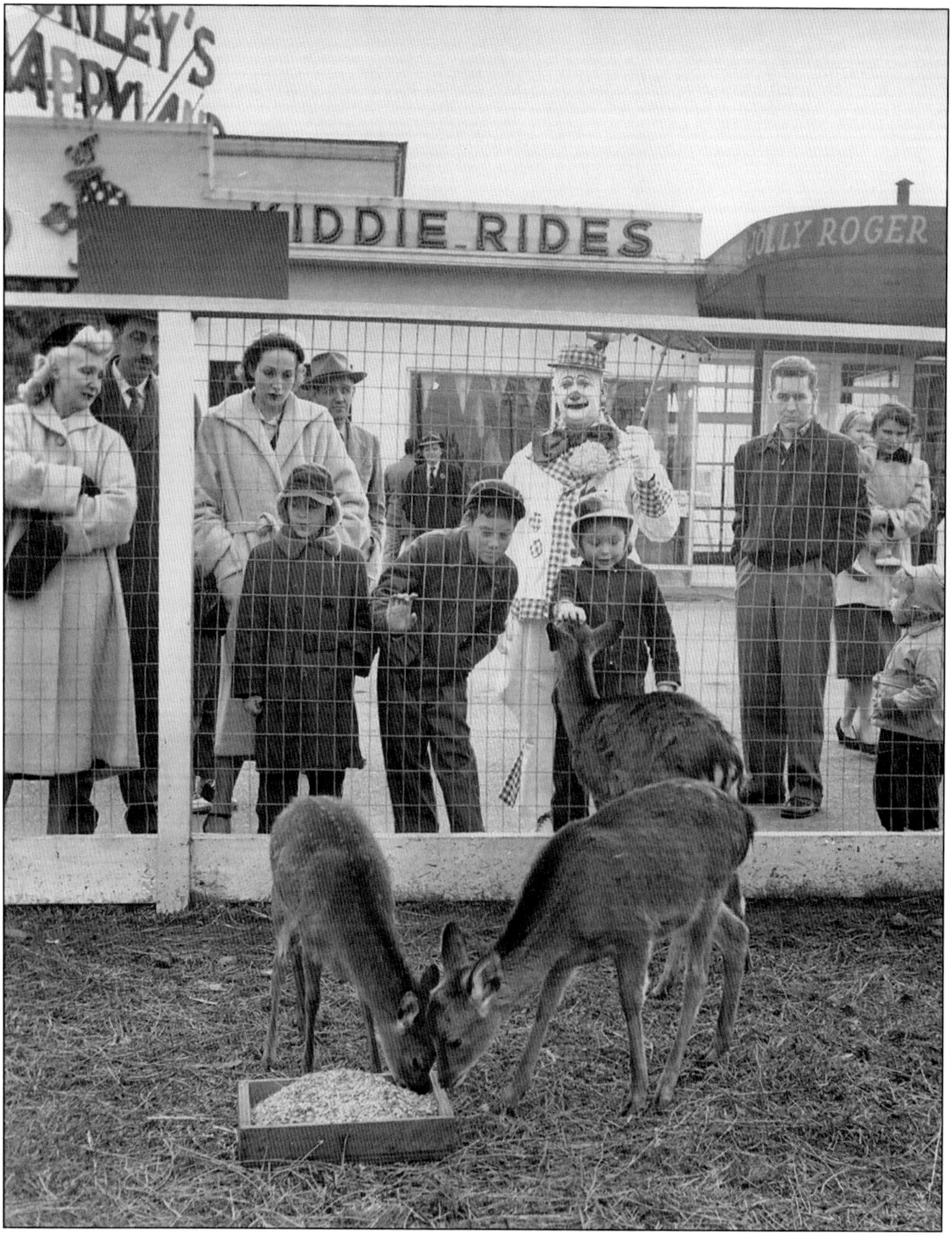

The popular Jolly Roger restaurant changed names to Robin Hood in 1974. The restaurant closed after two short years in 1976, and the amusement park followed two years after that. The carousel was auctioned off in November 1978. Today, the site is home to a strip mall. (Courtesy of Dennis Ciccone Jr.)

Two

The Life of the Park

The best part about Nunley's was that its only purpose was for fun. Once a child realized they were heading to the park that day, the excitement was palpable. The property that made up Nunley's was not large, less than four acres; it is easy to grasp the size today driving past the former site, wondering how all of the rides fit into that tiny space. However, to an excited child at the time (and in their memories later), the park was colossal. As a visitor turned south into the parking lot from Sunrise Highway, numerous features jumped out. The carousel building was the most iconic element, and the pavilion that housed it was the first thing that came into view when approaching the park. The carousel was the first component of what would become Nunley's Amusement Park. In 1947, various additions were made and rides were added. The final large element of the park, the miniature golf course, was added in 1961.

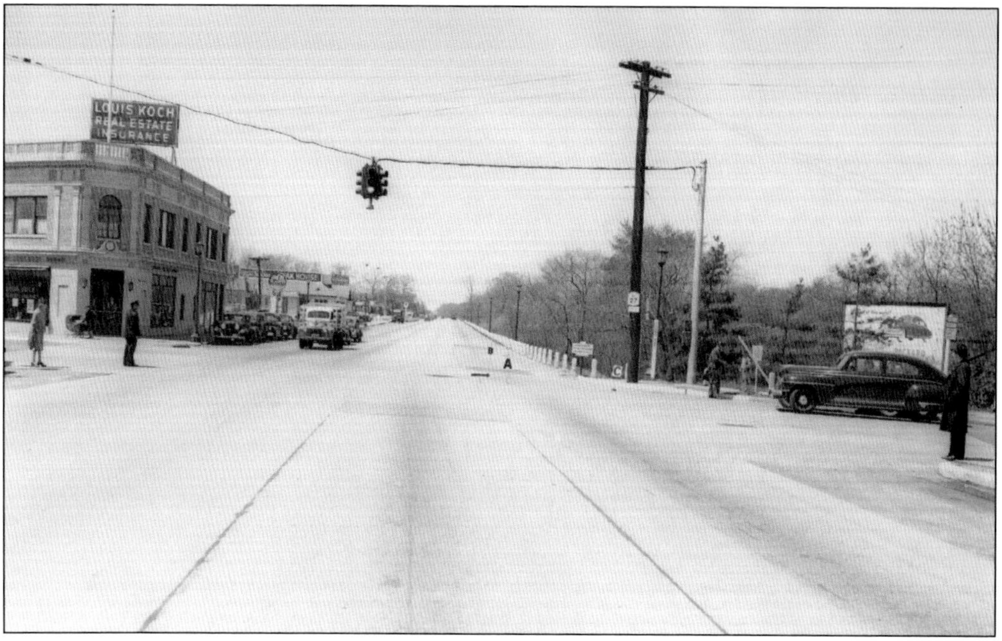

William Nunley chose a small lot in Baldwin for his next, and most famous, kiddie park. Ideally situated, it was directly across from a Long Island Rail Road (LIRR) station and was on Sunrise Highway, a highly-traveled road from Queens to Suffolk County. This 1948 image looks west down Sunrise Highway, a block past Nunley's park. (Courtesy of Queens Borough Public Library, Long Island Division, Illustrations Collection—Baldwin.)

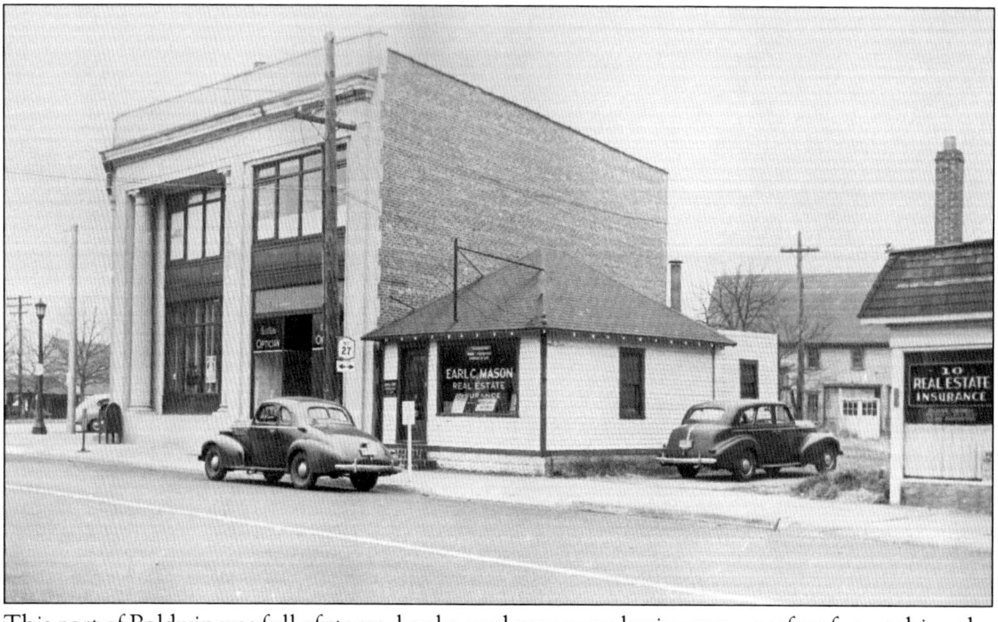

This part of Baldwin was full of stores, banks, and numerous businesses—perfect for catching the attention of residents and commuters alike. This 1947 image shows the southeast intersection of Grand Avenue and Sunrise Highway. The LIRR Station is visible at far left, before the track was elevated and on the north side of Sunrise Highway. Also pictured is Sunrise National Bank. (Courtesy of Nassau County Department of Parks, Recreation & Museums, Photo Archives Center.)

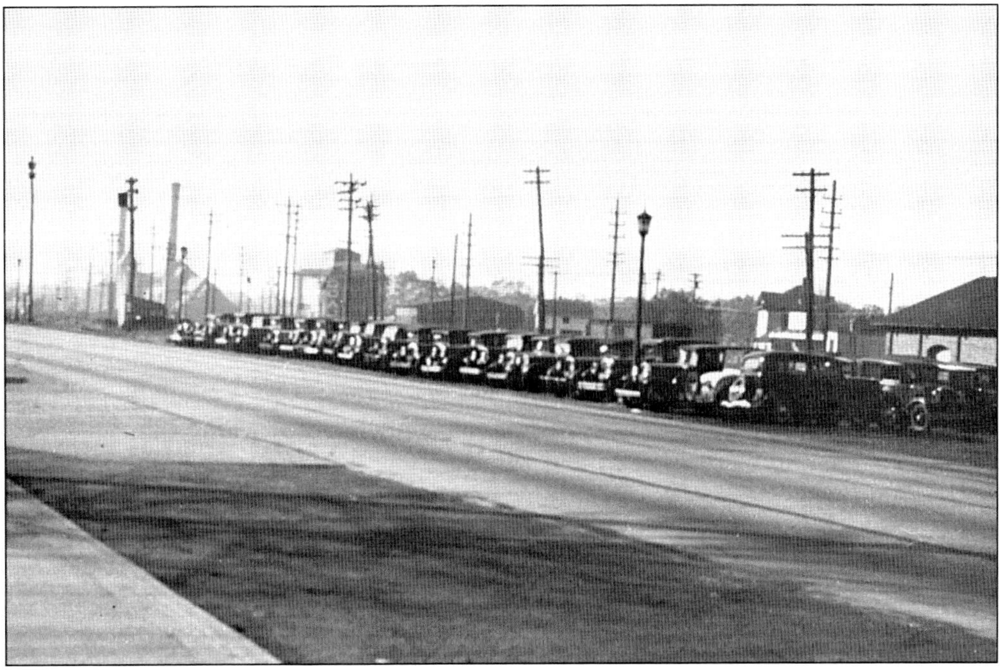

These two pictures show how much this area of Baldwin was changing around the time William Nunley opened his amusement park. The photograph above, taken around 1935, shows the railroad parking area along Sunrise Highway. The 1946 image below shows the same area after the beautification program was put into place. During this time, numerous trees were planted along the highway, including 68 Oriental planes, 50 dogwoods, 95 white pines, and 44 American elms. (Both, courtesy of Nassau County Department of Parks, Recreation & Museums, Photo Archives Center.)

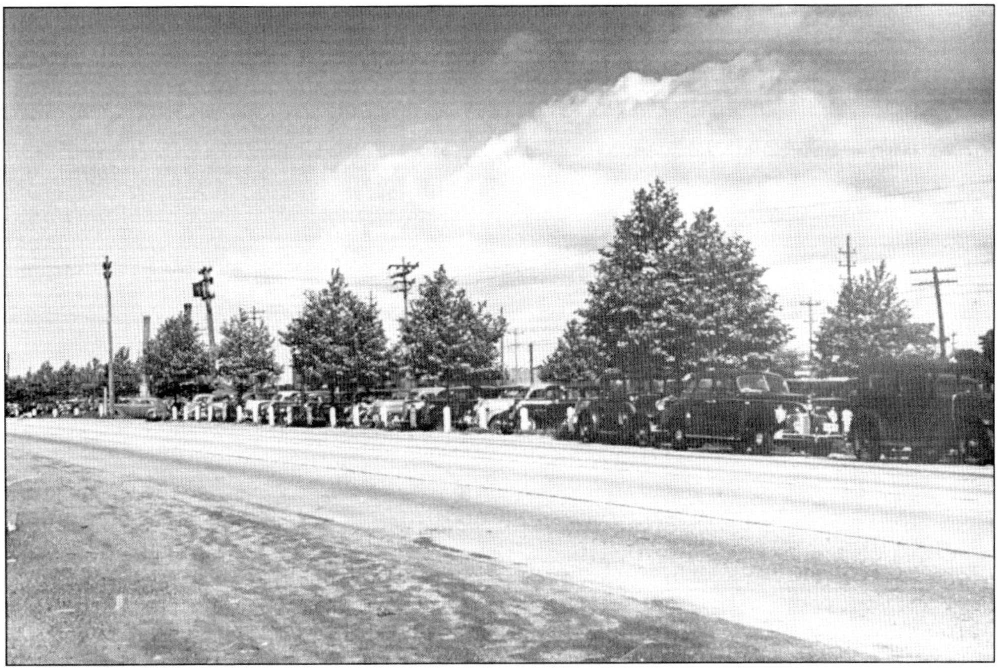

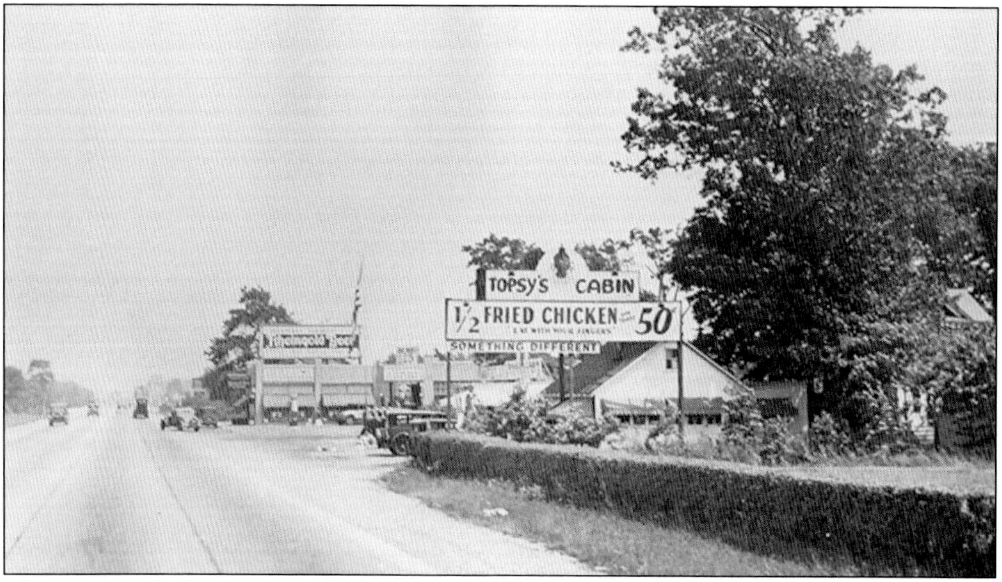

The area also had numerous popular restaurants. This photograph, looking east down Sunrise Highway in 1933, shows Topsy's Cabin. The restaurant was on the south side of Sunrise Highway, west of Rockwood Avenue. The building may look familiar to some, as it later became Raay-Noor's Cabin, a popular Long Island eatery, until it closed in the late 1990s. Today, it is an Ayhan's Shish Kebab Mediterranean restaurant. (Courtesy of Nassau County Department of Parks, Recreation & Museums, Photo Archives Center.)

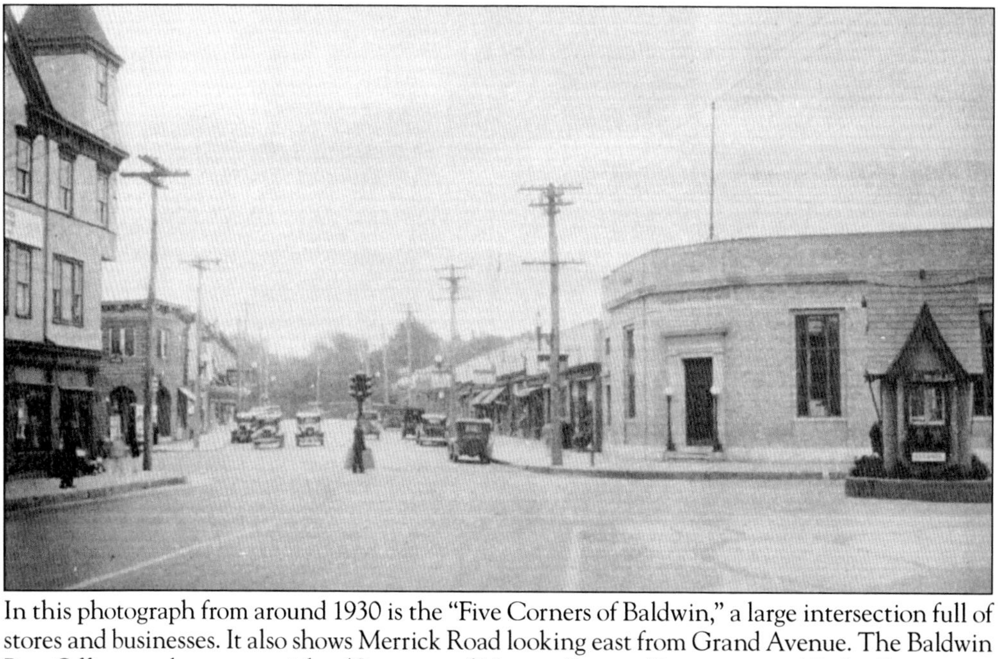

In this photograph from around 1930 is the "Five Corners of Baldwin," a large intersection full of stores and businesses. It also shows Merrick Road looking east from Grand Avenue. The Baldwin Post Office can be seen at right. (Courtesy of Nassau County Department of Parks, Recreation & Museums, Photo Archives Center.)

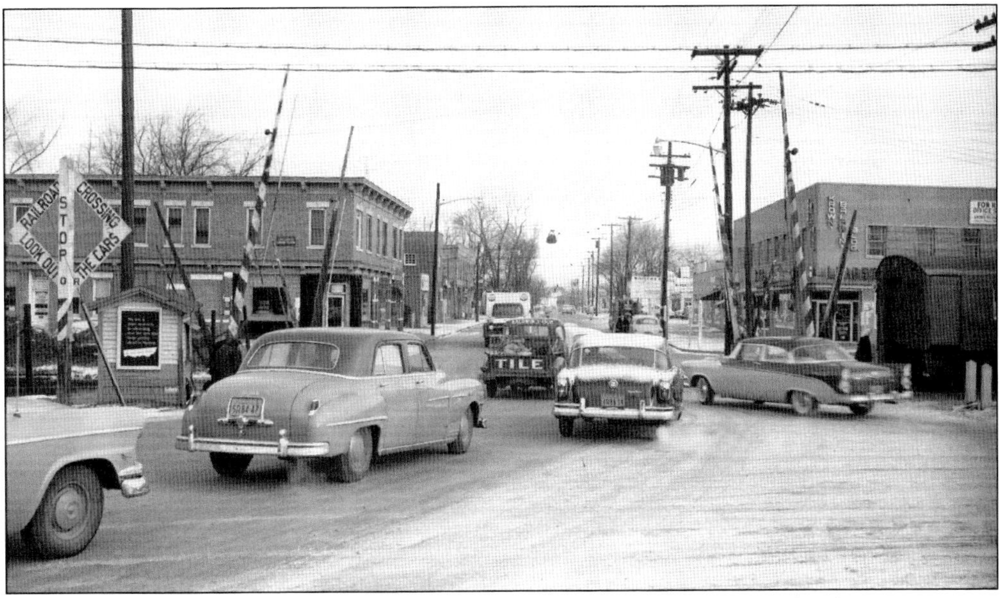

In 1956, the Long Island Rail Road was still at ground level in Baldwin. Pictured is the train crossing at Grand Avenue, just north of Sunrise Highway. However, just a few short years later in 1959, new elevated train platforms and tracks were already in operation for much of the Babylon train line. These elevated tracks eased congestion and were safer for drivers and pedestrians. The image below shows the new escalator at the Baldwin LIRR station leading up to the tracks. (Both, courtesy of Queens Borough Public Library, Long Island Division, Illustrations Collection—Baldwin.)

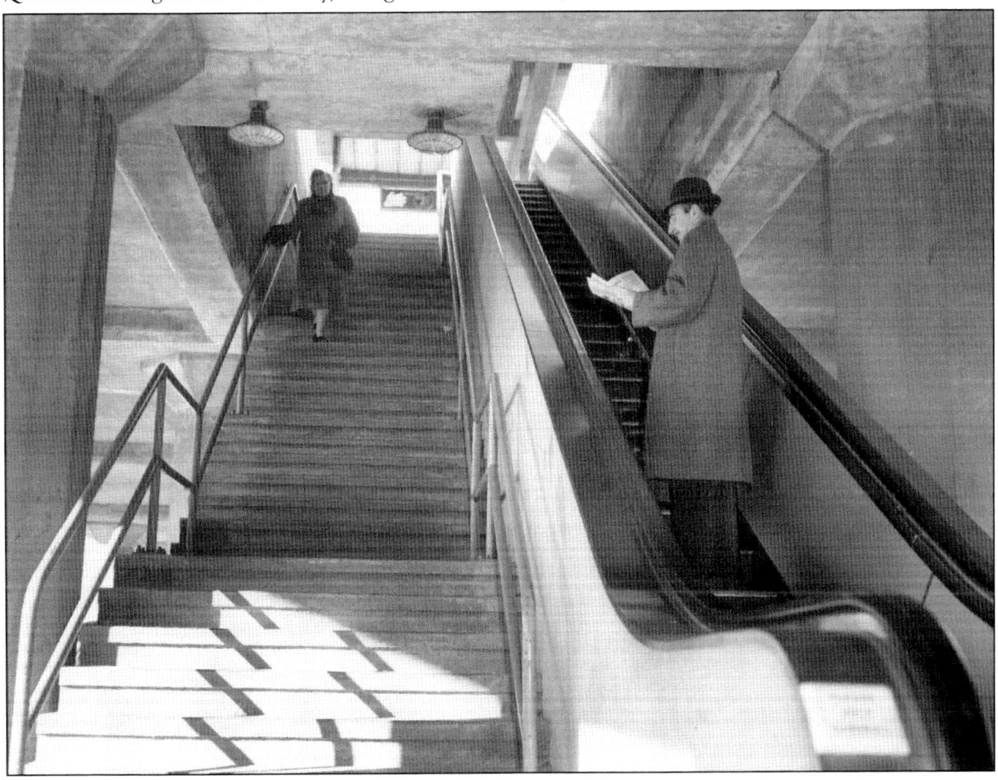

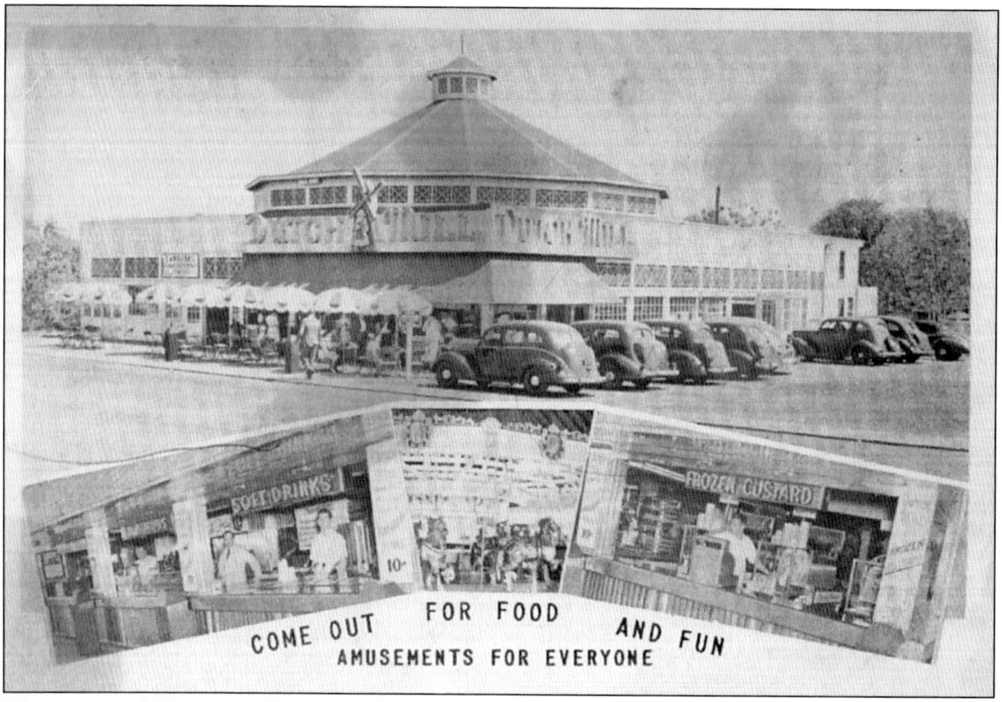

This postcard from 1939 shows the Dutch Mill restaurant, the location of Nunley's carousel and future site of the amusement park. At this point, the carousel was the only ride at the site. The restaurant boasted that it was "Famous for our All Beef Frankfurters, Fresh Fruit Drinks and Frozen Custard made with pure cream." (Courtesy of Northland Photo Co. Inc.)

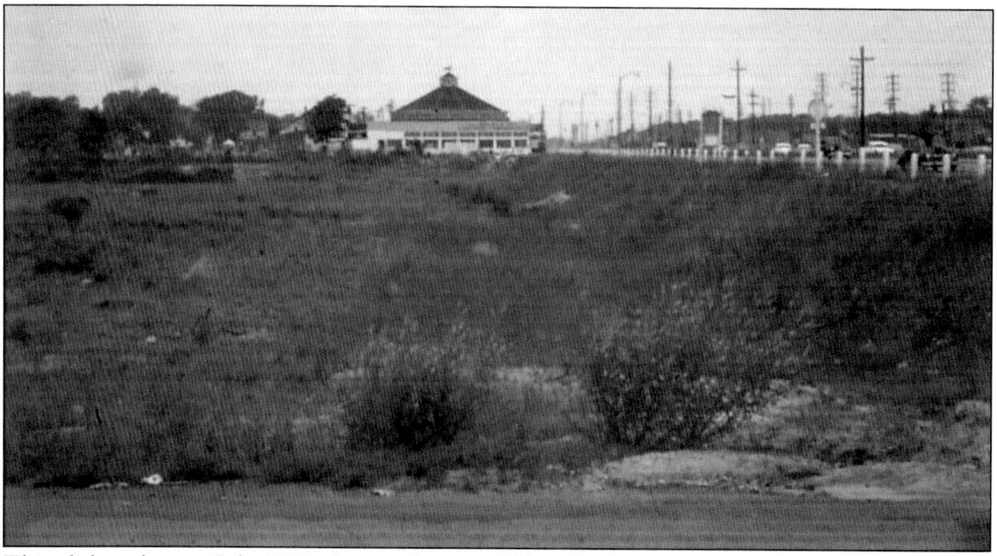

This slide, taken in July 1956, shows what would be the future site of the new Freeport High School. The photograph looks west on Sunrise Highway from Brookside Avenue. Nunley's carousel building can be seen in the distance. For many who remember Nunley's, it is difficult to imagine a time when the area surrounding the park was so desolate. Just a few years after the school was finally completed, dozens of new stores and offices popped up. Today, there is barely an open lot to be found along Sunrise Highway. (Courtesy of Freeport Memorial Library.)

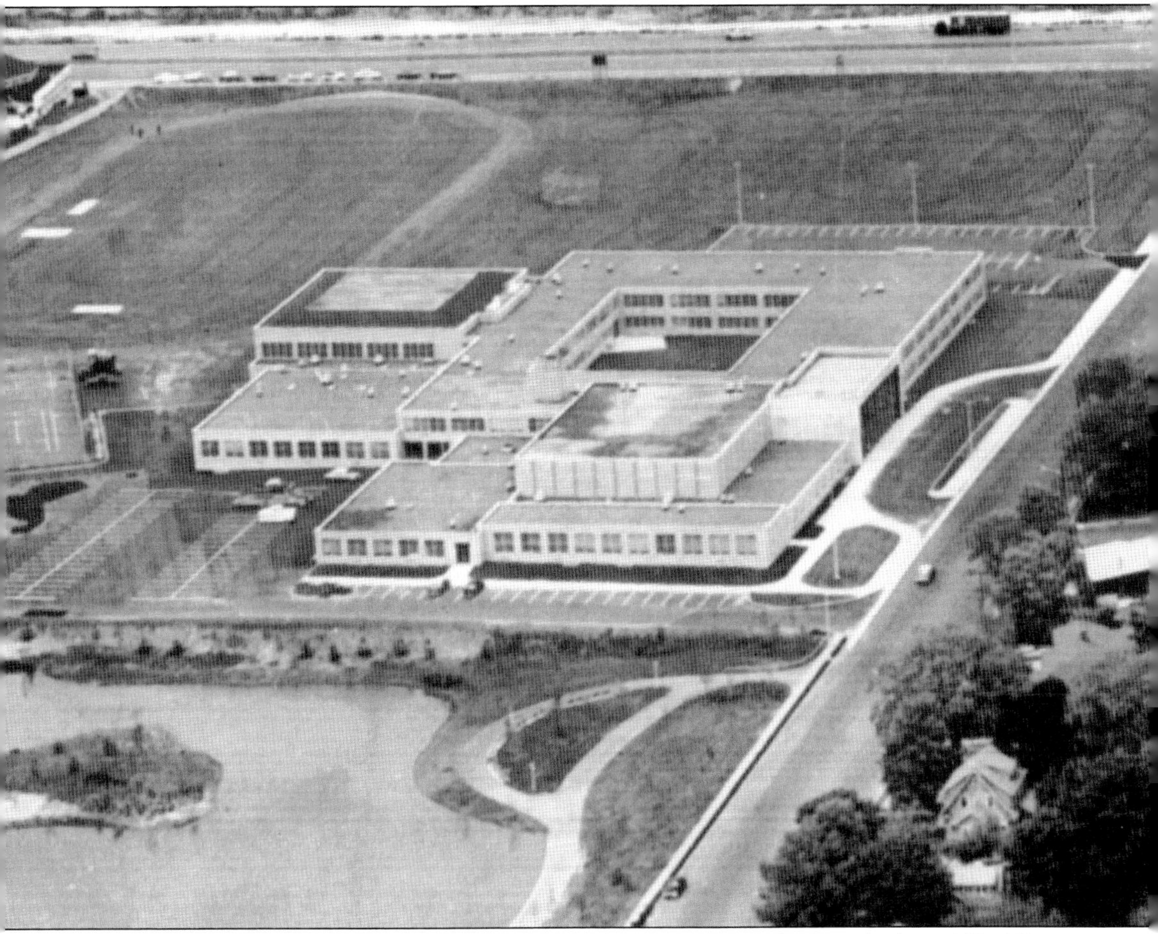

Freeport High School, located just east of Nunley's park property, was rebuilt in the late 1950s. This aerial view of the school property was taken in April 1957 for the school's dedication brochure. Nunley's carousel building can be seen at the top left. It is fitting that Nunley's was included in this picture of the school, as it was such a significant part of daily life for students. Randy Hassell, who graduated in 1986, has fond memories of trips to Nunley's for lunch: "The first thing you heard was one of the men yell 'Drop Fries, Nick!' in the thickest Greek accent. This meant that the lunch rush was on. We would buy french fries from Nick in a brown paper lunch bag, which became soaked with oil and salt, along with the best root beer known to mankind. They sold them faster than Nick could cook them. The place had a smell that if you smelled it today, it would bring you back in time." (Courtesy of Freeport Historical Society.)

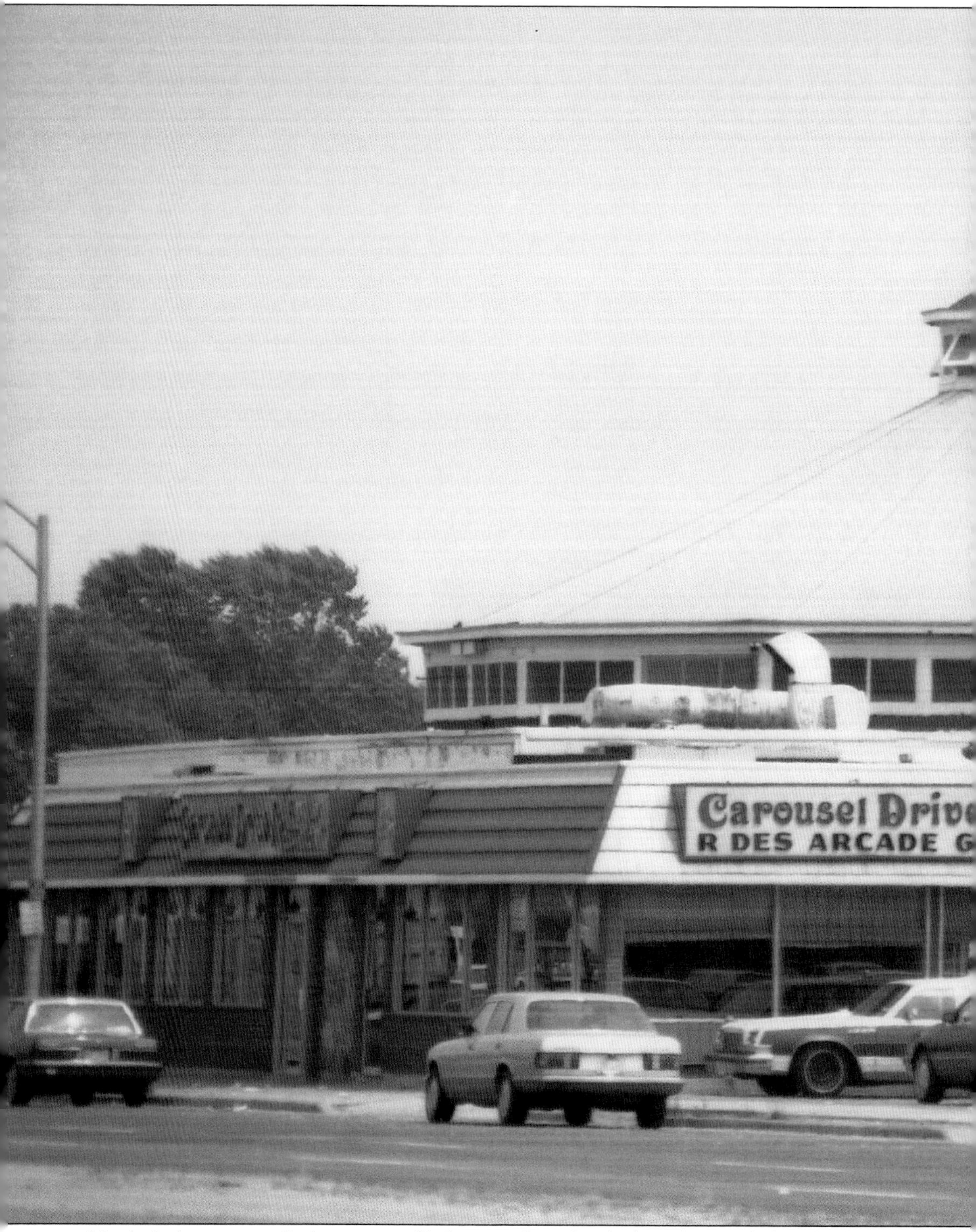

Nunley's Amusement Park was a small place on the side of a heavily traveled road. This 1988 photograph shows the park from Sunrise Highway. The restaurant, the carousel building, and the Ferris wheel can be seen. It may not seem like much, but for those who loved the park, it became

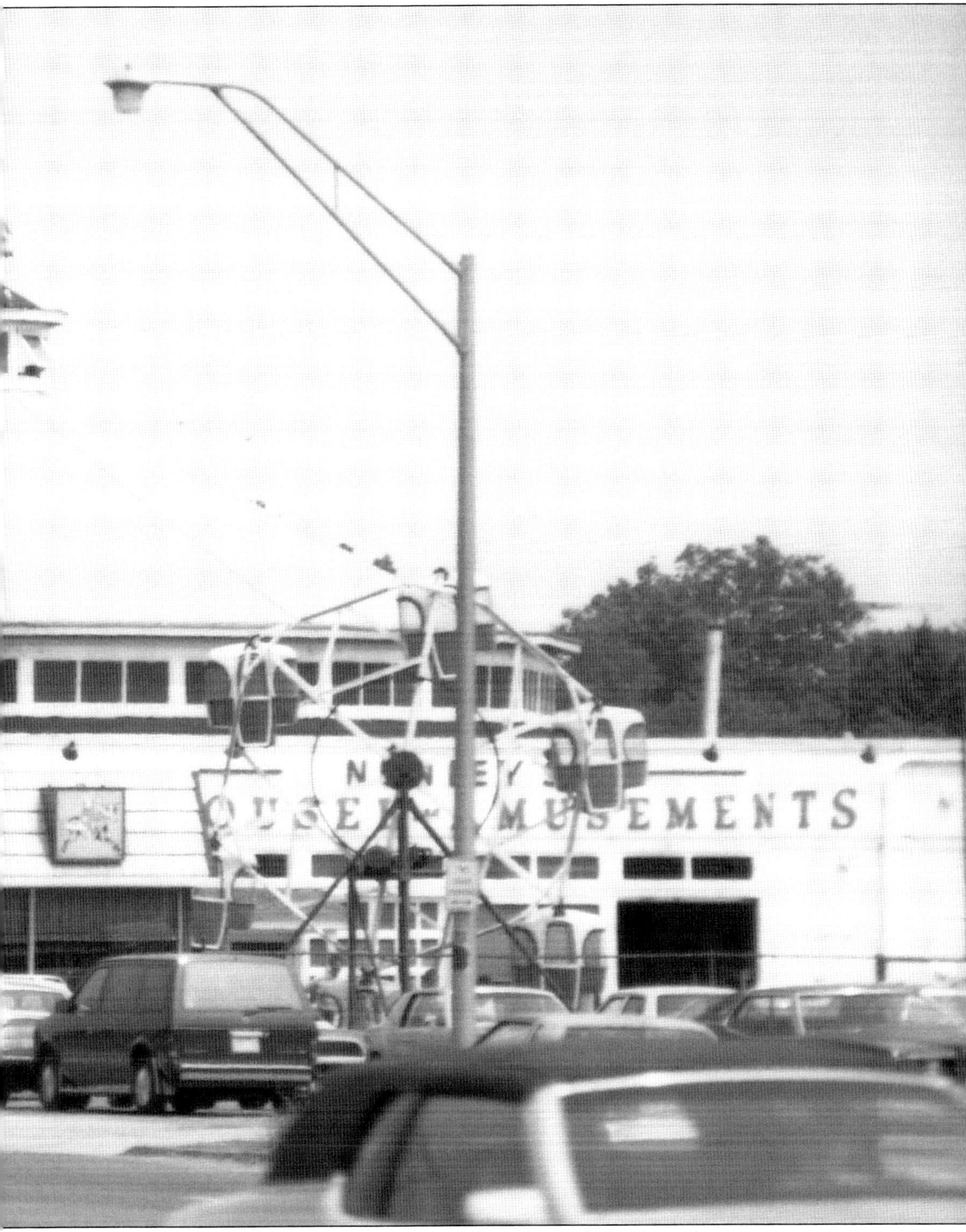

a magical place once the car turned into the parking lot; a place where the entire point was to just have fun and be with friends and family. (Courtesy of Gary Monti.)

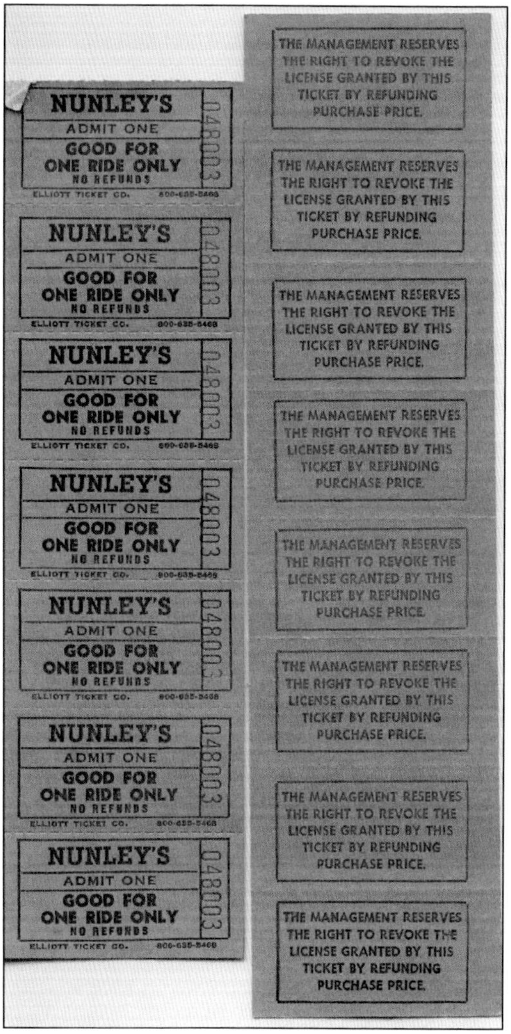

Pictured are regular ride tickets, as well as a book for 16 carousel tickets. After running frantically through the parking lot to get to the gates, standing there struggling to decide which ride to go on first, one would always have to be reminded that the ticket booth was the first stop. Most of the rides required one ticket each, so the visitor would have to try and calculate how many rides he or she wanted to go on. Most likely, however, that choice was made by whoever was actually purchasing the tickets. (Both, courtesy of Dennis Ciccone Jr.)

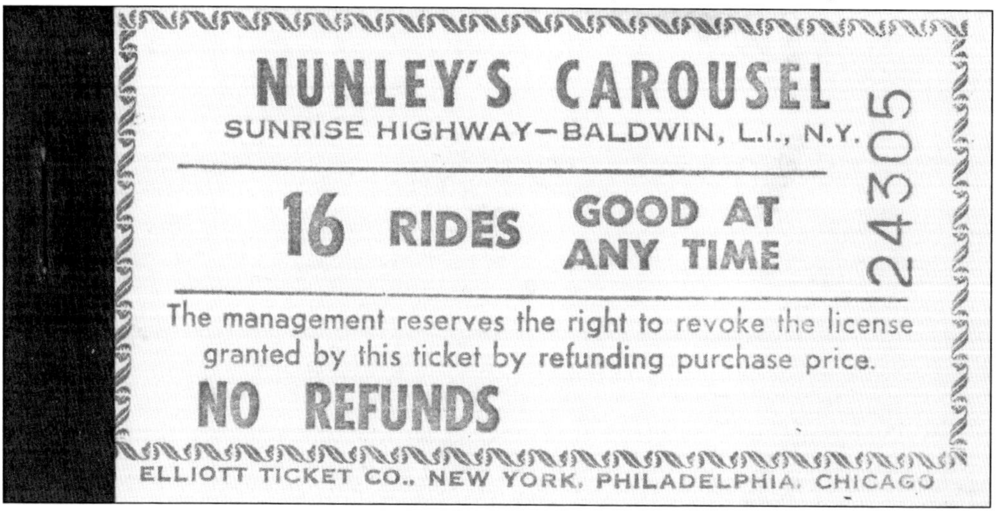

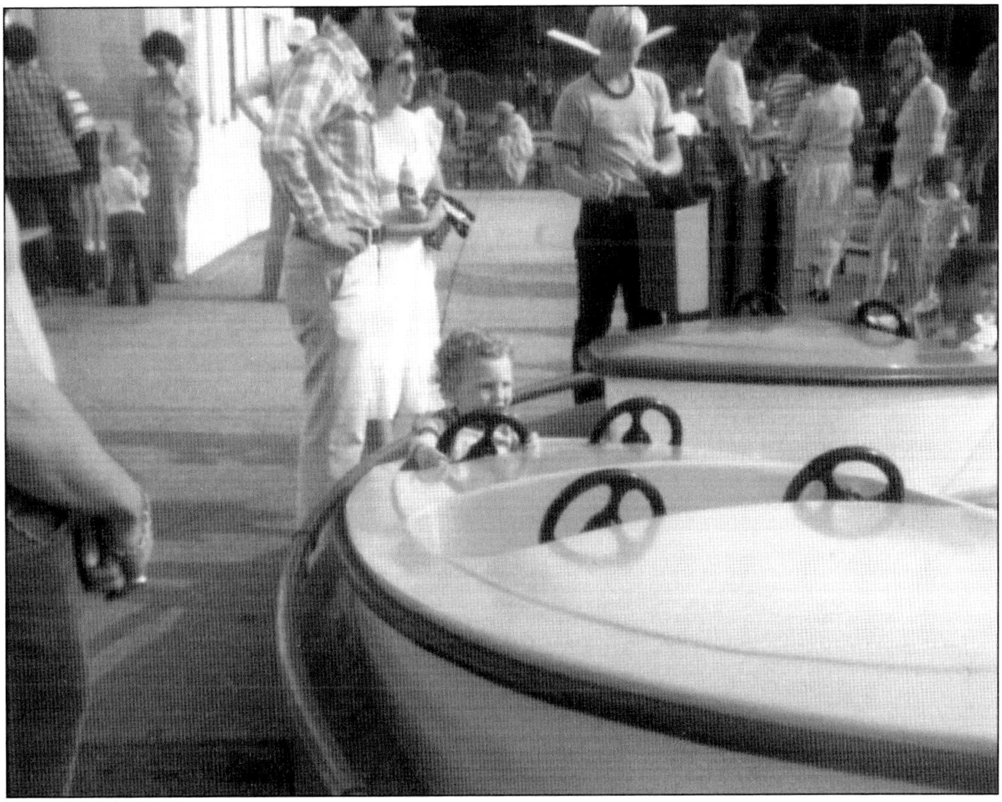

The first ride seen upon entering the park was the Schiff wet boat ride. A simple ride meant for young children, it was made up of six boats that could hold up to four riders in each. The boats were designed by B.A. Schiff & Associates, who also designed the park's Ferris wheel and roller coaster. The design of many of the rides at Nunley's allowed for each child to have their own steering wheel, so there was no fighting over the best seat. Below, the Ferris wheel and restaurant are visible in the background. (Above, author's collection; below, courtesy of Price family.)

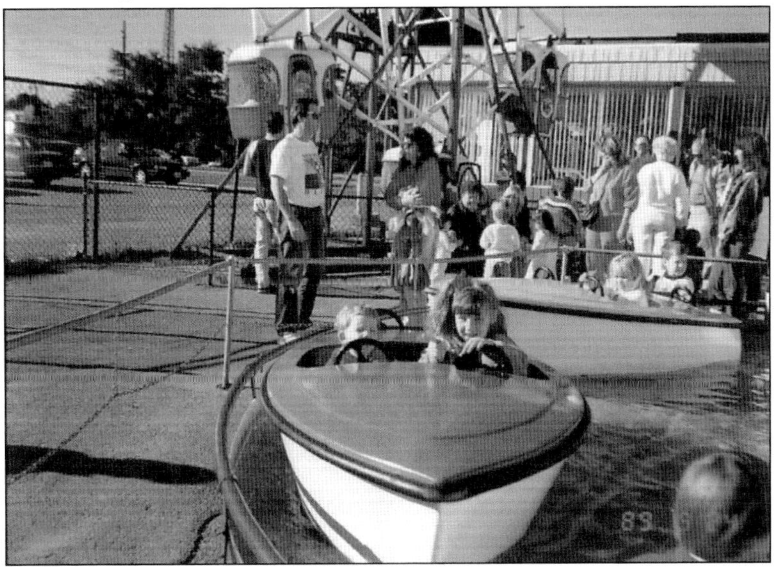

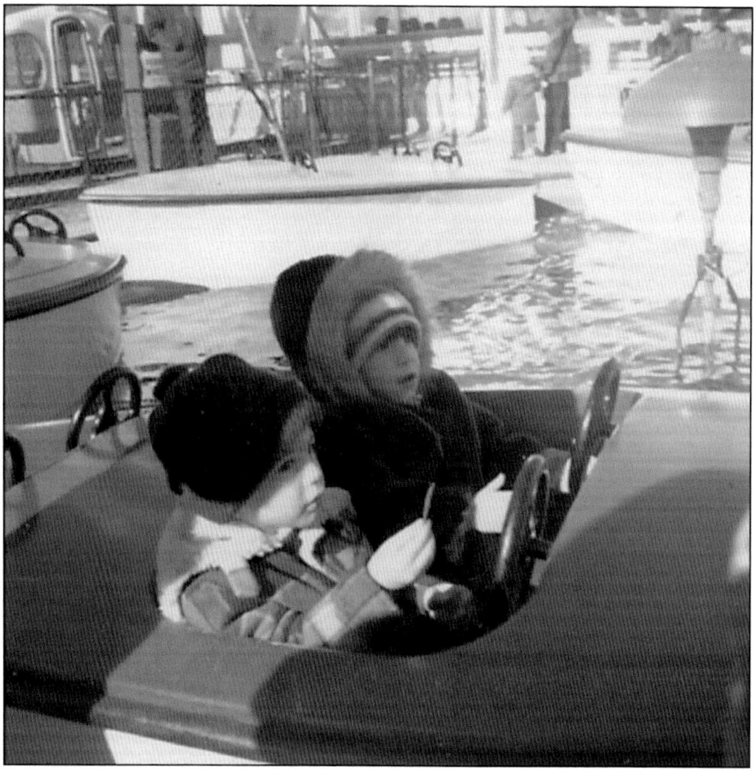

Connected to a central motor, the six multicolored boats would slowly move around a low circular pool that was full of shallow water. Nunley's Amusement Park was seasonal because almost all of the rides were outdoors, with the exception of the carousel. This 1976 photograph was taken close to the end of the season, as indicated by the heavy clothing of the riders. (Courtesy of Chuck Egbert.)

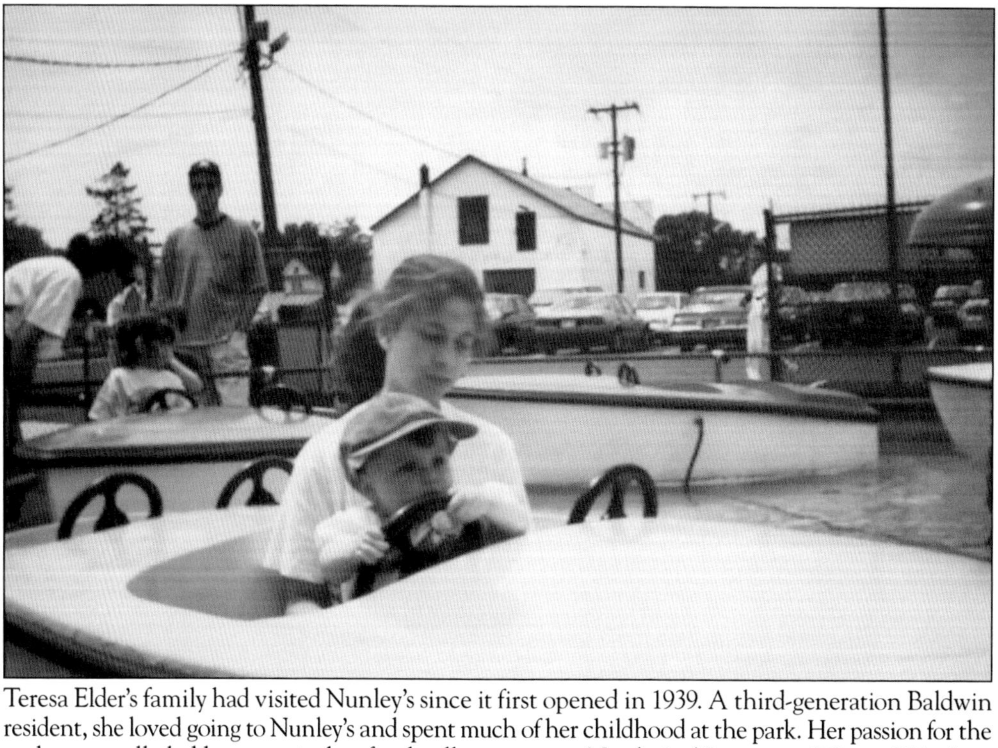

Teresa Elder's family had visited Nunley's since it first opened in 1939. A third-generation Baldwin resident, she loved going to Nunley's and spent much of her childhood at the park. Her passion for the park eventually led her to write her final college essay on Nunley's. (Courtesy of Teresa Elder.)

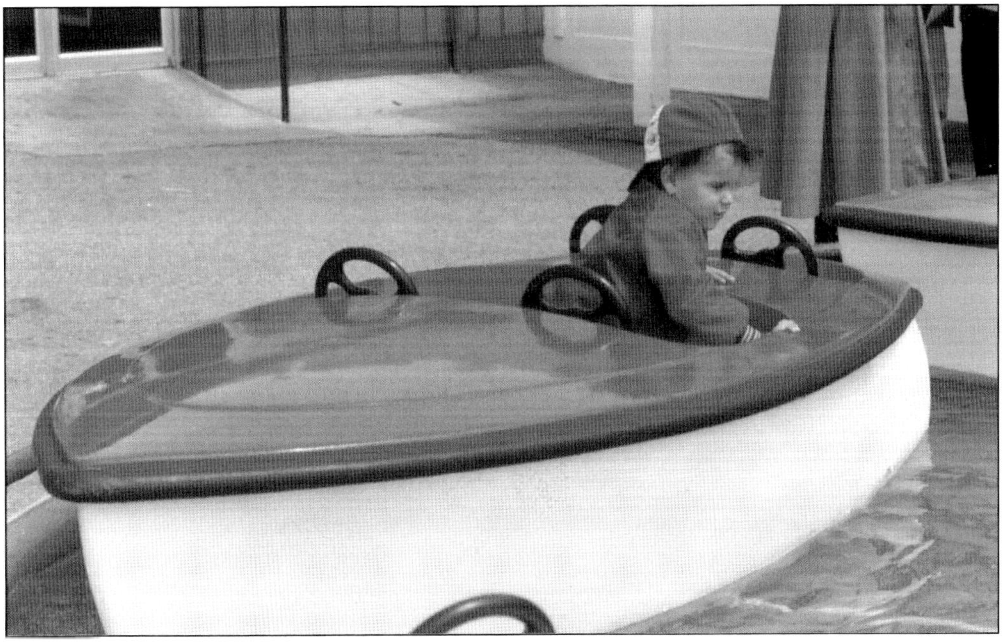

It wasn't uncommon to see perplexed toddlers in the boat ride. This ride was one of the easiest in the park to photograph children in, due to its small size and slow rotations. Almost every visitor to Nunley's has at least one posed shot from the boat ride in their family albums, according to the number of photographs collected from various sources showing this ride. (Above, courtesy of Dennis Ciccone Jr.; below, courtesy of Donna Cappello.)

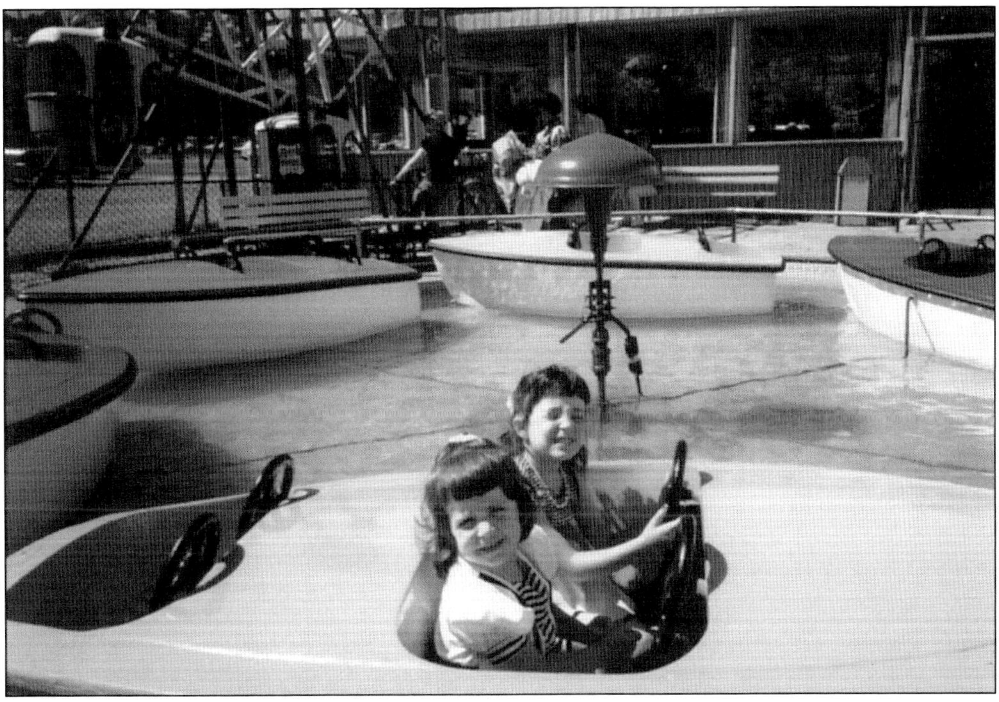

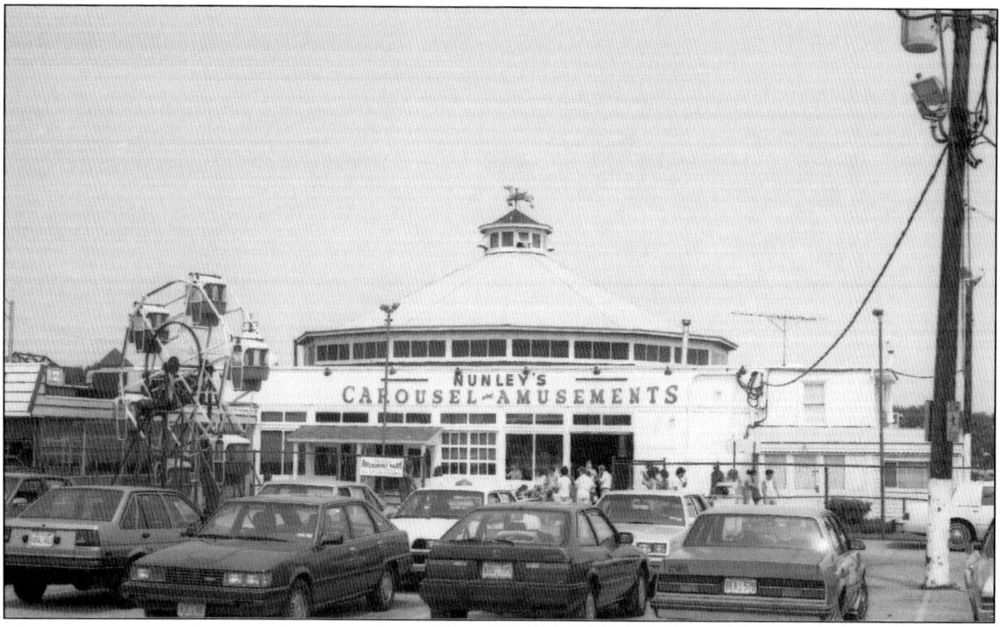

The next stop on the tour through the park is the Schiff Ferris wheel. The Ferris wheel was the tallest ride and offered the best views of the entire park. At around 25 feet tall, the ride was made up of six multicolored cages that could hold two riders each. (Courtesy of Gary Monti.)

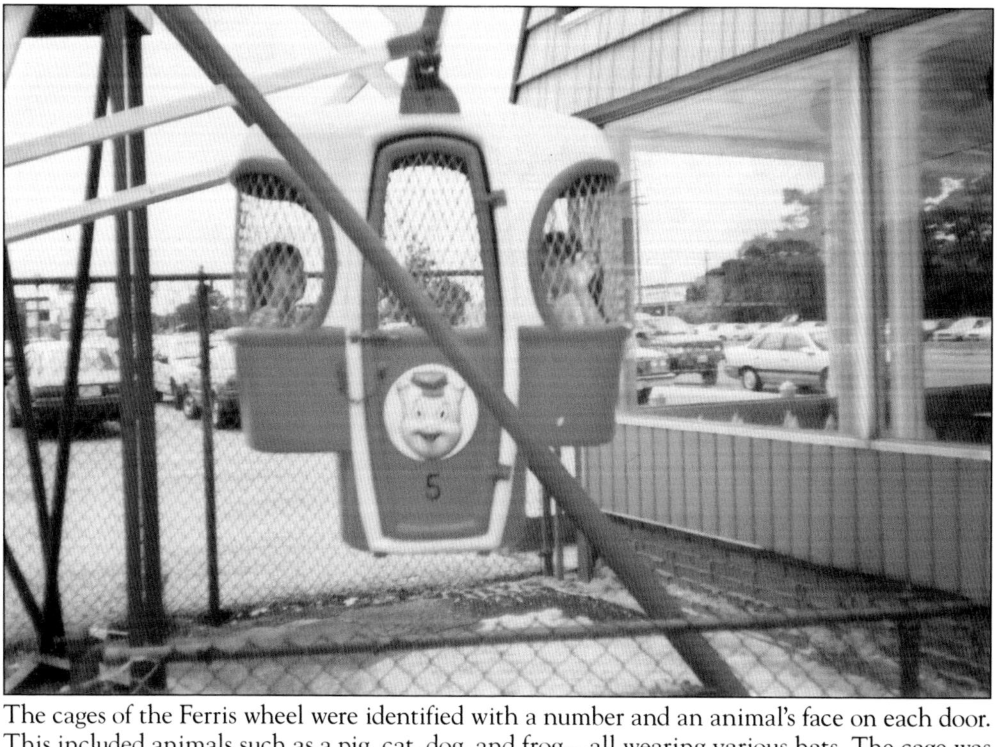

The cages of the Ferris wheel were identified with a number and an animal's face on each door. This included animals such as a pig, cat, dog, and frog—all wearing various hats. The cage was completely enclosed and had minimal swinging during its rotations, so it was suitable for young riders. (Courtesy of Kristen Williams.)

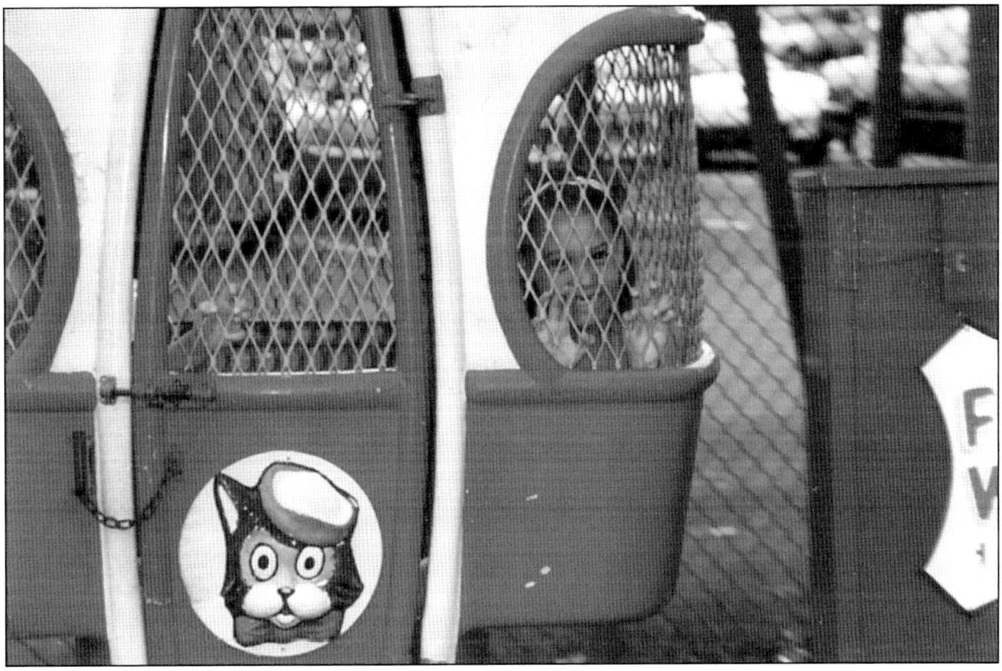

Although this tiny Ferris wheel was completely safe, there was still a slight fear for its younger riders. Parents could not accompany their children on the ride and were left to watch from below, hoping that their child would not panic when their cage halted at the very top. (Courtesy of Nancy Radecker.)

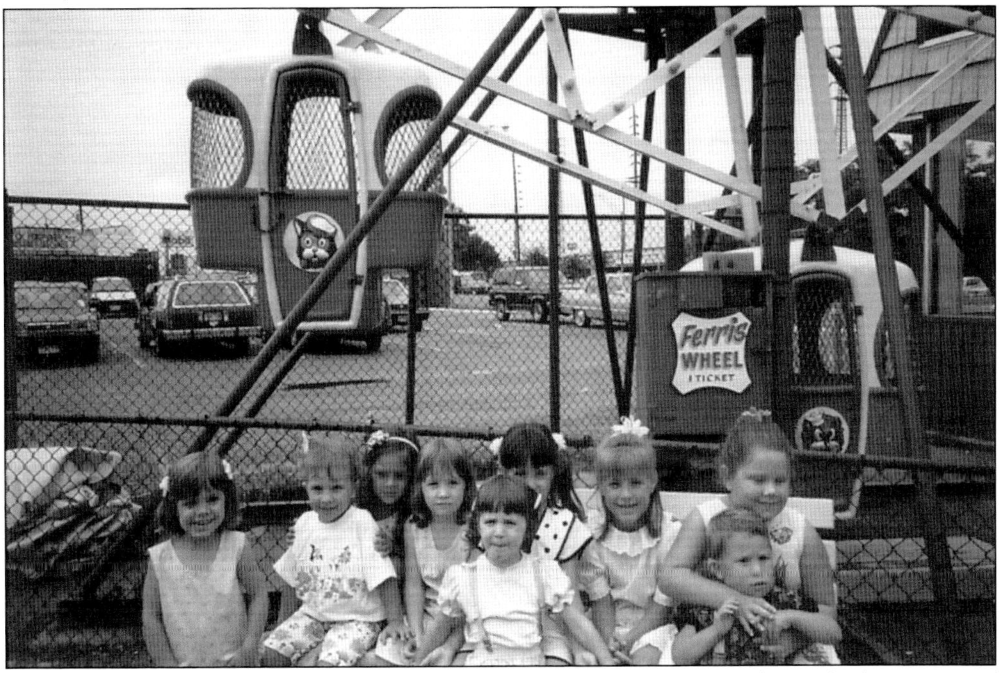

The six cages all had white tops and either red, blue, or green bodies. Each cage had two types of locks: a deadbolt and a heavy metal chain, both of which were on the exterior. This photograph shows Nunley's parking lot in the background. (Courtesy of Donna Cappello.)

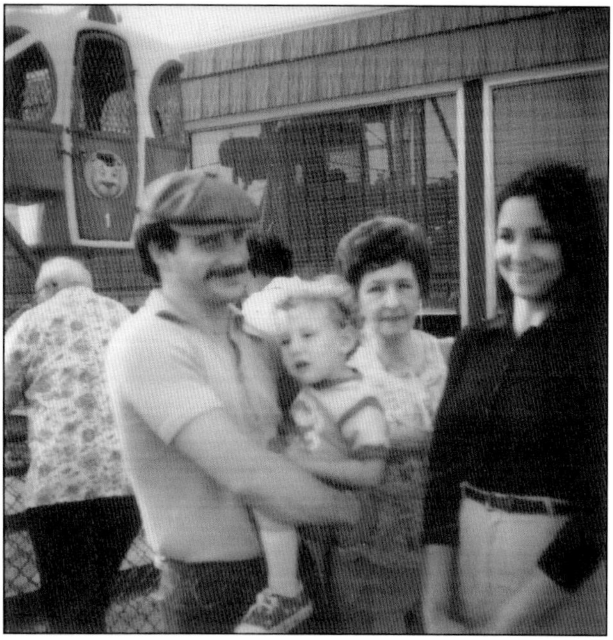

Riders of the Ferris wheel can recall that it was located right next to the restaurant. One of the most entertaining aspects of the ride was that one could see not only the whole park, but also the roof of the restaurant and carousel pavilion. (Author's collection.)

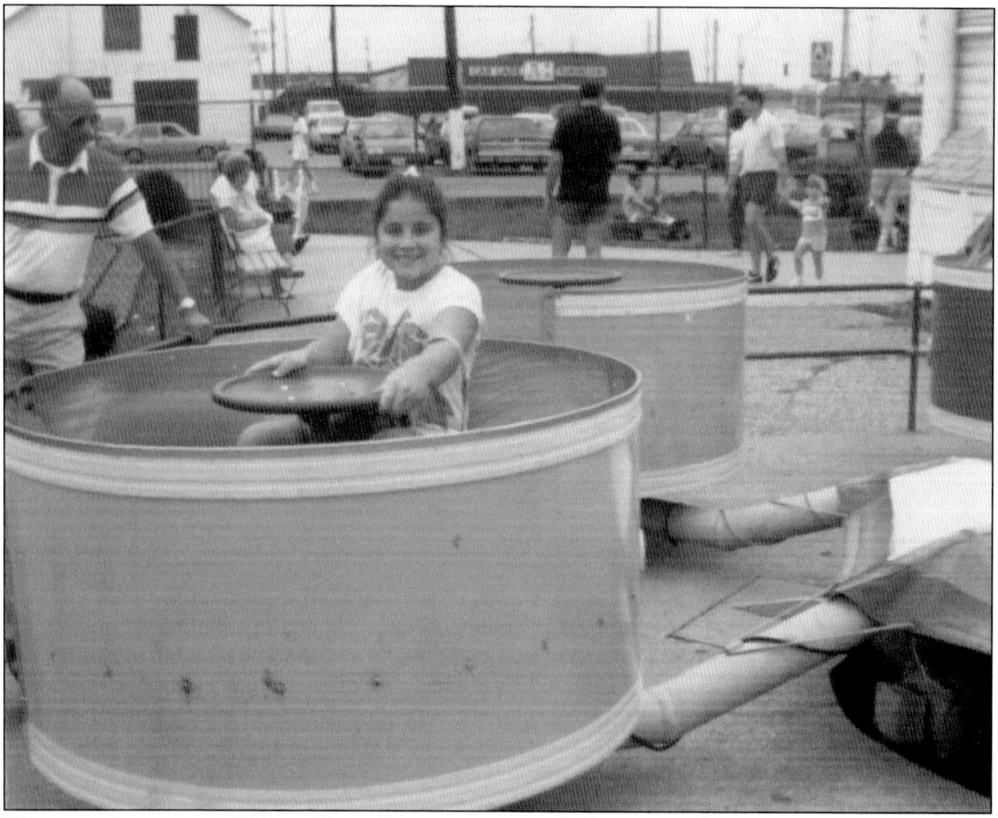

Hampton Amusement Tubs-o-Fun ride, more commonly known as the "teacups," was a ride with passenger-controlled spinning tubs. The entire ride could hold 24 children or 16 adults. Each of the eight cars was numbered and multicolored. (Courtesy of Michele Di Rico.)

Each tub had a central wheel that, when turned by riders, caused the ride to spin. All of the tubs were connected to a central unit that revolved, causing further rotations of each one. This resulted in lots of spinning and high-pitched squeals. (Courtesy of Chuck Egbert.)

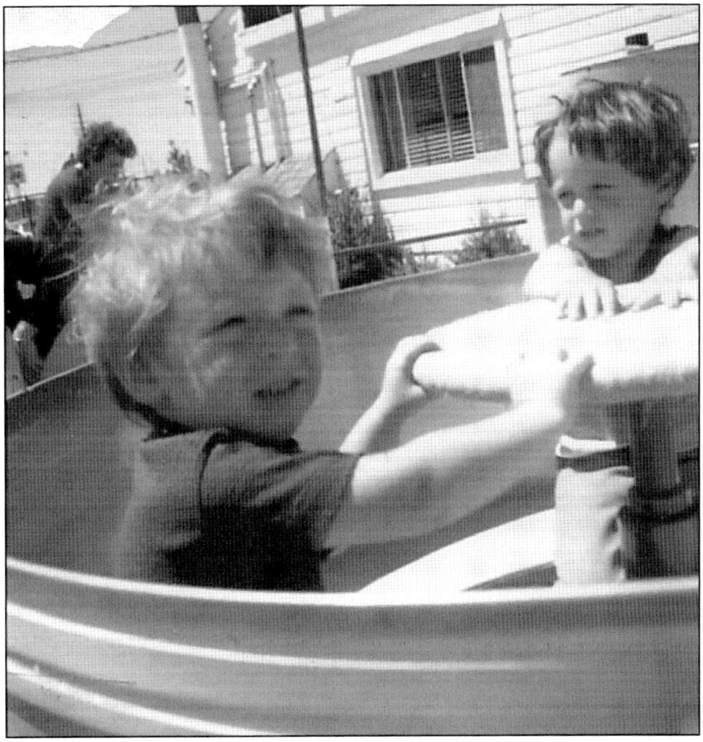

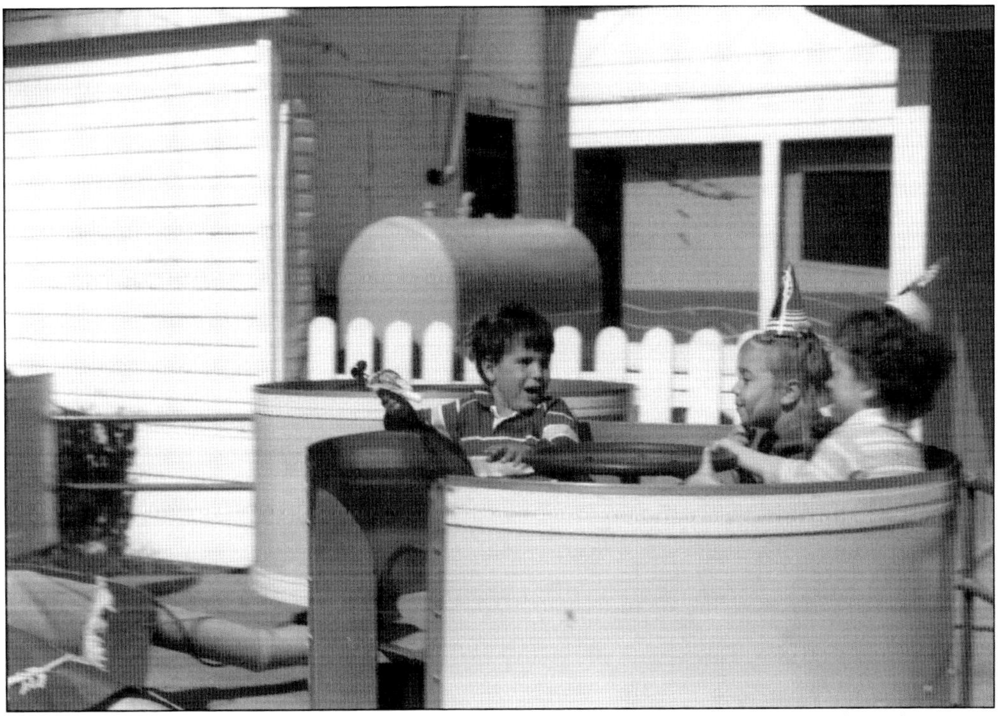

Although riders could be as young as five, it still could be an intense experience. The Tubs-O-Fun ride probably caused more upset stomachs than any other ride in the park—especially for riders with older sibling who refused to slow down the spinning. (Courtesy of Dennis Ciccone Jr.)

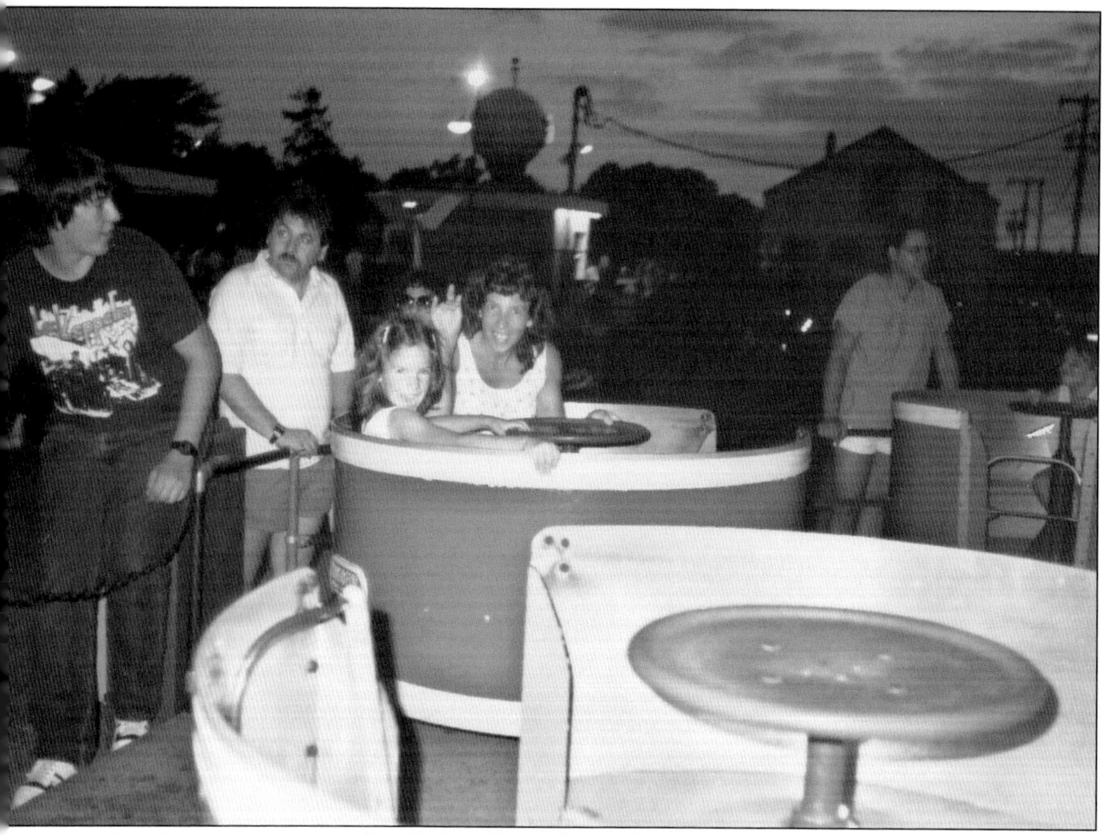

Another unique aspect of the Tubs-o-Fun ride was the fact that adults could ride with or without their kids. This was a novelty since the majority of the rides had tiny seats and were unable to hold the weight of the average adult. That being said, adults are probably more susceptible to bouts of vertigo than children, so this may have not been the best ride. When it comes down to it, this ride was never a good idea, and yet, these photographs show smiling, excited faces. (Courtesy of Kristen Williams.)

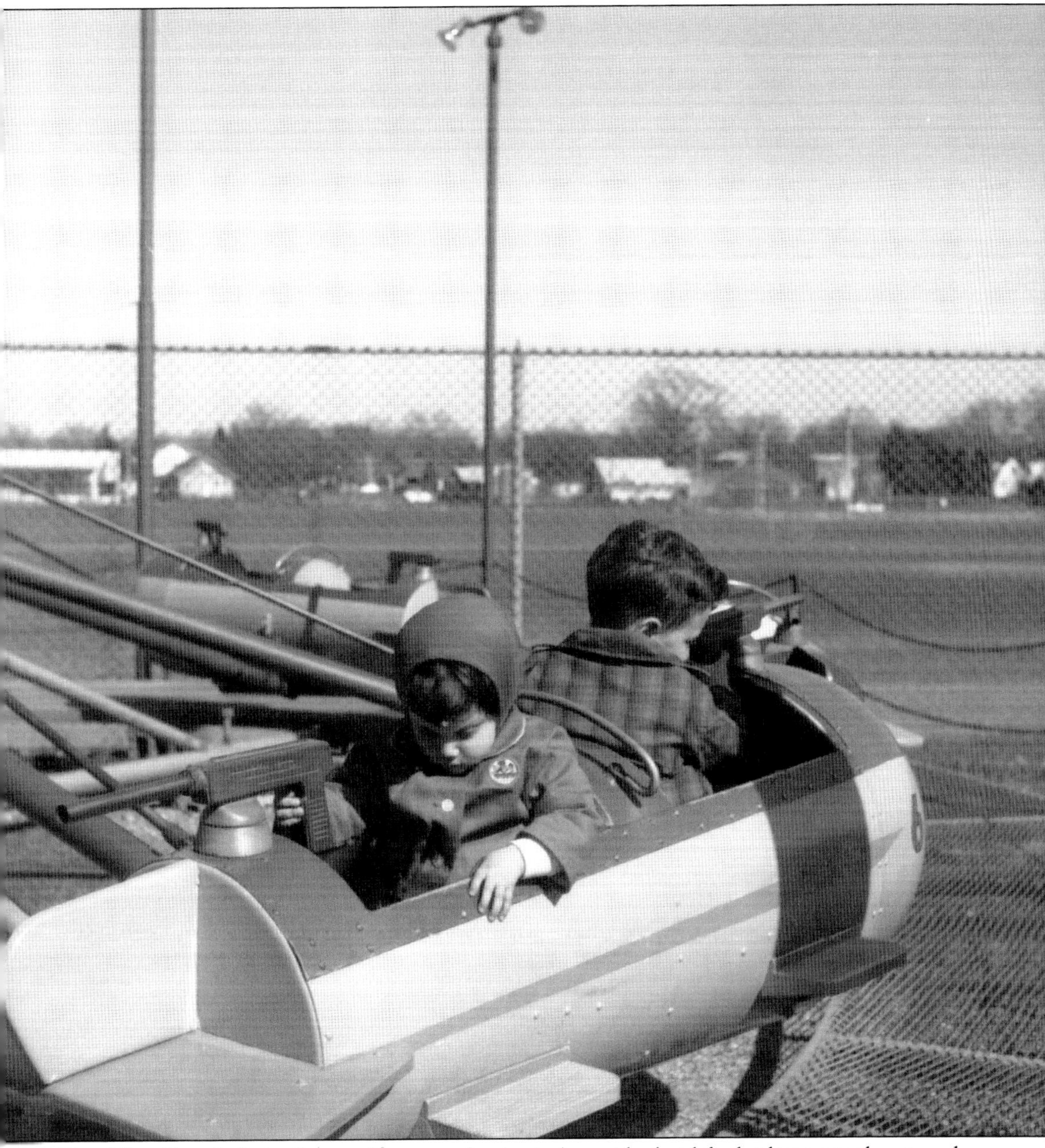

The Allan Herschell sky fighter ride was a classic airplane ride that lifted riders up in the air and back down while rotating. The planes each had two steps to aid the child while climbing into the cockpit. Each plane could hold two passengers back to back, and each had their own mounted gun that could swivel. Due to the novelty of being able to play with a gun the entire ride, many family photographs taken of these rides show the riders completely focused on the swiveling gun instead of waving to those holding the cameras, as usual with the other rides. This ride offered eight planes that were either blue and yellow or blue and red and were individually numbered. A striped cloth tent covered the centrally located motor. (Courtesy of Larry Estrin.)

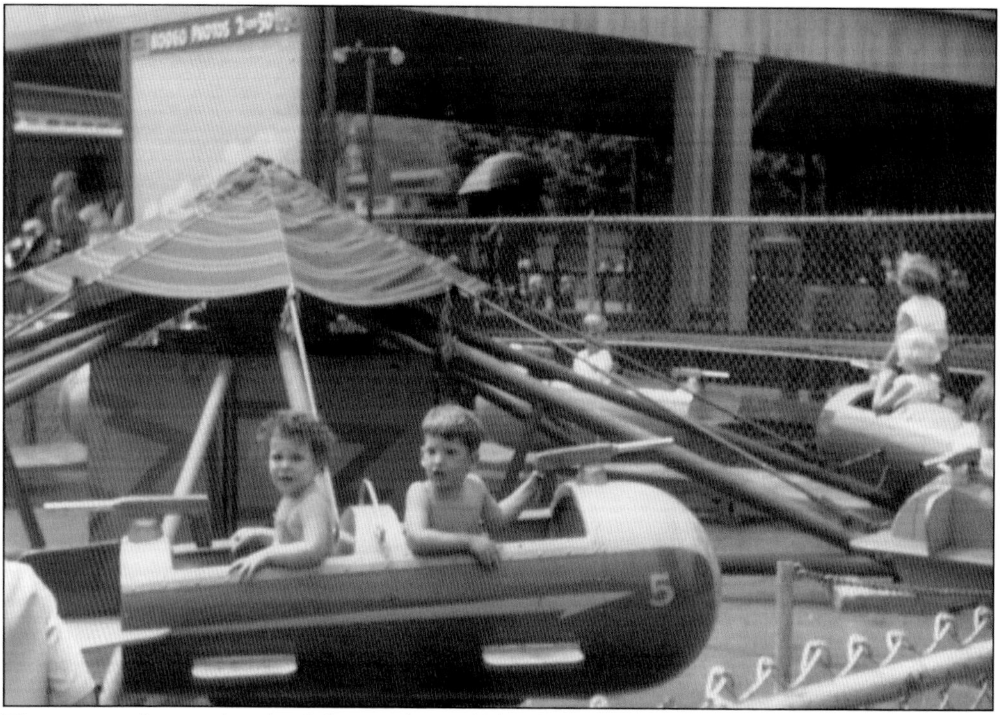

The extremely popular sky fighter ride could be found at amusement parks throughout the country. The popularity of this ride was probably due in part to World War II interest. Here is an almost identical ride from Kennywood Amusement Park in Pittsburgh, Pennsylvania. (Author's collection.)

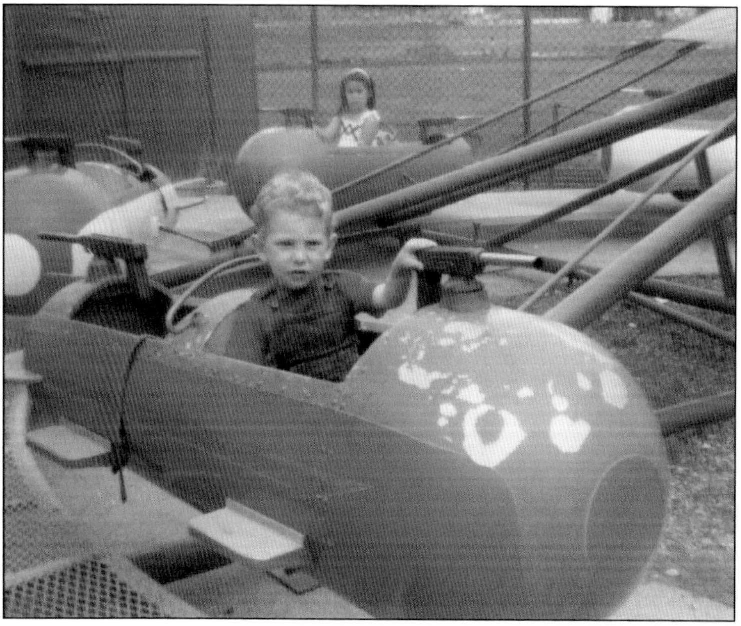

The sky fighter was one of multiple rides that were right up against the east fence that went along the length of the park property. The Freeport High School's football field and track are visible in the background. A metal ramp with a chain fence surrounds this ride. (Author's collection.)

While the sky fighter ride remained relatively unaltered throughout the course of Nunley's park life, the paint detailing definitely changed over the years. Although there was a mounted gun for each rider, one person would be riding backwards the entire ride, possibly causing arguments over who got which seat. (Right, courtesy of Hollywood family; below, courtesy of Mary Disanto.)

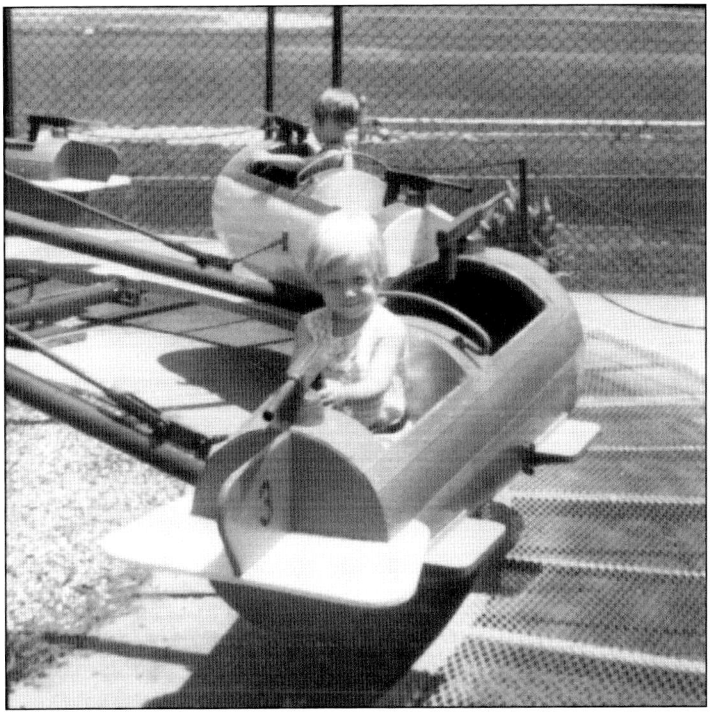

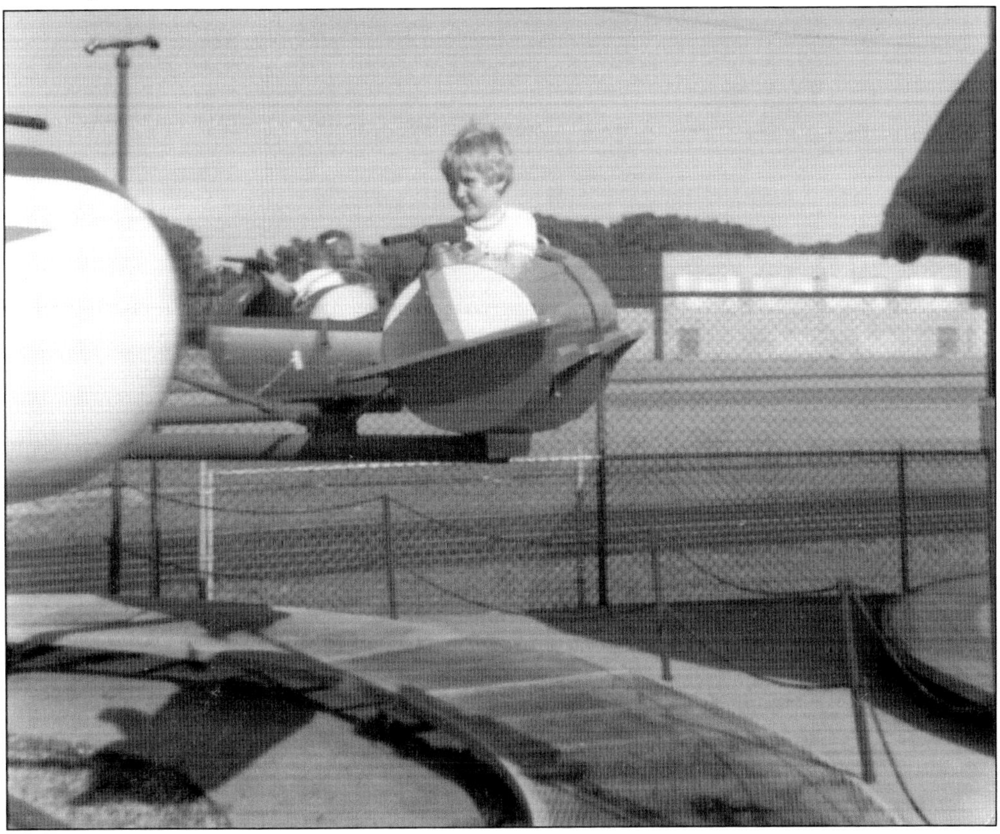

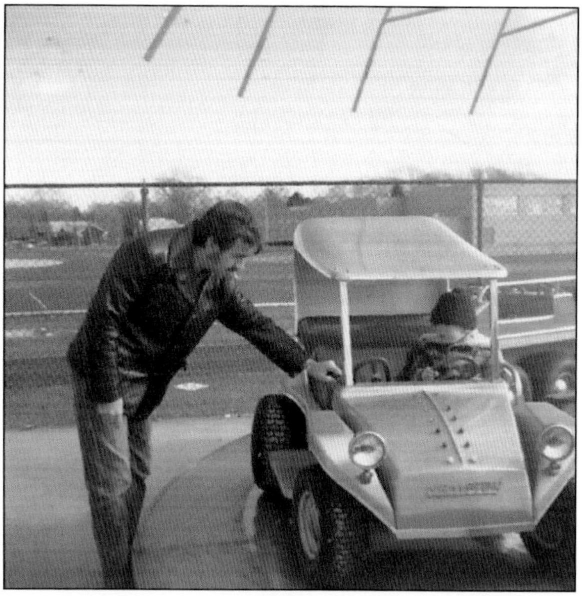

The Hampton dune buggy umbrella ride was made up of various styles of cars and trucks that could hold up to four riders depending on the car, each with their own steering wheel. There were dozens of lights all over the cars and the central umbrella supports. (Courtesy of Chuck Egbert.)

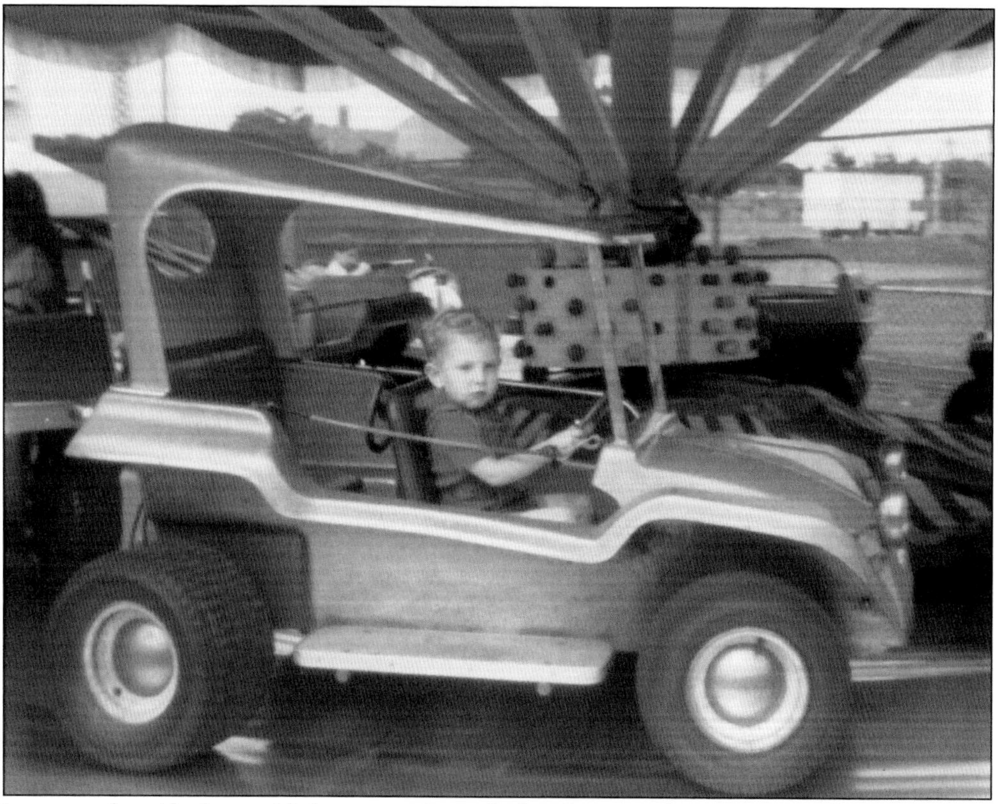

It was another ride that enabled easy snapshots of riders due to its slow rotations and cars remaining grounded, which also made it good for very young riders. The vehicles had horns that made loud buzzing sounds, obviously a delight to riders, but irritating to both parents and ride operators. Operators had the ability to turn this feature off, which may be why it might not sound familiar to some visitors. (Author's collection.)

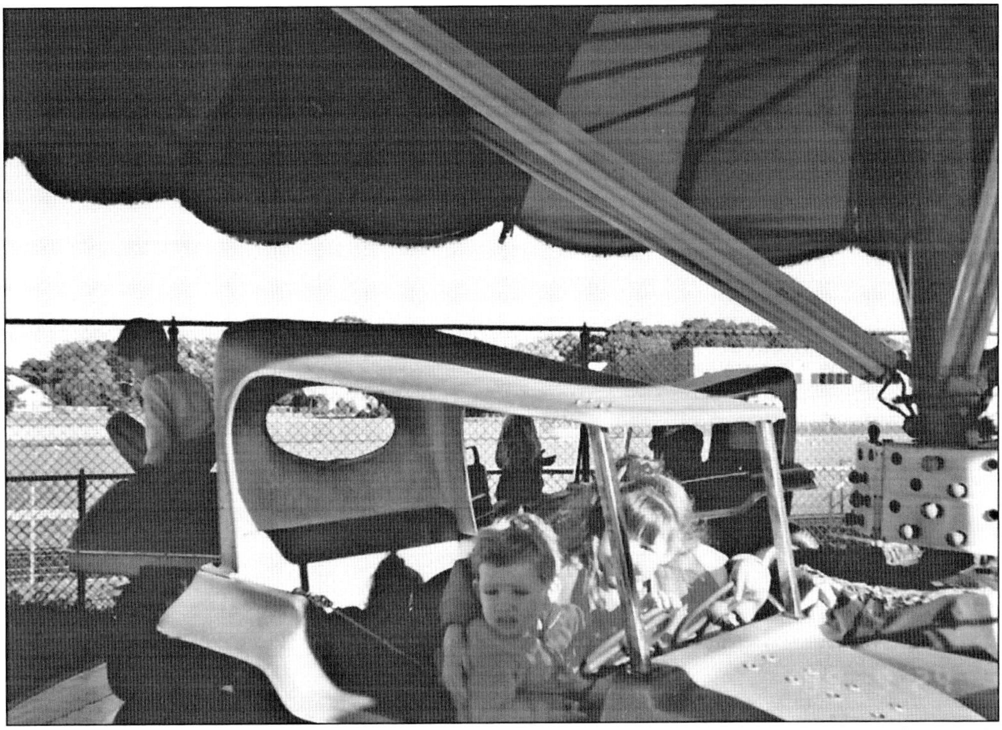

The umbrella that covered the dune buggy ride was made up of brightly colored stripes that made the ride visible beyond the park, even though it wasn't very tall. This was one of the safest rides in the park, so it was able to handle the youngest occupants riding on their own. (Both, courtesy of Price family.)

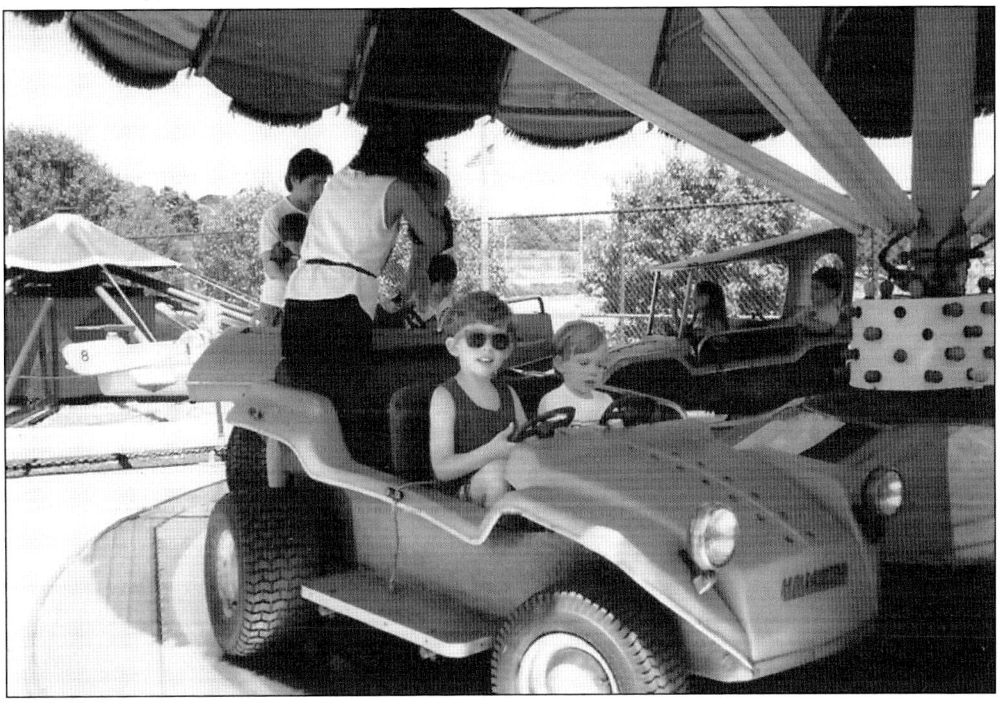

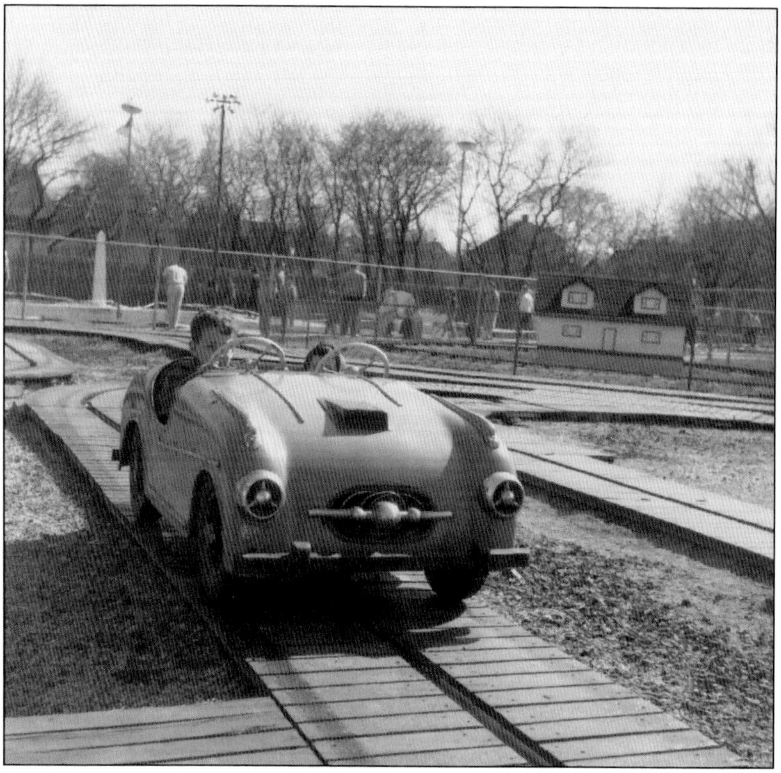

The next stop in the park was the beloved hot rod ride. On this attraction, two children drive their very own car around a large and winding track. Both riders have their own steering wheels, but the car moves on its own along a track. The cars were all a similar style but came in a variety of colors, such as orange, red, green, and yellow. (Courtesy of Larry Estrin.)

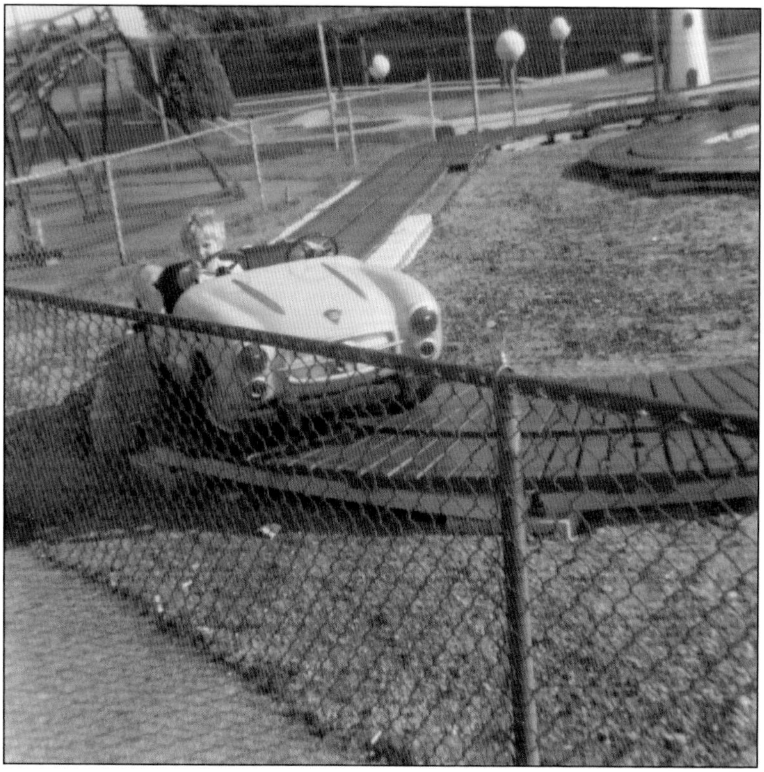

This ride, a crowd favorite, made it a little more difficult to get a good shot of riders unless the car was right along the fence. Many photographs captured riders blocked by shrubbery or the chain link fence that enclosed the ride. Children adored this ride because they actually got to drive a car, even though they had no control of the vehicle. (Courtesy of Mary Disanto.)

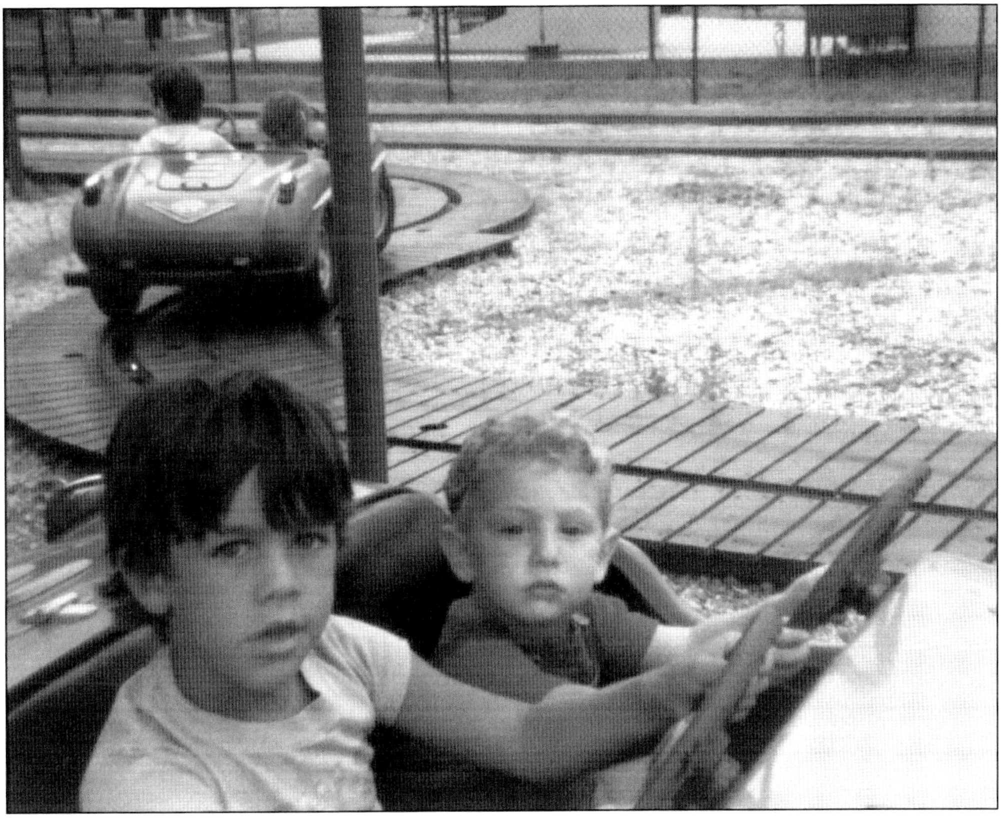

One commonly forgotten aspect of Nunley's is how riders shared tight quarters with complete strangers. Visitors looking over old family photo albums eventually come to a photograph where they do not recognize the person sitting next to them. This usually involves everyone passing the image around, trying to think of who it could be, before someone finally realizes that it was just another random visitor. (Author's collection.)

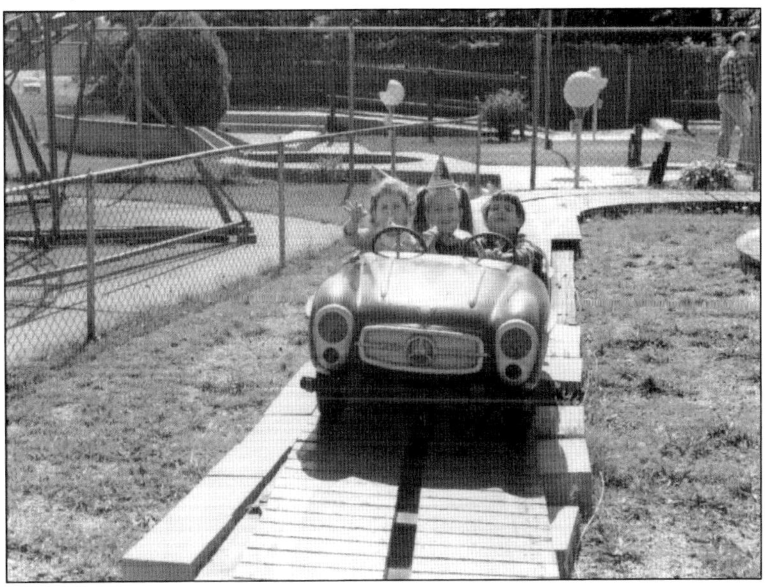

In this shot, three tiny riders are crammed into one car, which was probably against the rules. These cars were small, and past visitors to the park remember the quick sharp turns from this ride as it wound around the track, jostling its riders. (Courtesy of Dennis Ciccone Jr.)

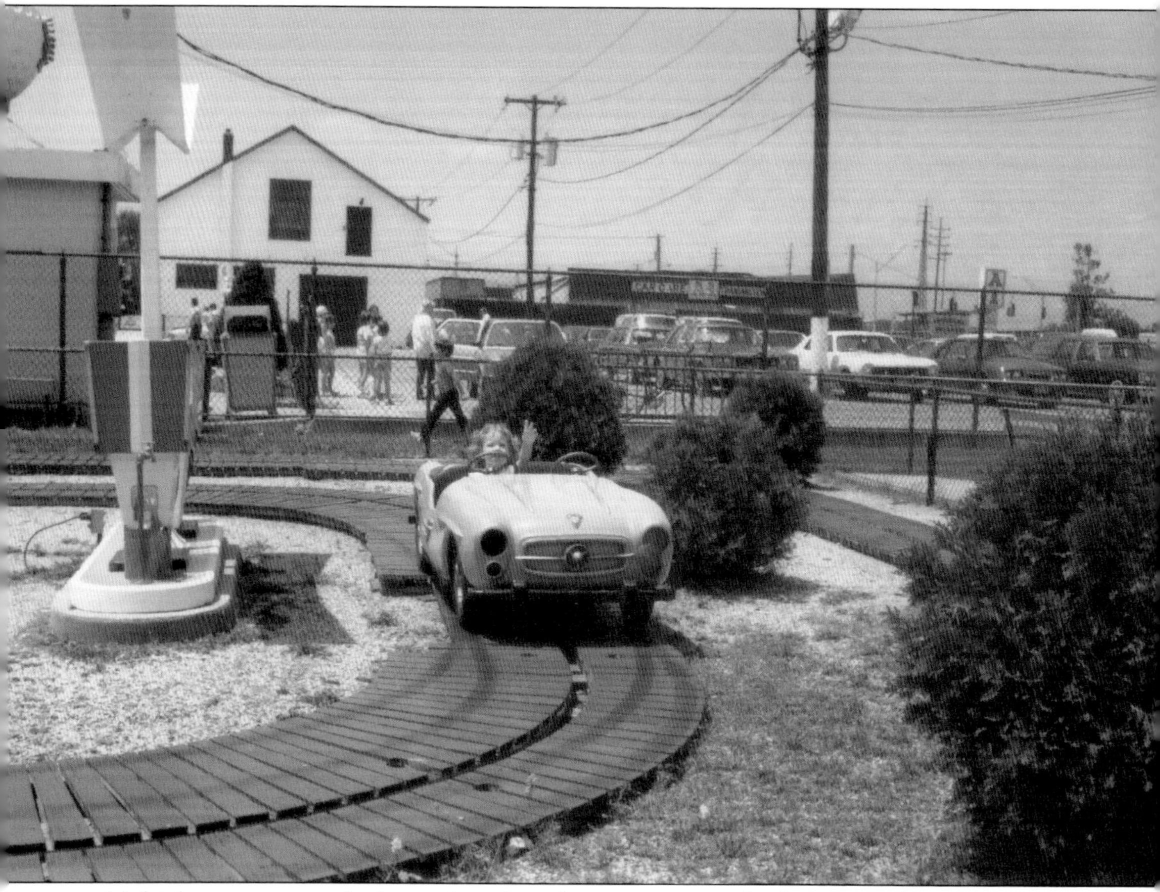

Multiple cars were on the hot rod track at the same time, and riders enjoyed great views of the park. Riders could see much of the miniature golf course that was along the eastern side of the park and even passed two tiny gas pumps along their journey, but there was no stopping. In this shot from the late 1980s, the mini-golf hut can be seen directly behind the gas pumps. Also visible are some nearby stores farther west on Sunrise Highway, as well as parked cars in the lot behind the park. Many visitors recall having a favorite color car that they would always insist on waiting to ride. (Courtesy of Kristen Williams.)

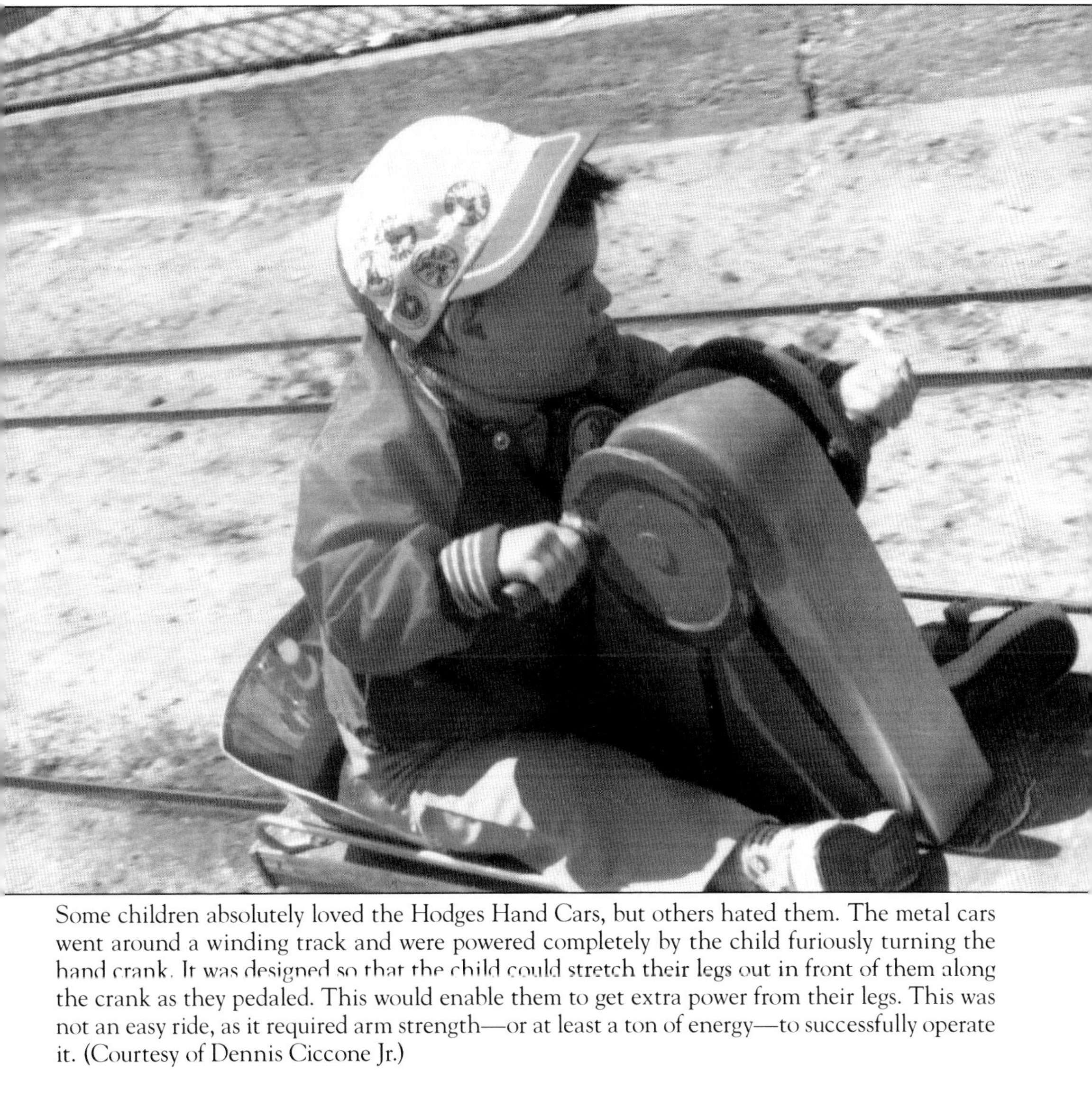

Some children absolutely loved the Hodges Hand Cars, but others hated them. The metal cars went around a winding track and were powered completely by the child furiously turning the hand crank. It was designed so that the child could stretch their legs out in front of them along the crank as they pedaled. This would enable them to get extra power from their legs. This was not an easy ride, as it required arm strength—or at least a ton of energy—to successfully operate it. (Courtesy of Dennis Ciccone Jr.)

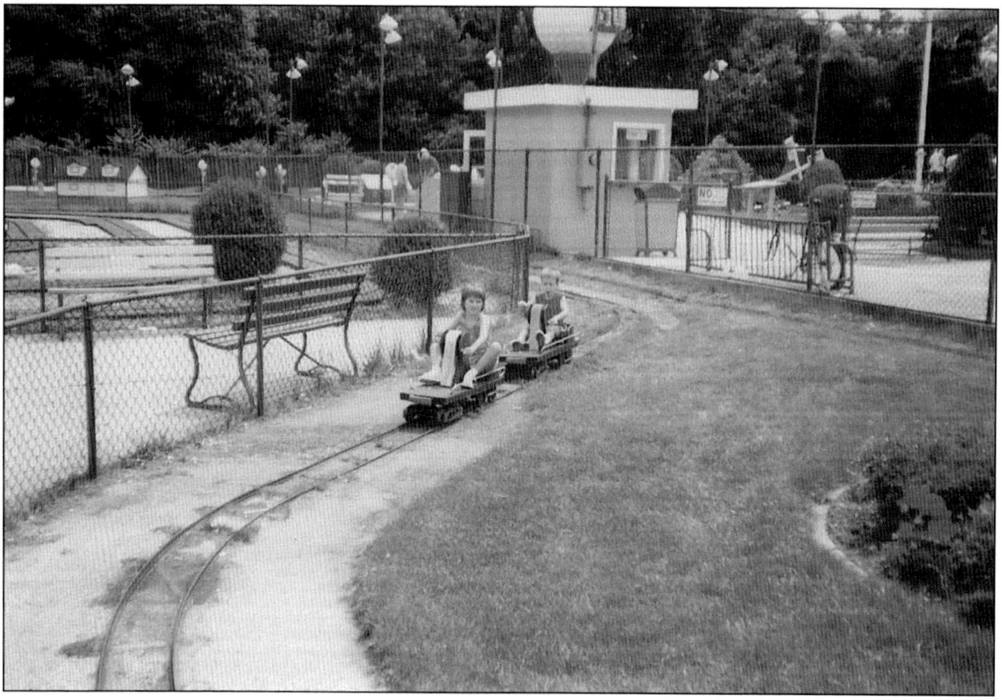

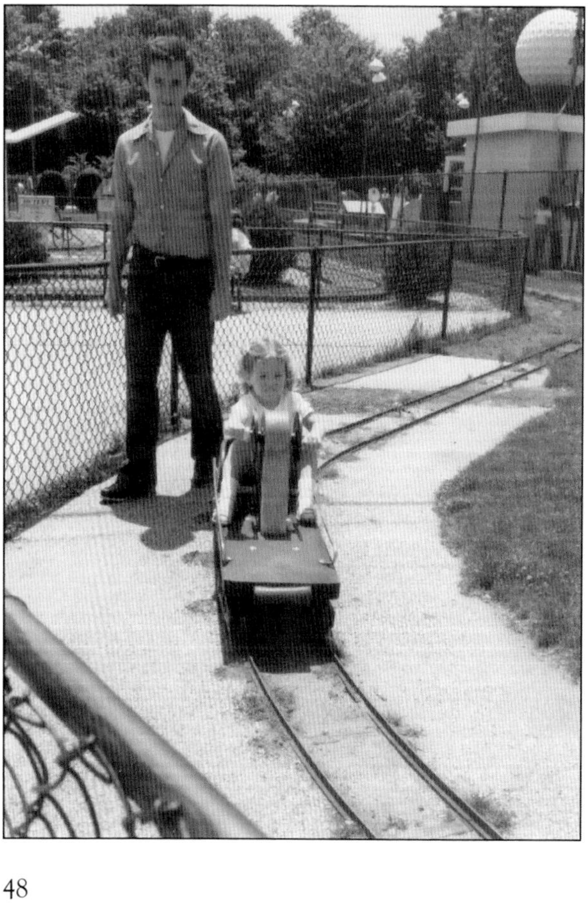

For the bigger and stronger kids, this was a fun ride, but for the younger ones who were constantly causing traffic jams because they were going too slow, it was awful. Some of those weaker kids may remember the feeling of being rear-ended by the car behind them, or when the ride operator would have to give them a push when they got stuck. The above image captures the moment before a fender bender occurs. In the picture below, a Nunley's ride operator warily looks on as a girl struggles with the crank. Many times, operators would have to follow behind the younger children for most of the ride, giving them much needed pushes to get through. (Both, courtesy of Kristen Williams.)

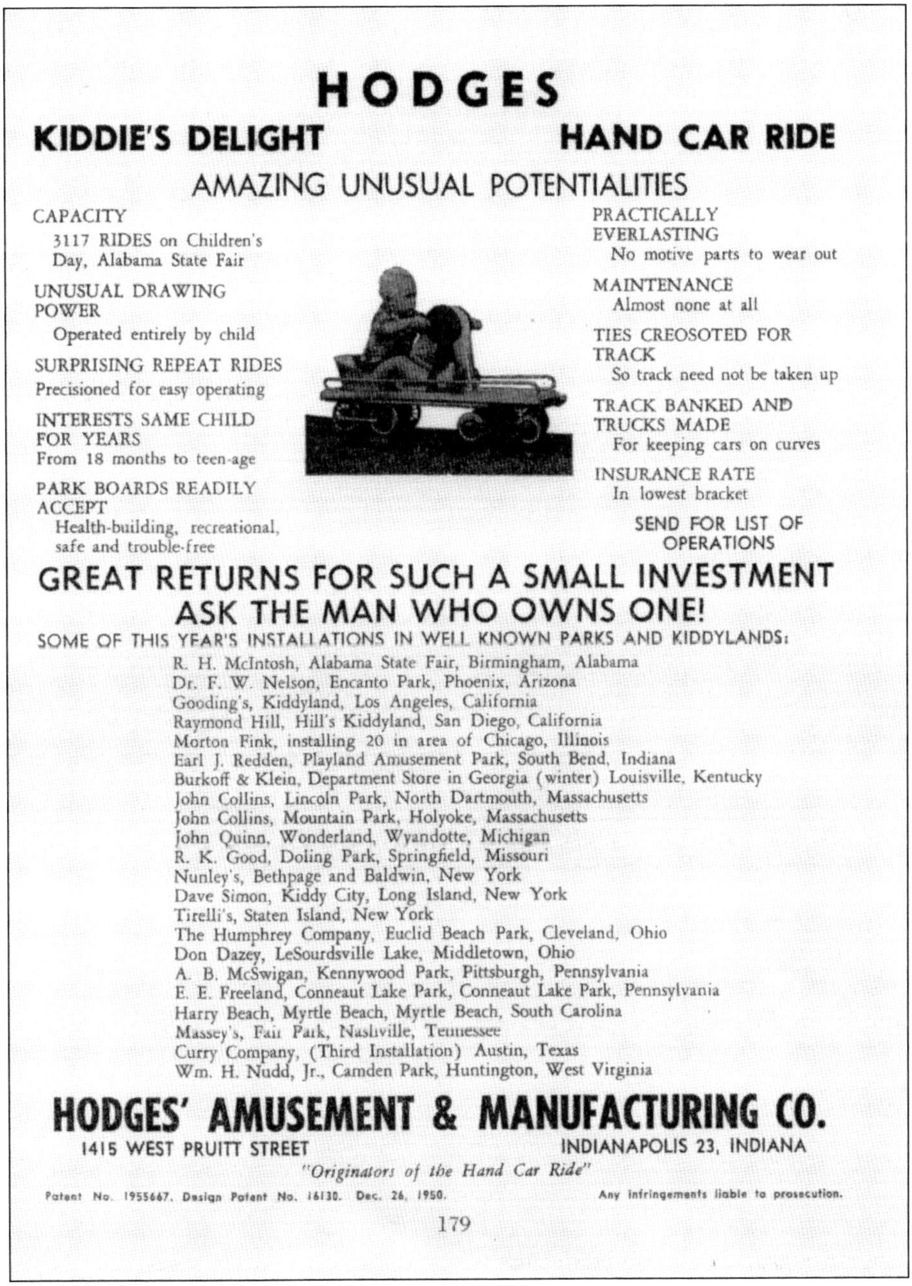

In this advertisement by Hodges Amusement & Manufacturing Co. for their hand car ride, the company highlights numerous reasons why amusement park owners should purchase this for their visitors. It boasts that it promotes "health-building" and only requires low insurance rates. In a smart ploy to gain business and make themselves clear as a national distributor of these unique goods, the company also listed other amusement parks that had already purchased the ride. The list at the bottom of the page includes both the Baldwin and Bethpage Nunley's parks. The company was based out of Indianapolis, Indiana, but the parks listed in the advertisement were from all over the country. The only other New York–based park that was on the list is referred to as "Kiddie City, Long Island." (Courtesy of Dennis Ciccone Jr.)

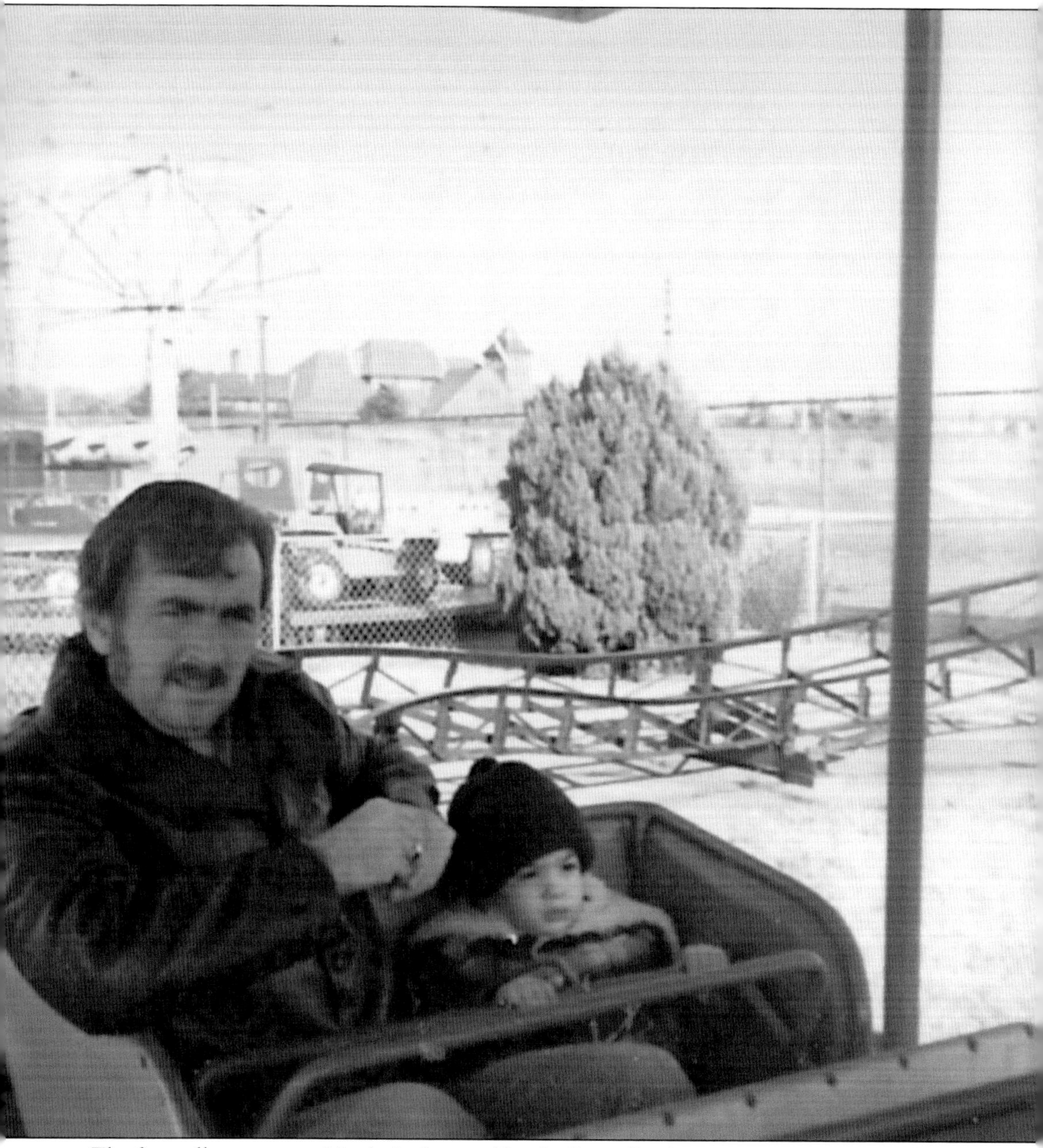

The first roller coaster at Nunley's, designed by the Pinto Brothers, was in operation at the park until some time after 1953, when the company went out of business. It was replaced with a new coaster that was a Schiff. The Miami-based B.A. Schiff & Associates built over 50 roller coasters before they went out of business. They used single-road wheels that were fixed to the car bodies. The coaster at Nunley's was on an oval track, and it was right up against the property border of the amusement park and Freeport High School. The cars were made of fiberglass, and eventually, they were altered so that they had white frames with a rainbow design on the front and along the sides. (Courtesy of Chuck Egbert.)

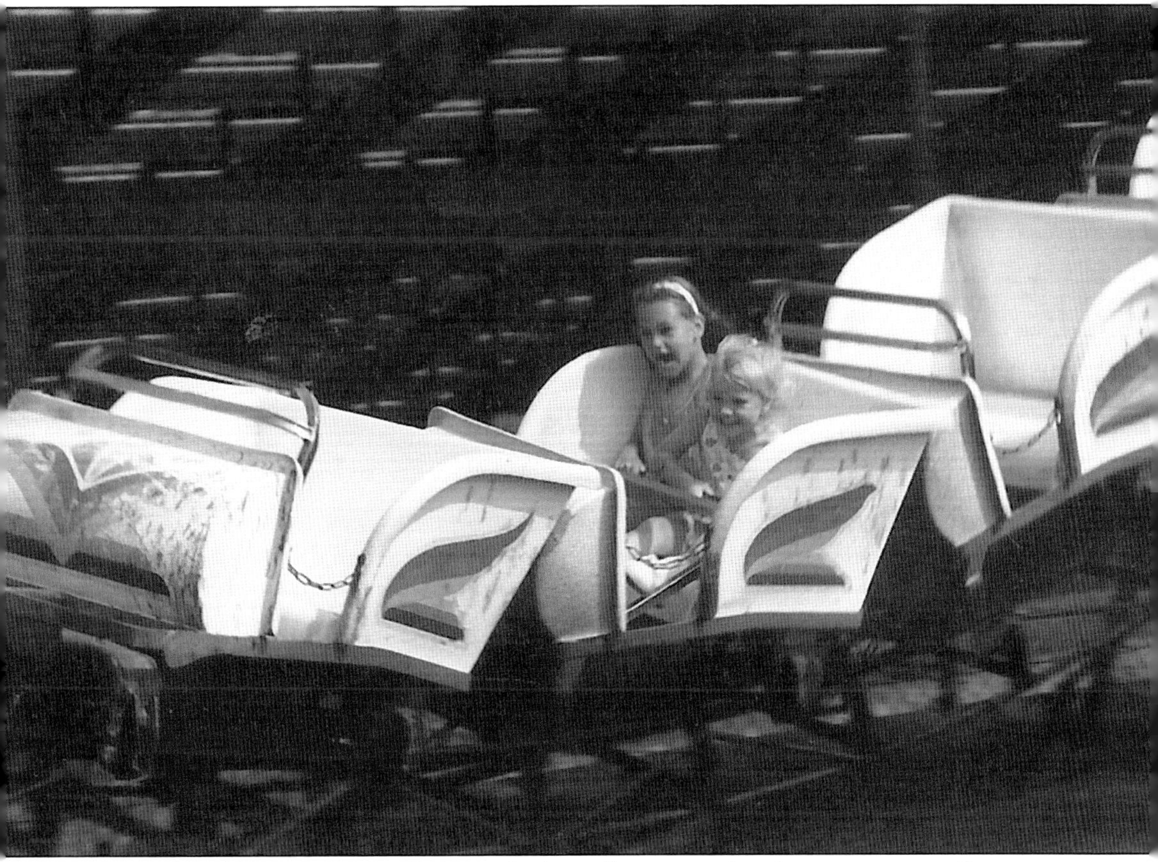

For many, the roller coaster at Nunley's was the first roller coaster that they ever went on. For some, it was the last roller coaster they ever went on after their traumatic experience. Almost everyone who visited Nunley's has a story about someone they know or a friend of a friend who screamed and cried so loud on the roller coaster, the ride had to be stopped. Amusement park connoisseurs considered this an incredibly mild coaster, even for a kiddie park. There were no loops, huge drops, or even any twists. Even though this wasn't for those seeking a big thrill, the ride was definitely rough. The sharp turns and uncomfortable seats made the turns that much harder, causing the coaster to painfully bounce its passengers around. (Courtesy of Nancy Radecker.)

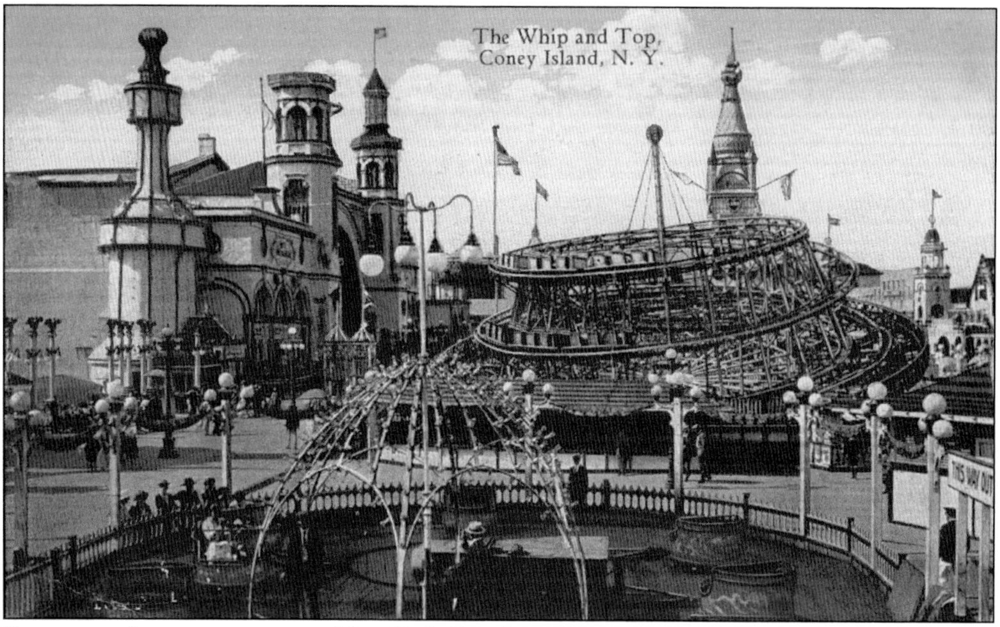

Four years after immigrating to New York City from Germany, 20-year-old William F. Mangels opened his own factory in Coney Island producing carousels. Beyond carousels, Mangels designed more than 40 types of amusements, including the Whip in 1914. His company also developed some of the first children's rides. This postcard shows the Whip at Luna Park, in the foreground. (Courtesy of Manhattan Post Card Co.)

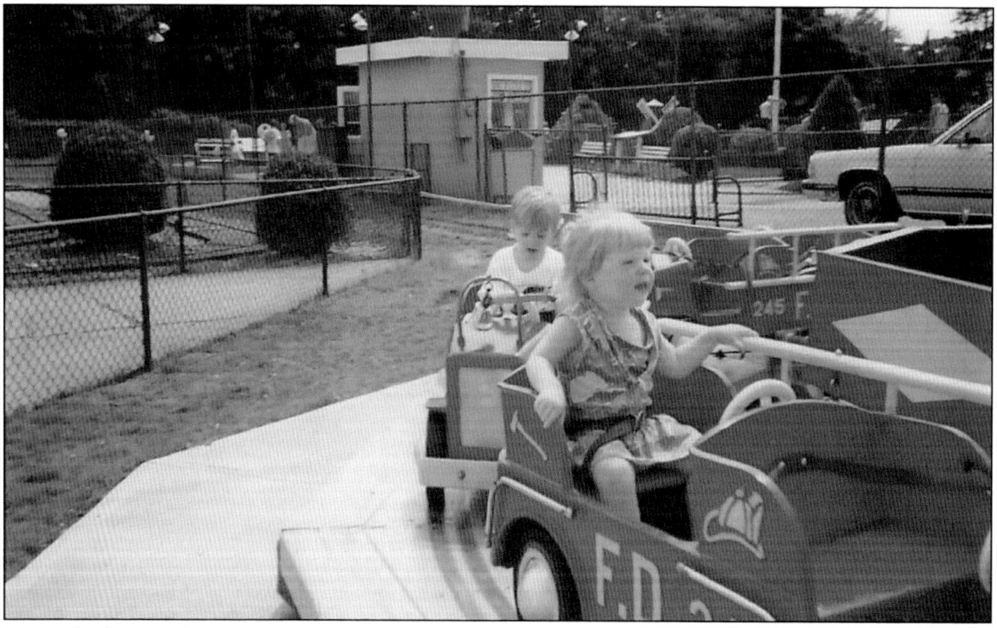

Mangels designed numerous amusement park rides during his career, including the fire engine ride. Nunley's visitors may not remember this ride at Baldwin Park. The ride was found at both Nunley's Rockaway Park and Nunley's Happyland in Bethpage, but it was a later addition to Nunley's in Baldwin. The fire engines replaced the hand car ride at the park in the 1990s. (Courtesy of Price family.)

Three

Nunley's Famous Carousel

The most iconic element of Nunley's Amusement Park was and always will be the beloved carousel. This 1912 Stein & Goldstein carousel is a cherished landmark for Long Islanders, but its importance goes way beyond the towns surrounding its Baldwin home. During the golden age of amusement parks in the late 1800s, there were more than 6,000 hand-carved carousels across the country; today, there are fewer than 200. When family-run parks shifted to corporate theme parks, it began a slow demise of the traditional carousel. As the number of carousels in the country began to decrease, the carousel became less of an amusement feature and more of a cherished relic. The carousel began to be looked at like artwork and became more appreciated for its traditional craftsmanship. Soon, carousels began to be broken apart so that individual horses could be sold off to collectors. The carousel that once stood at Nunley's Amusement Park has had multiple homes in its journey throughout New York.

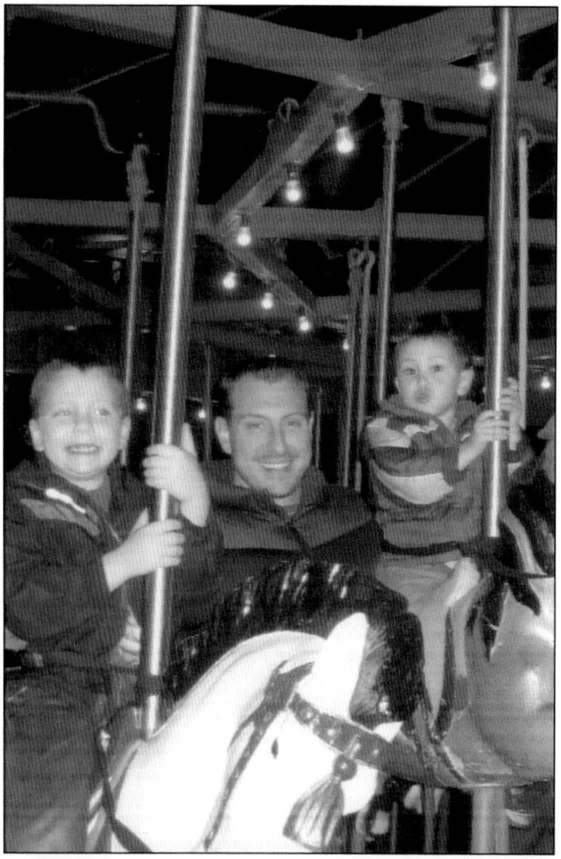

According to the National Carousel Association, there are 48 carousels still in operation in New York State, 11 of which are within the five boroughs, but most of them can be found within public parks. There are three carousels on Long Island: Nunley's in its new location in Museum Row; one in Mitchell Park, Greenport, designed by Herschell-Spillman and dating to 1920; and an M.C. Illions and Sons carousel in Hempstead State Lake Park, West Hempstead, from around 1914. The image at left shows the museum at Greenport, and below is the carousel found in Hempstead State Lake Park. (Both, author's collection.)

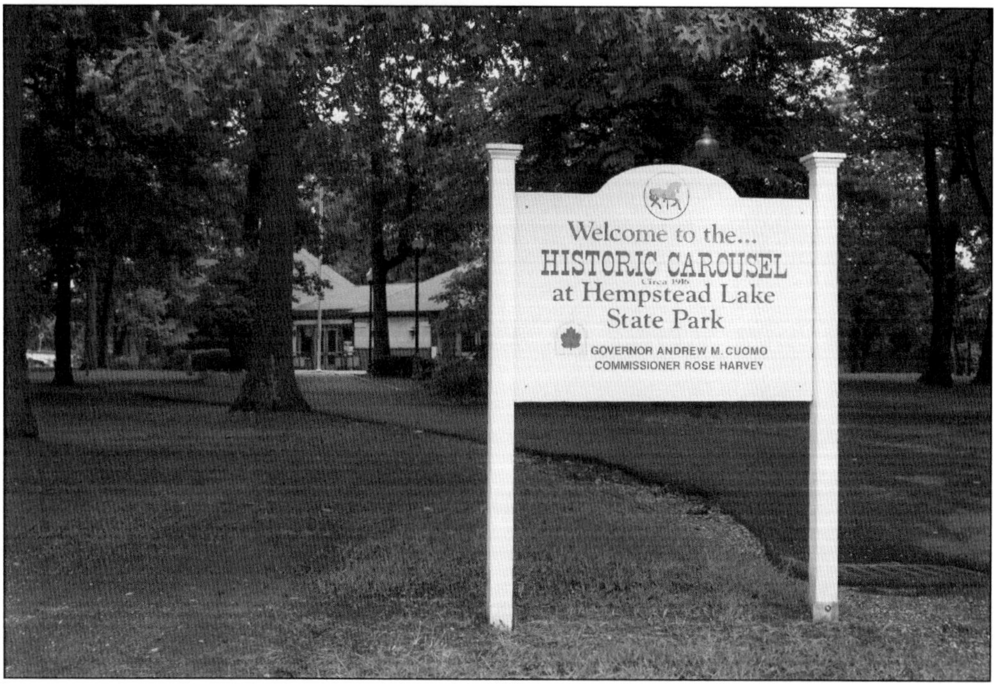

The partnership of Solomon Stein and Harry Goldstein began in Brooklyn around 1905 when they were working at Mangels Carousel Works. They established their own business, the Artistic Carousel Manufacturing Company, on Hopkins Street. This sticker is on a support beam on the interior of the Nunley's carousel. Their carousels are referred to as "Stein & Goldstein" by historians, and are described as being incredibly lifelike. (Courtesy of Steven Lercari.)

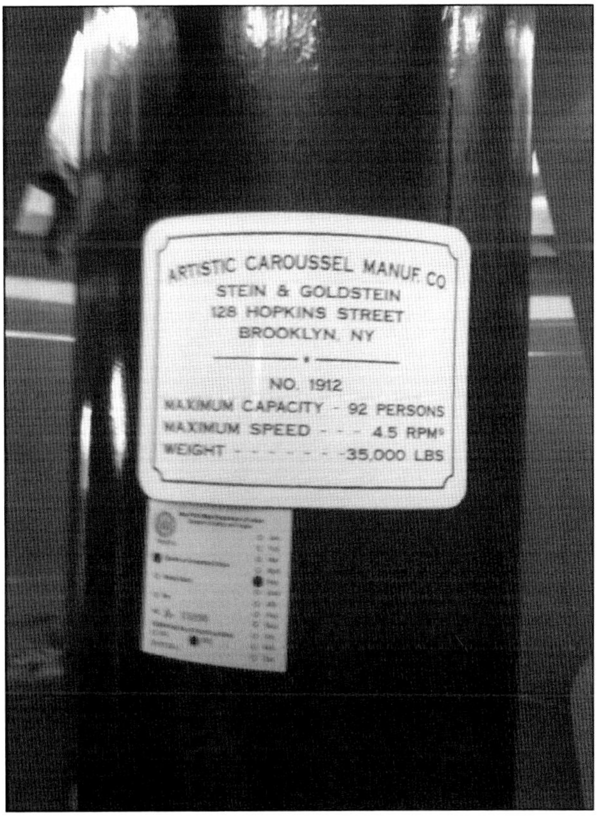

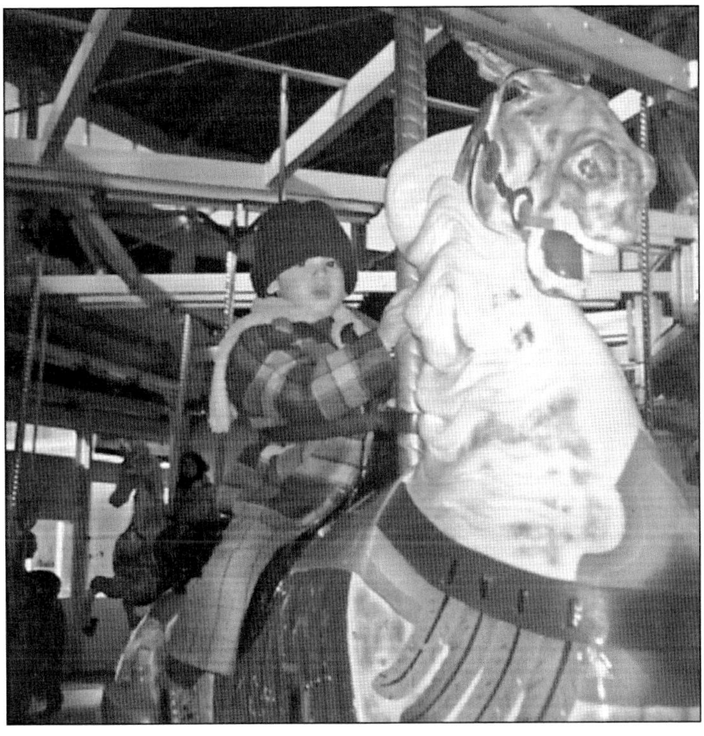

Their horses are large and muscular with big heads and bared teeth. Designers softened the look of these warhorses by adding flowers and ribbons. Trademark designs are buckles and the absence of forelocks, the part of the mane that falls between the ears. Stein & Goldstein carousels are considered to be the Coney Island style, along with W.F. Mangels, Charles Looff, M.C. Illions, and Charles Carmel. This picture shows a Nunley's horse in 1976. (Courtesy of Chuck Egbert.)

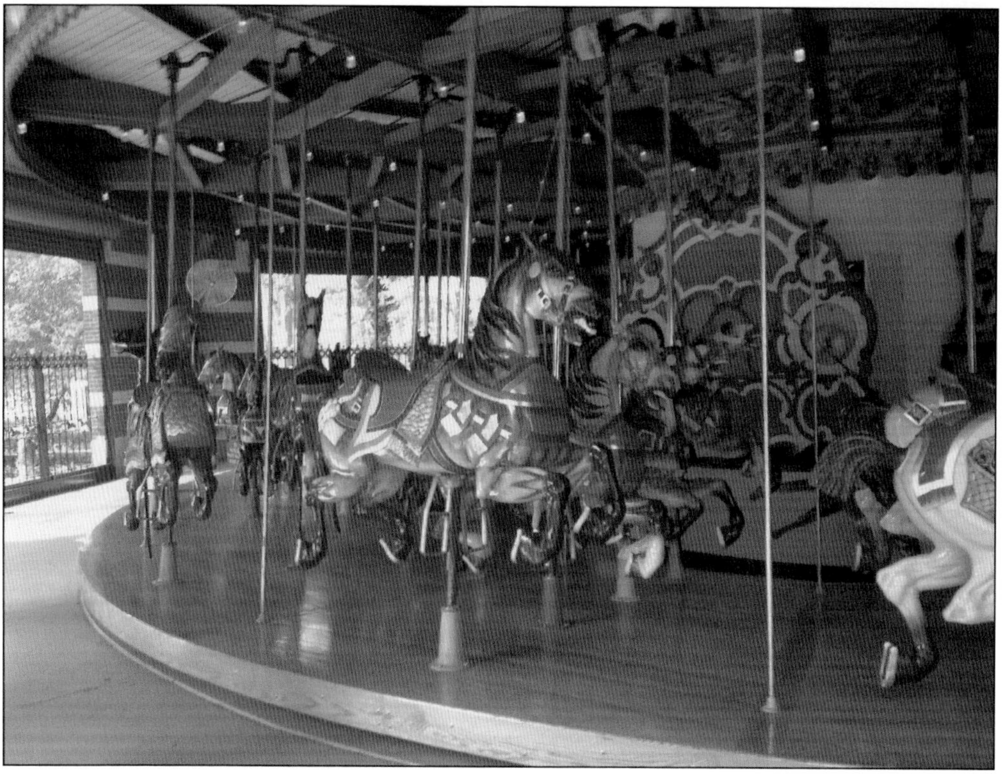

There are only four Stein & Goldstein carousels still operating throughout the country, two of which are in New York: Nunley's, and the carousel in Central Park. The Central Park carousel, seen above, began its life in Coney Island, where it operated from 1908 until 1951. It then moved to Central Park, where it has remained since. This carousel is one of the largest in the entire country. It is made up of 52 jumping horses, five standing horses, and two chariots over four rows. (Above, courtesy of Jim Henderson; below, courtesy of Hollywood family.)

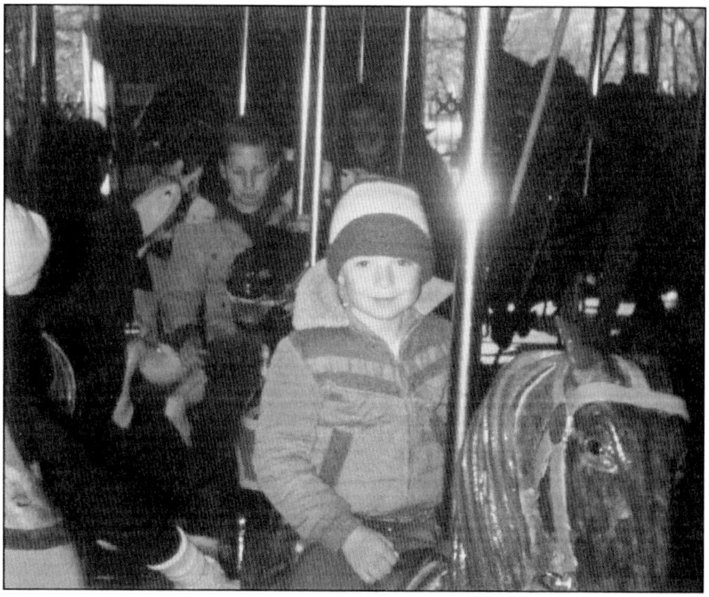

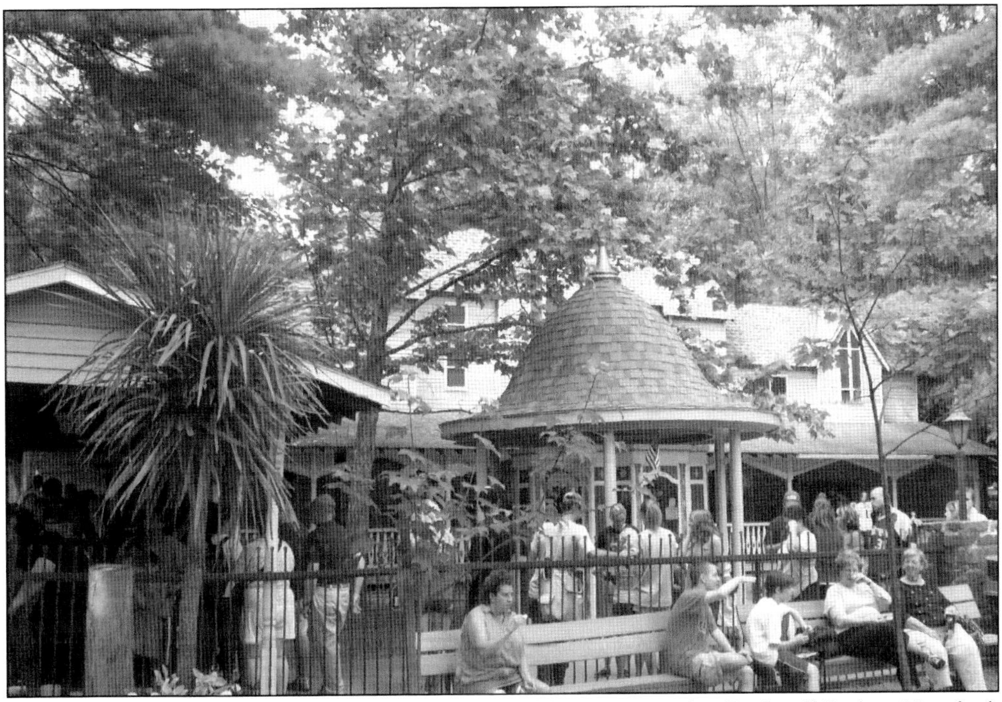

Outside of New York State, there is one Stein & Goldstein carousel in Bushnell Park in Hartford, Connecticut, dating back to 1914, and one in Knoebels Amusement Resort in Elysburg, Pennsylvania, from around 1910. Many of the carousels still in operation today can be found in municipal parks or other public properties. Above, the Knoebels carousel celebrated its 100th anniversary in 2012. Below, Bushnell Park, which was the first municipal park in the country, has its carousel in a beautiful enclosed building. (Above, public domain; below, courtesy of Library of Congress.)

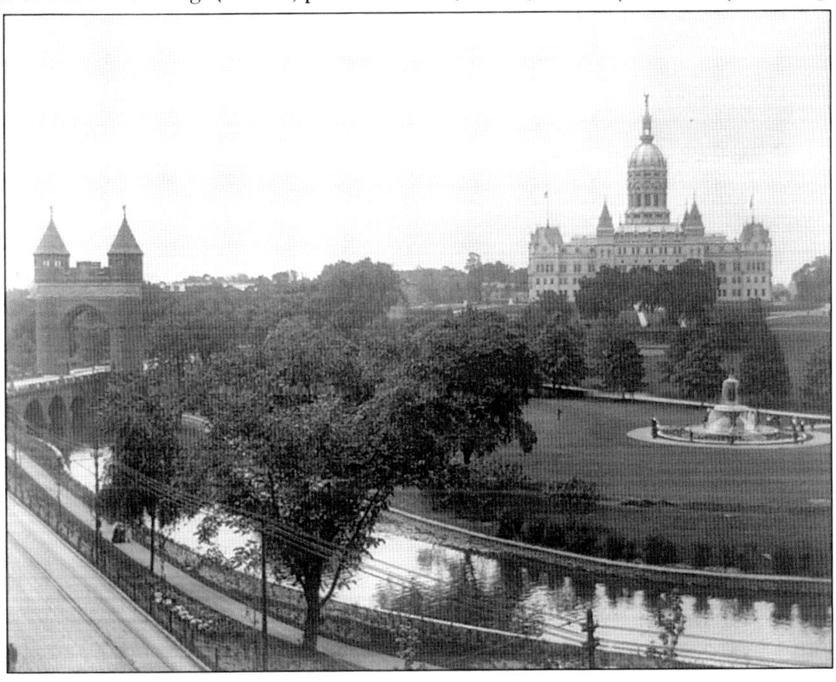

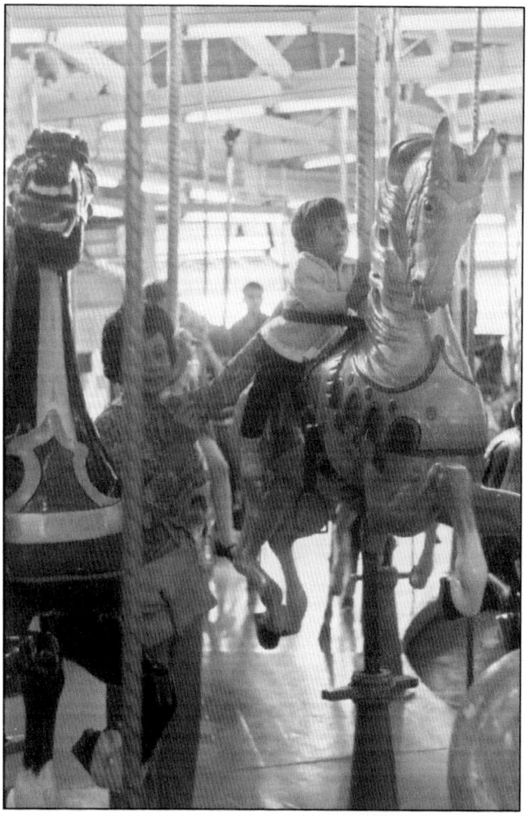

The Nunley's carousel, first known as "Murphy's Carousel," was brought to Baldwin by William Nunley in 1939. It falls into the carousel class of classic wood and is made up of 16 sections. In its three-row composition, it features 30 jumping horses, 11 standing horses, one lion, and two chariots. (Courtesy of Larry Estrin.)

One of the most beloved features of the Nunley's carousel is its music, which was provided by a band organ—specifically, a Wurl 153 w/MIDI. (Courtesy of Gary Monti.)

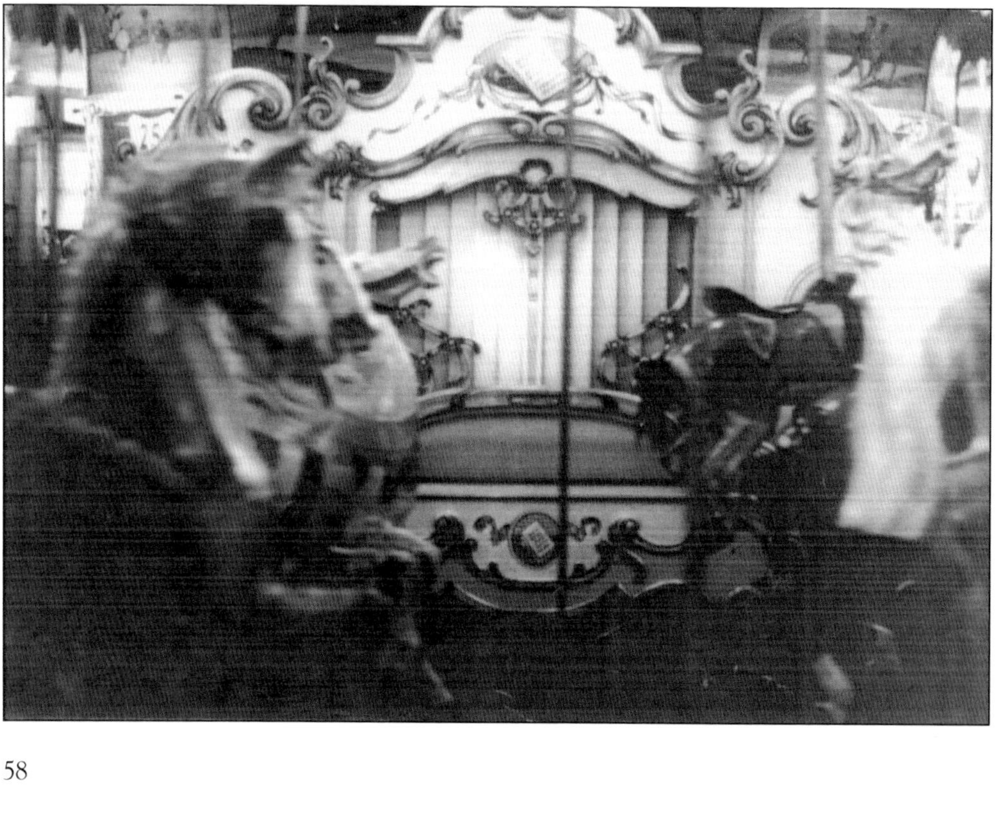

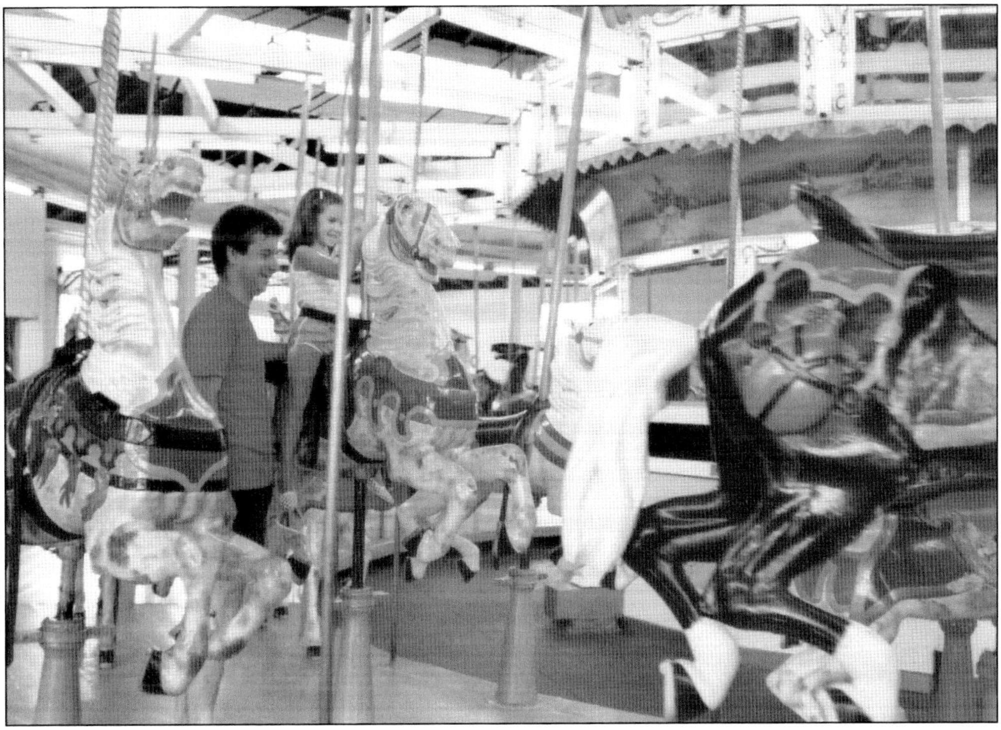

The carousel has both stationary horses, as well as horses that jump. It has always been referred to as a Stein & Goldstein carousel, and it does, in fact, have 24 horses and two chariots that were carved by the Stein & Goldstein Manufacturing Company in Brooklyn. (Courtesy of Kristen Williams.)

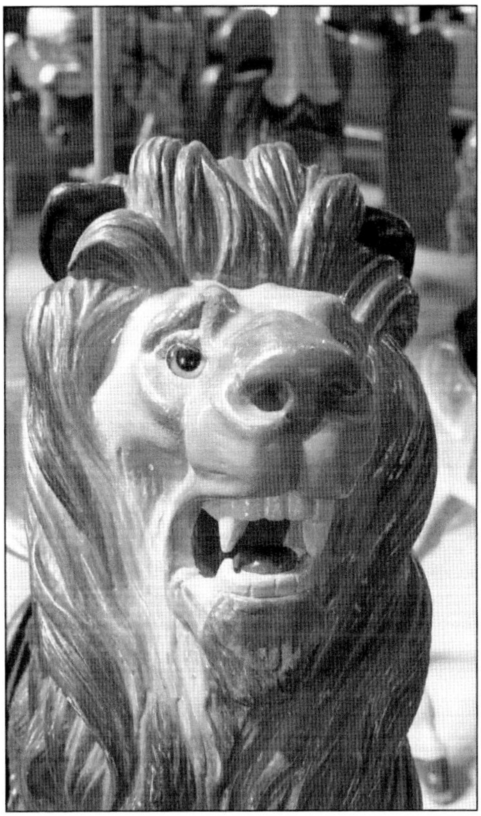

Not all the components were found to be by Stein & Goldstein, however. The lion and three standing horses were by the Dentzel Company of Philadelphia, and there are 10 jumping horses and three stationary horses that were carved by M.C. Illions and Sons of Coney Island. (Courtesy of Gary Monti.)

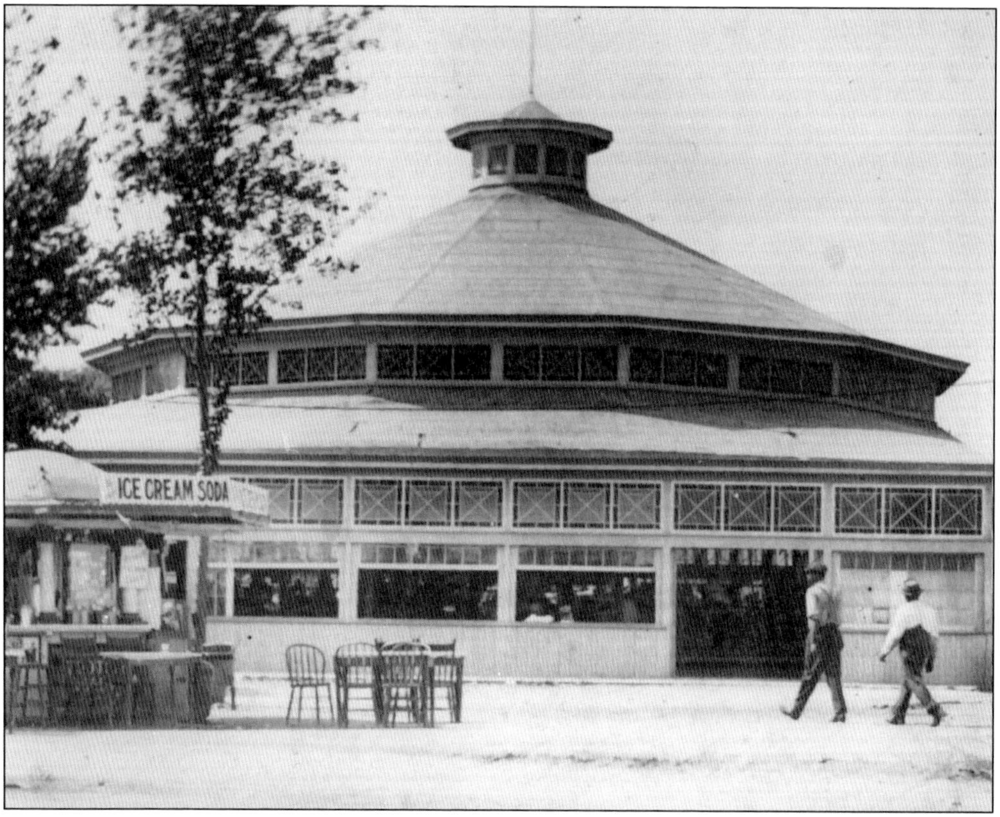

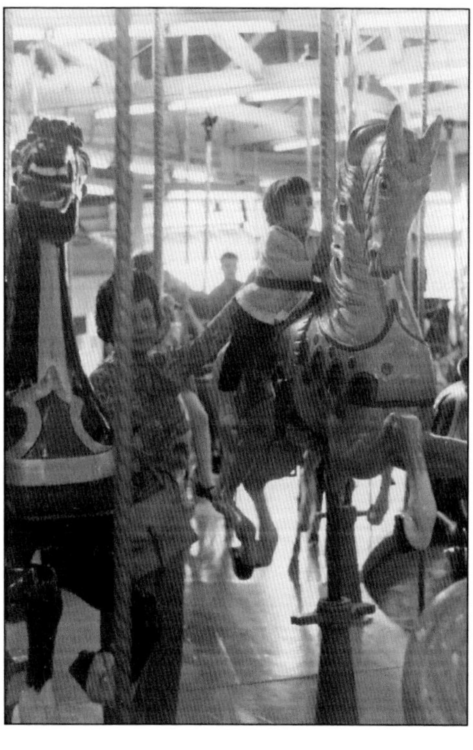

The carousel began its life in Canarsie, Brooklyn—specifically, Golden City Park. This amusement park was built in 1907 to rival those found in Coney Island. Located around Jamaica Bay, it was closer to Manhattan, with elevated trains and trolley routes nearby. The park featured dozens of rides, a bandstand, shows, and even a circus. The carousel remained in this location from 1912 until the park closed in 1938. (Courtesy of Gary Monti.)

In 1939, the carousel journeyed to its new home at what would become Nunley's Amusement Park in Baldwin; it remained until the park closed in 1995. Originally, when the carousel first moved to the Baldwin location, the carousel building was attached to a restaurant called the Dutch Mill. The carousel pavilion was the same that had housed the ride in Golden City Park—the building was dismantled and reconstructed in Baldwin. (Courtesy of Larry Estrin.)

The most memorable feature of the carousel was, without a doubt, its ring arm. Children could reach out and (hopefully) snatch a ring. If they were lucky enough to catch a brass ring, it won them a free ride. Being old enough, or at least tall enough, to finally reach the ring was a rite of passage for Nunley's patrons. To the chagrin of many, the ring arm was deactivated around 1986 due to insurance liability concerns. Tom Hollywood brought his seven children to Nunley's from 1970 until the park closed. He witnessed firsthand as each child strove to catch this trophy, marking the beginning of adulthood. Here, his youngest son, Matt, finally gets a chance to reach for the ring. (Author's collection.)

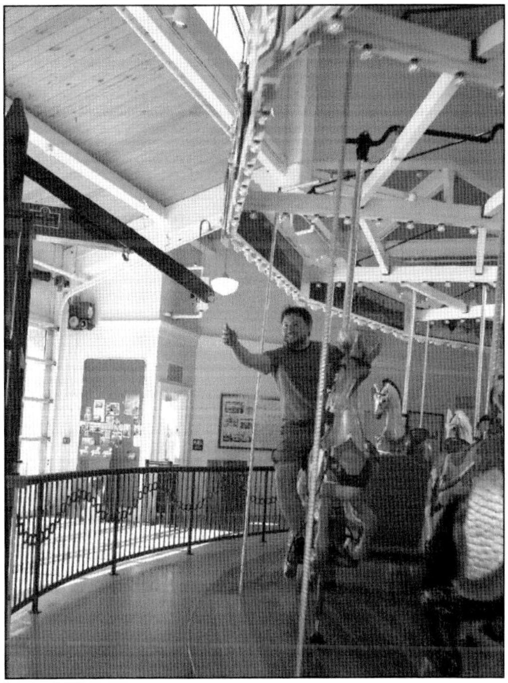

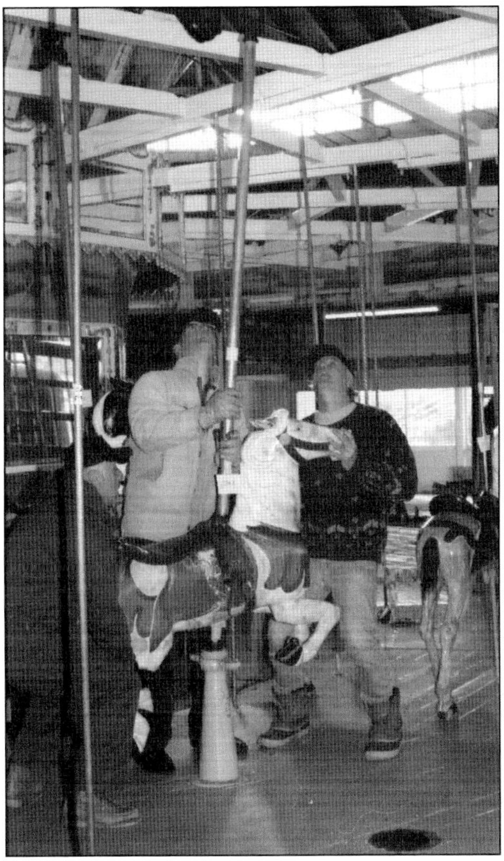

When Nunley's closed down in 1995, the fate of the carousel was uncertain. Eventually, it was documented, broken down, and packed up, and then it remained in storage with the Nassau County Department of Parks and Recreation from 1995 until 2007. (Courtesy of Gary Monti.)

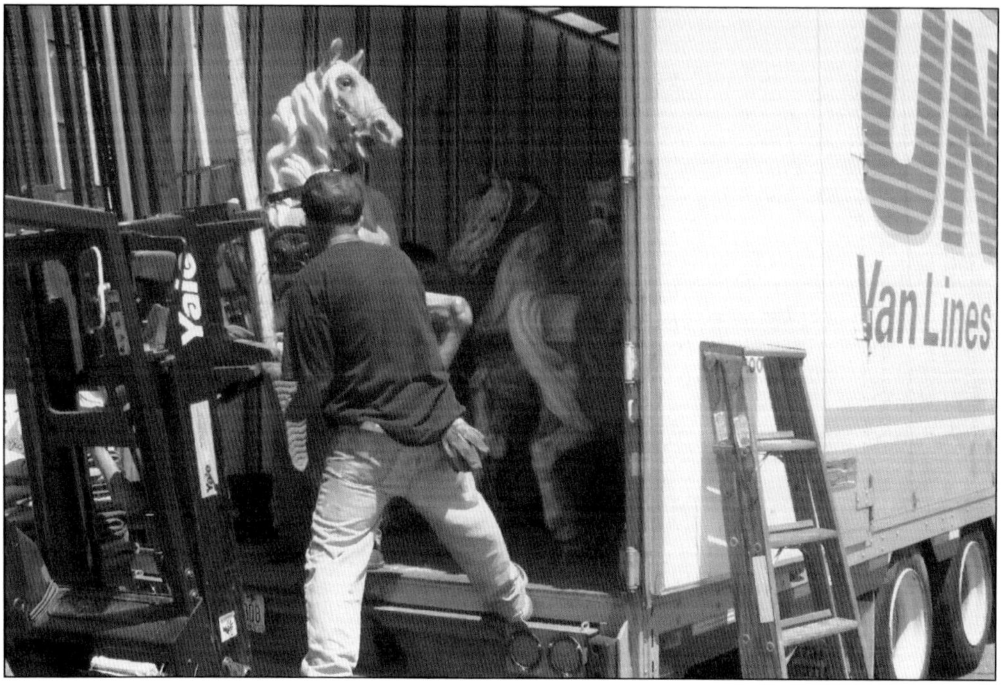

In 2007, it was time once again for the carousel to take a journey; however, this time, it was a much farther trip. The carousel headed to Ohio for restoration by The Carousel Works. It remained there from 2007 until 2009. (Courtesy of Dennis Ciccone Jr.)

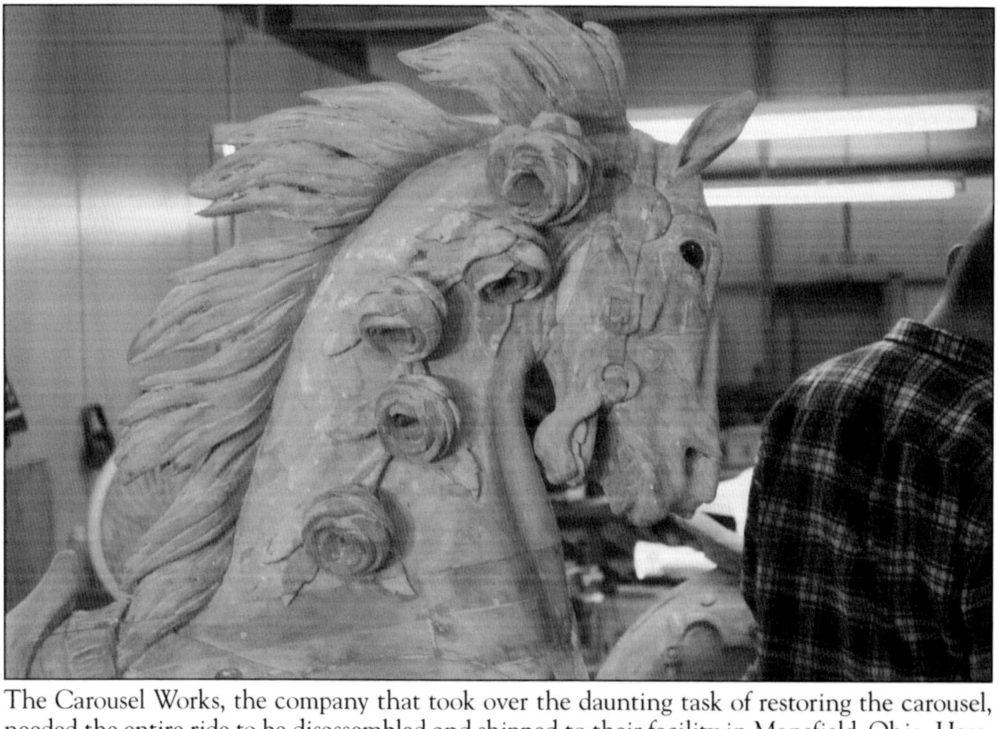

The Carousel Works, the company that took over the daunting task of restoring the carousel, needed the entire ride to be disassembled and shipped to their facility in Mansfield, Ohio. Here, a horse has been stripped of its paint and cleaned. (Courtesy of Kate Blakely.)

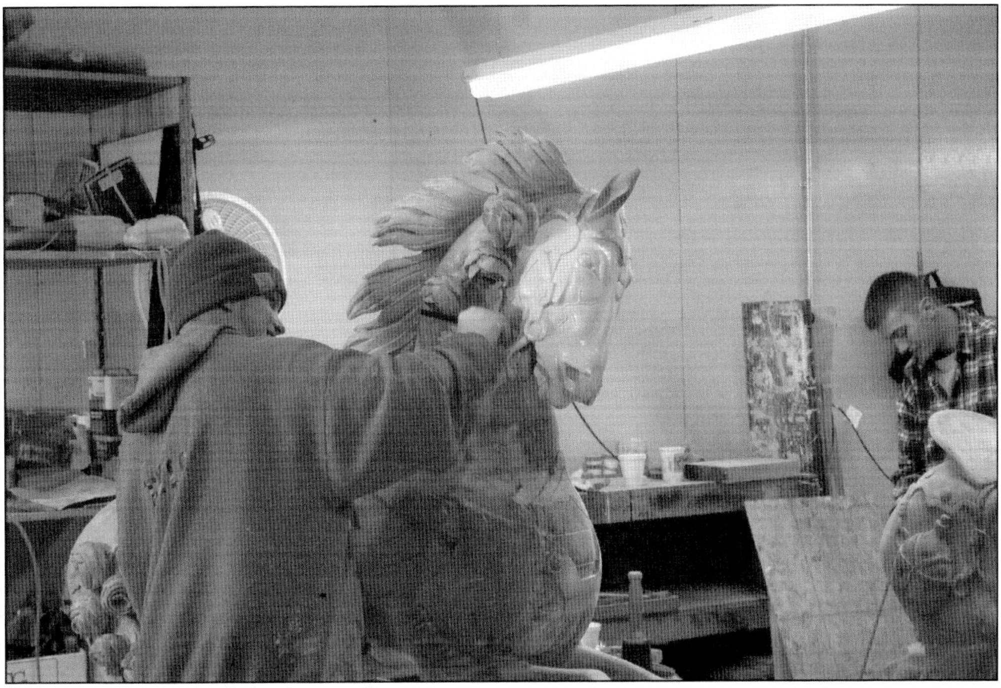

The next step after all the layers of paint were stripped was to sand the wood on each piece in preparation for future painting, as well as to complete any repairs that might be needed. After that, the wood was coated with primer. (Courtesy of Kate Blakely.)

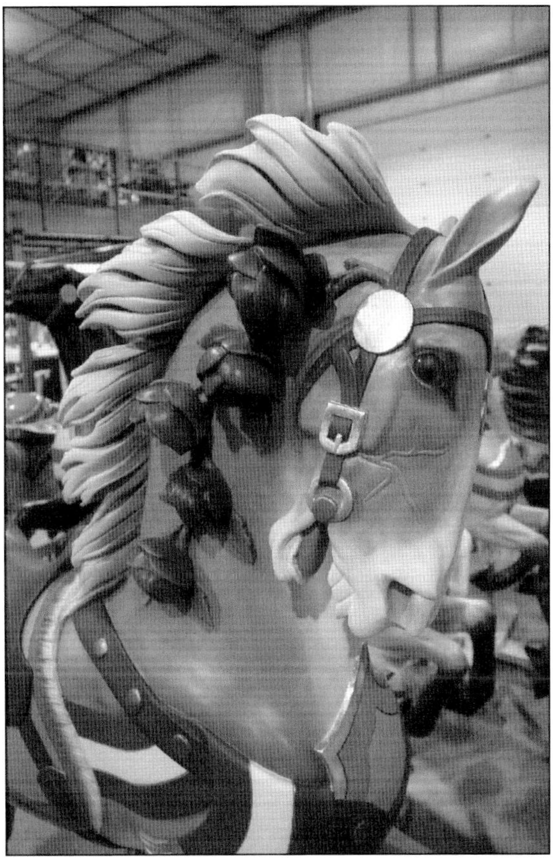

The final stage of the restoration process was to repaint each piece. This was no easy task and required the work of a skilled painter to replicate the depth and detail of each large piece. Most of the horses, as well as the lion and carriages, had elaborate designs decorating them. (Courtesy of Kate Blakely.)

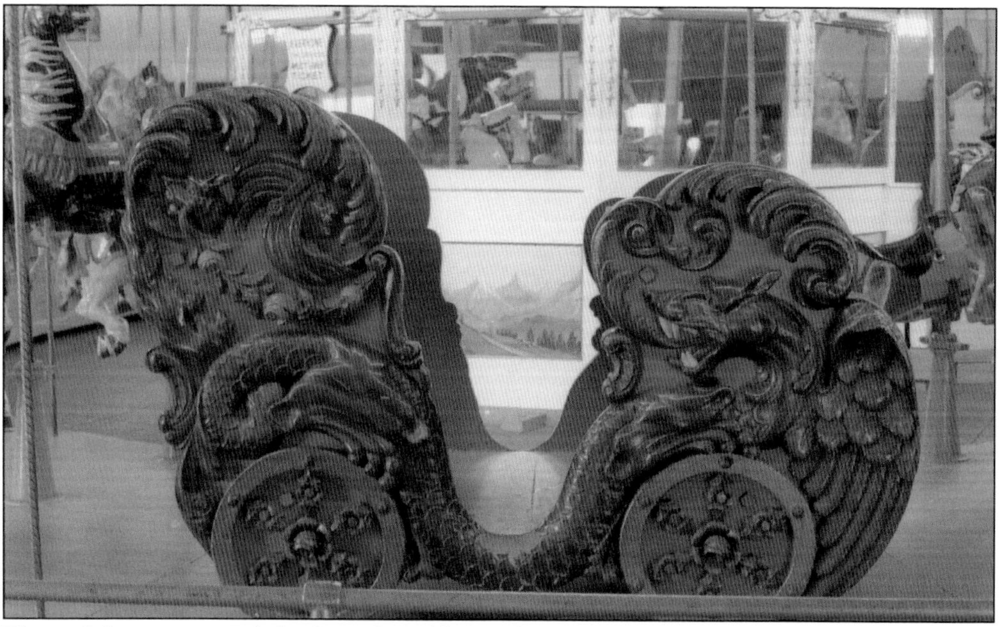

This red chariot was made by Stein & Goldstein about 1910. It has an intricate carving of a large dragon draped along the lower edge, with wings extending to form the front of the chariot. The tongue of the dragon becomes a garland of Stein & Goldstein trademarked cabbage roses. This piece, sponsored by Tony Vourou of E&A Restoration Inc. during restoration, was christened "Chief."

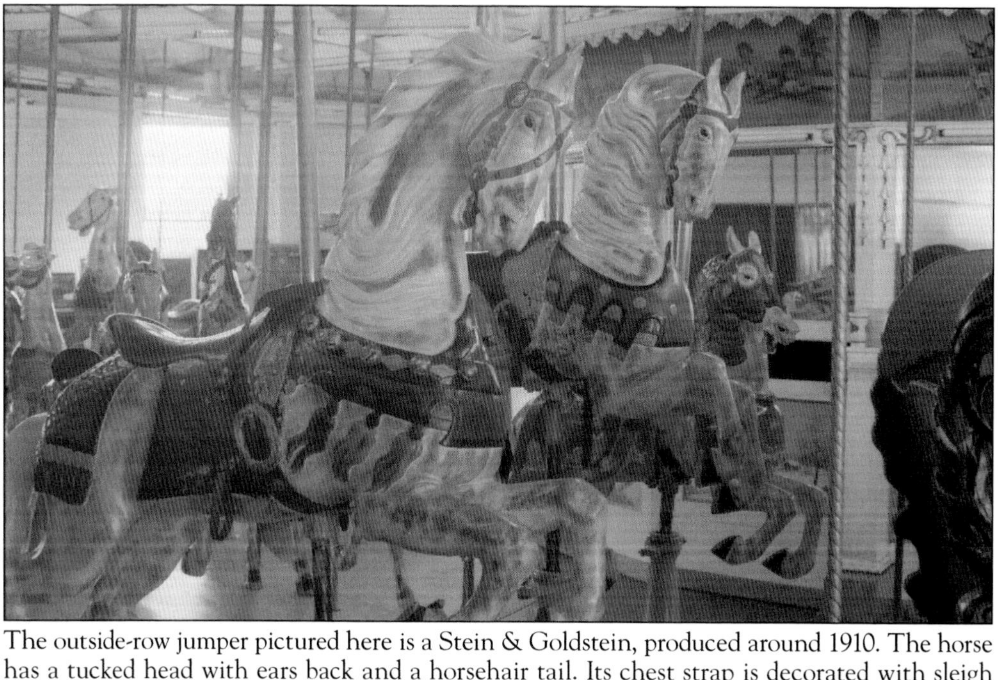

The outside-row jumper pictured here is a Stein & Goldstein, produced around 1910. The horse has a tucked head with ears back and a horsehair tail. Its chest strap is decorated with sleigh bells, diamonds, and hanging tassels. It was sponsored by the Houser/Heiberg family, who named it "Sir Gabriel Full of Grace."

This c. 1910 second-row jumper was designed by Stein & Goldstein. The horse has a tucked head with its mane blowing forward on its right side, a plain saddle, and a fringed chest strap. It was sponsored by the Hewitt Elementary School in Rockville Centre, Long Island; the students dubbed it "Jennie E. Hewitt."

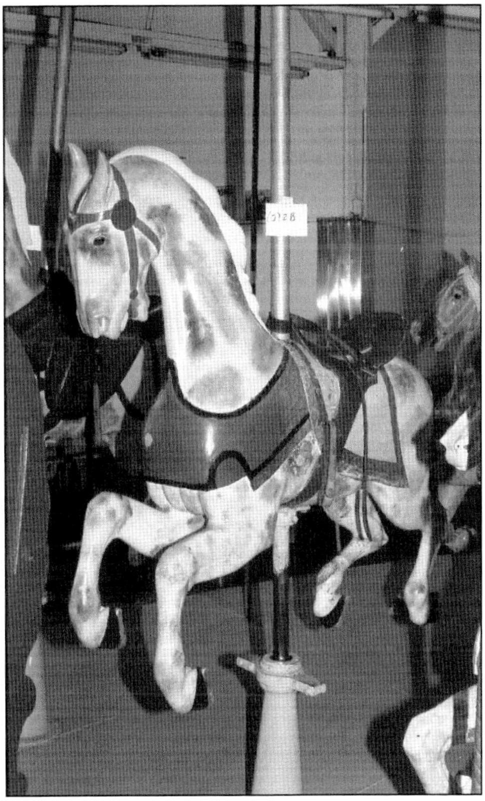

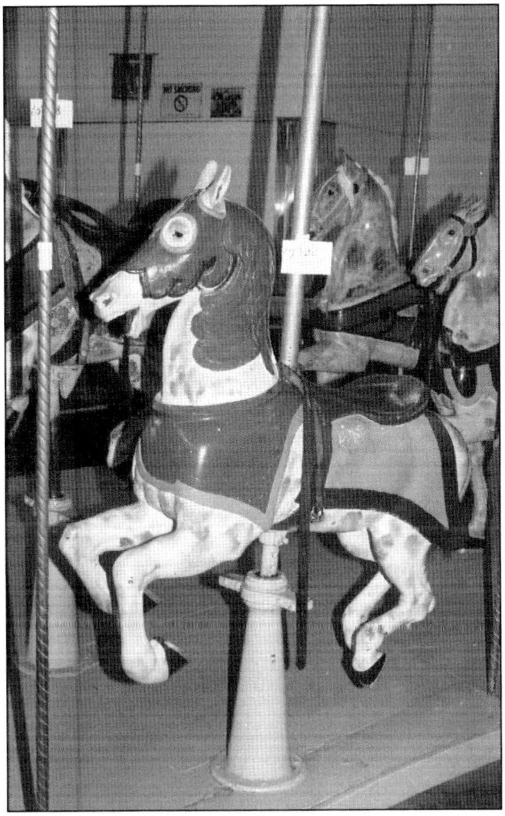

The inner-row armored jumper was created by M.C. Illions & Sons sometime between 1895 and 1900. The horse is in the Feltman style, where the head is upwards, and it has full armor on its neck and head. It also features carvings on the side showing a bearded man and a lion. The horse was sponsored by the Shubert Elementary School in Baldwin, Long Island, and the students named it "Shubert Student Council."

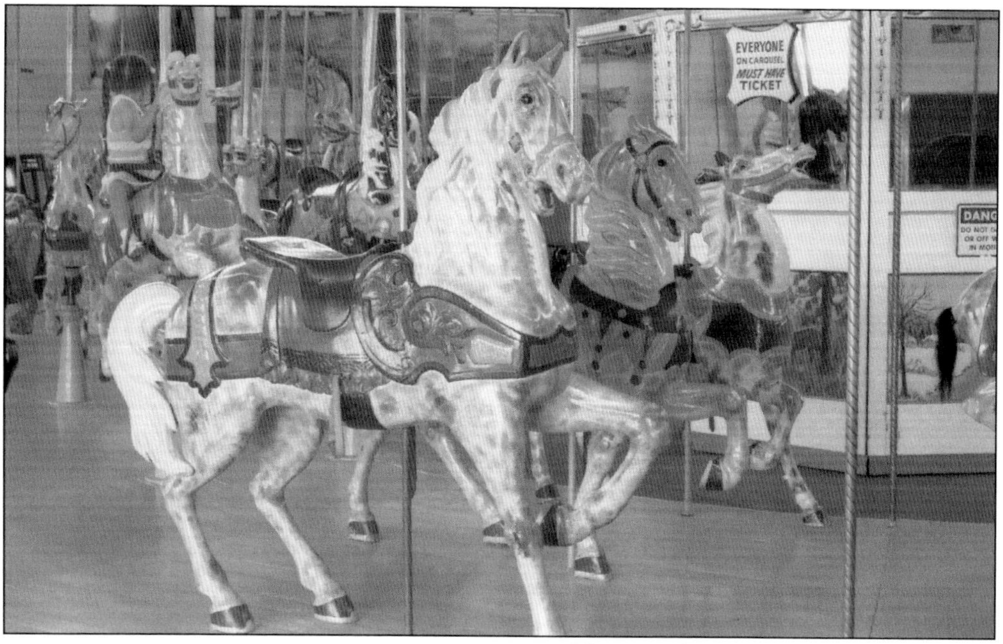

This outside-row stander was designed by Dentzel around 1910 to 1915. The horse is in the thoroughbred style created by Dentzel. It has a gentle face, long forelock, lengthy mane, and carved wood tail, and its strap is decorated with flowers and scrollwork. It was sponsored by Madracchia Sawmill Intermediate School in Commack, Long Island; their students christened it "Bailey."

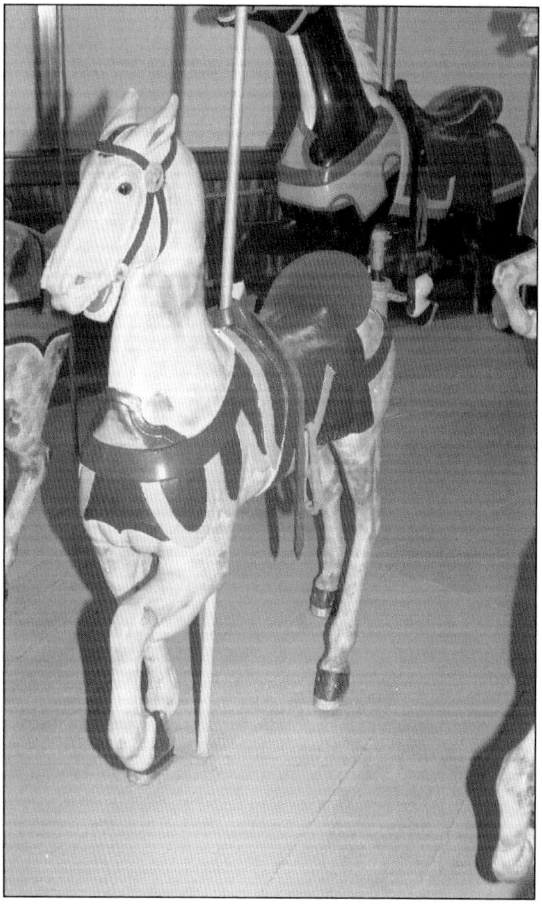

Pictured here, the second-row stander was produced by Stein & Goldstein in about 1910. The horse features a blown-forward mane, and has its head up, ears back, and an elaborately carved chest strap. This horse was sponsored by rock legend and Long Island native Billy Joel, who named it "Penny."

This inner-row stander was designed by M.C. Illions & Sons sometime between 1895 and 1900. The horse is in the stargazer position, with its head looking up to the sky, and a bird back saddle cantle. The horse was sponsored by Steve, Liz, David, Peter, and Stephanie Letzler, who dubbed it "Barbara Jean."

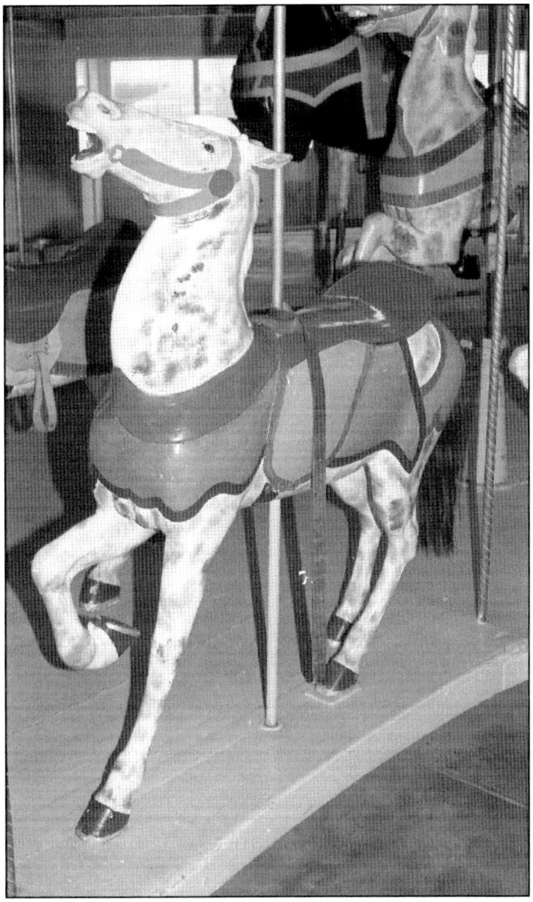

Here is a c. 1910 outside-row jumper that was designed by Stein & Goldstein. This horse is in the fierce pose this company is known for, with the horse looking ready to attack. The head is up with ears back, and the teeth are bared. Eagle feathers hang down the head, and a large shield covers the chest. It was sponsored by Pennies for Ponies, which named it "Mount Monti."

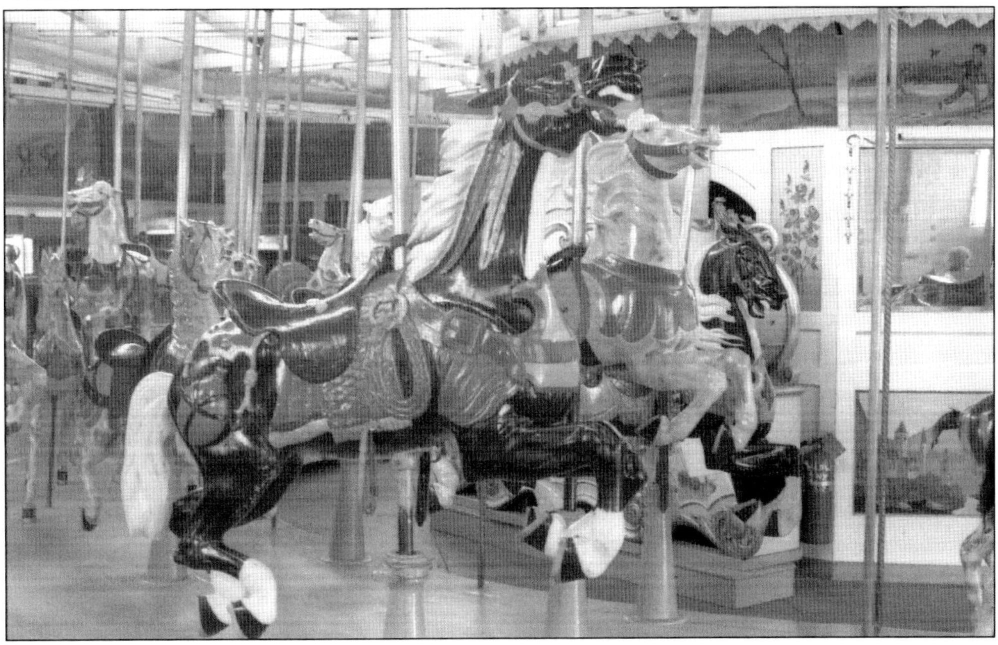

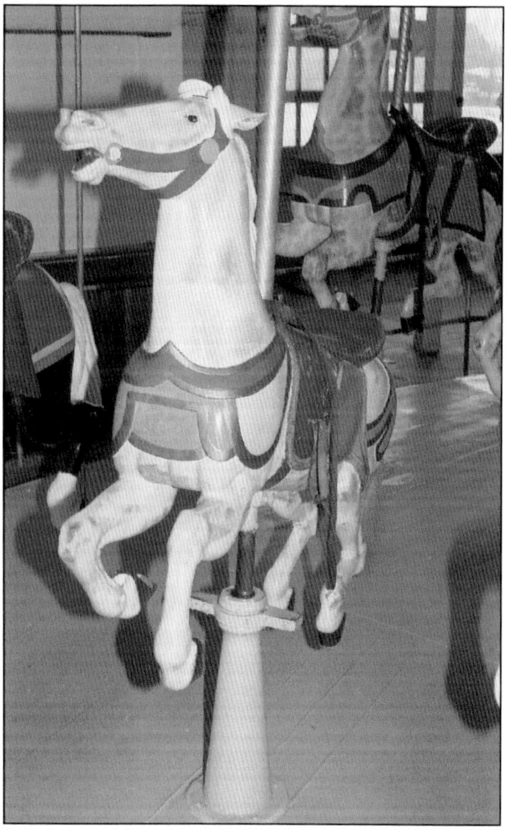

This second-row jumper was created by M.C. Illions sometime between 1895 and 1900. The horse has its head up, ears back, and mane flowing forward. Its saddle is plain, but it highlights carved chest straps and rump. It was sponsored by Reinhard Early Childhood Center in Bellmore, Long Island; it was christened "Reinhard Racer."

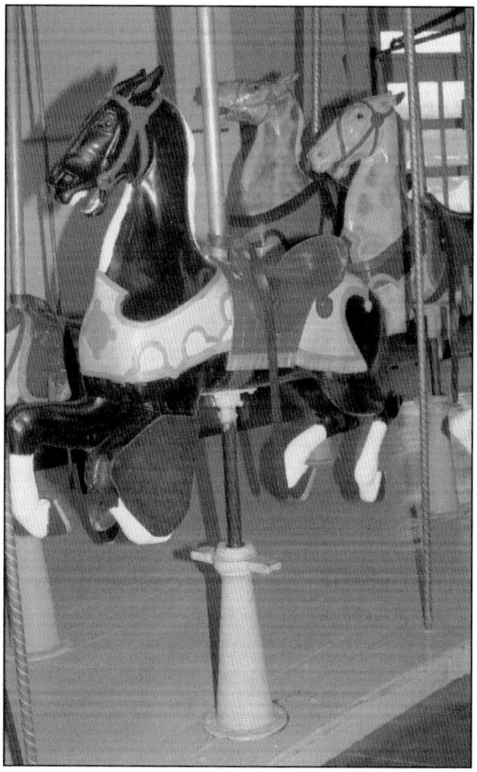

Here is an inner-row jumper produced by Stein & Goldstein about 1910. The horse has its ears back and mane blowing forward, and its head is at a slight angle upwards. The upper body features a large medallion, fringed blanket, and a wide chest strap. It was sponsored by Gail Gilbert, who named it "Darrin Lee."

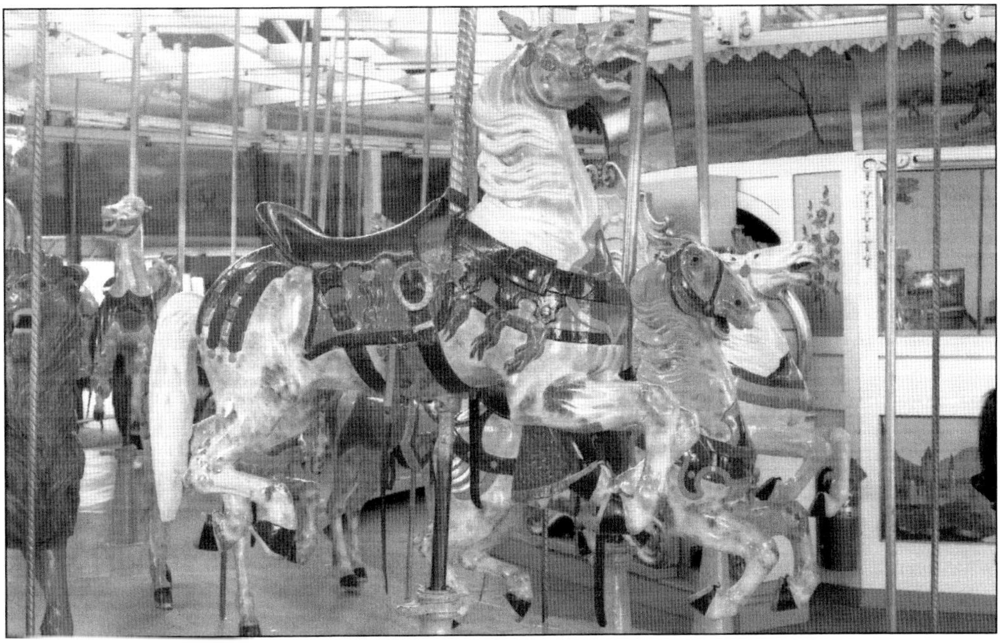

This c. 1910 outside-row jumper was designed by Stein & Goldstein. The horse has its head up, and wears a bridle covered with disks and buckle decorations. It also has a chest shield and a strap with a large buckle. The horse was sponsored by Milburn Elementary School in Baldwin, Long Island. The students gave it the title of "Martin's Milburn Pride" in honor of principal Deborah Martin, who retired in 2006.

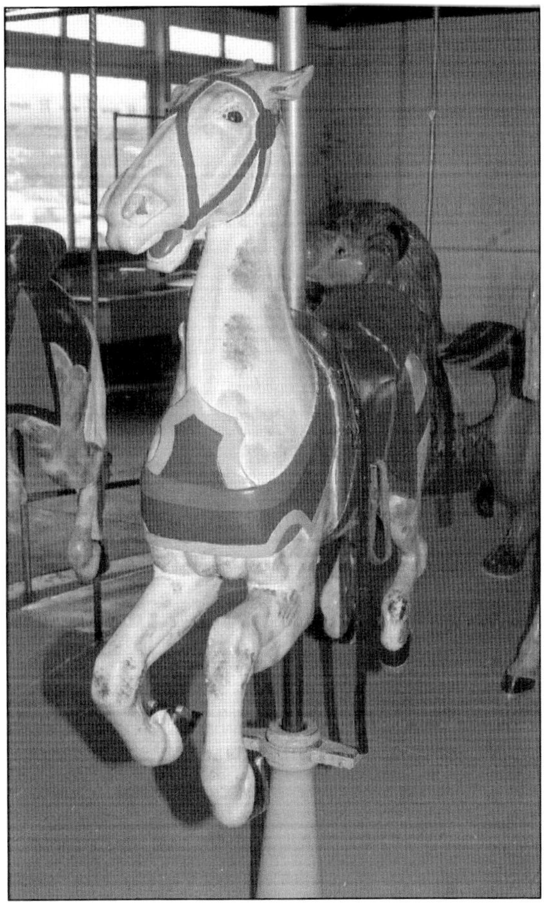

The second-row jumper pictured here was produced around 1910 by Stein & Goldstein. The horse's mane is blowing forward, and its ears are back. The bridle crisscrosses the face, and the chest has a large shield. It was sponsored by the Kadtke triplets, who named it "Triple Threat."

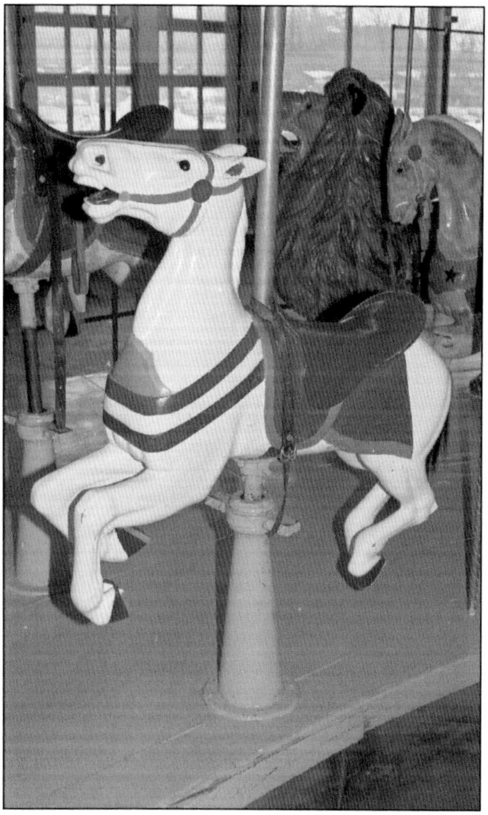

This inner-row jumper was designed by Stein & Goldstein in about 1910. The horse has its head up and ears back, and its mane blows forward. It has a chest shield, chest strap, and blanket. It was sponsored by Meadow Elementary School in Baldwin, Long Island, and the students dubbed it "Meadow."

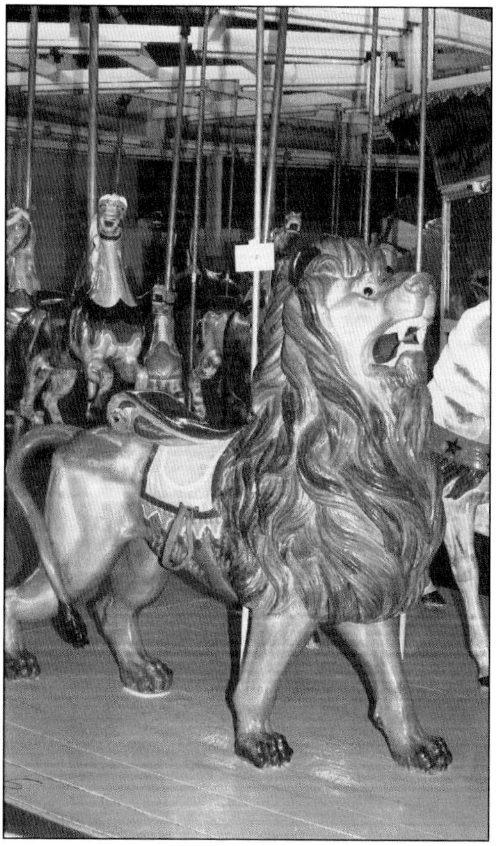

Here is the outside-row standing lion, which was created by Gustav Dentzel sometime between 1885 and 1895; it is considered the most unique piece of the carousel. The lion is in an upright stance with its mouth open as if it were roaring. It has a scooped saddle with two owl heads under the cantle. It was sponsored by Lakeside Elementary School in Merrick, Long Island. The students christened it "Lakeside Lion."

This second-row stander, by Stein & Goldstein, was produced around 1910. The horse has its head tucked with its mane blowing forward and ears back. The chest strap has hanging feathers and large carved stars. The horse was sponsored in memory of Fredric R. LaMarca Jr. (1974–1996), a beloved son and brother. It was named "Ernest."

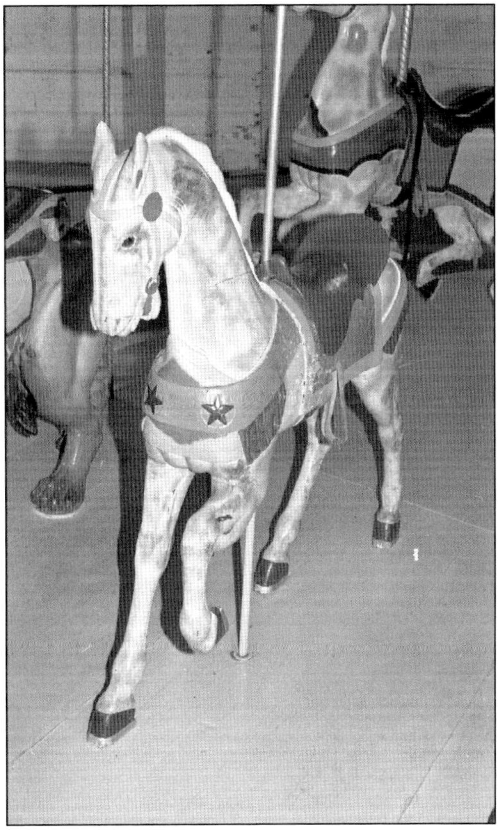

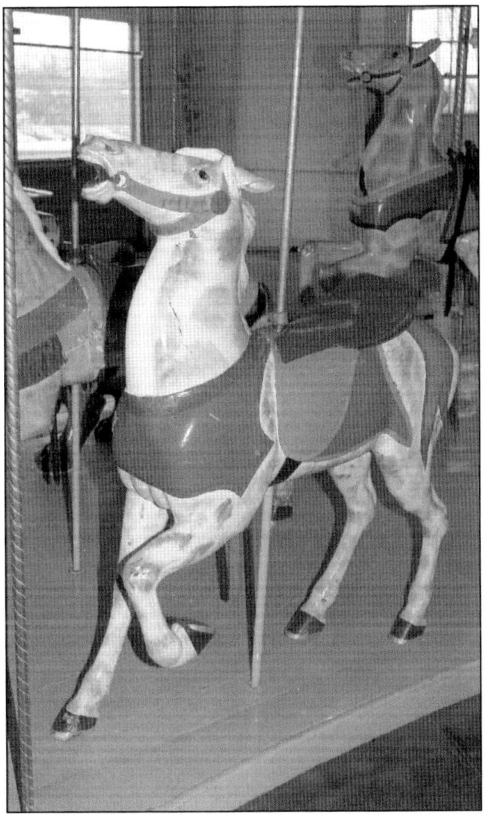

Here is an inner-row stander designed by M.C. Illions sometime between 1895 and 1900. The horse has its head up and a parted forelock. Both its chest and rump are draped, and it has a large saddle with a double bird back cantle. Sponsored by Long Beach Middle School in Long Beach, Long Island, it was dubbed "Lilly's Look."

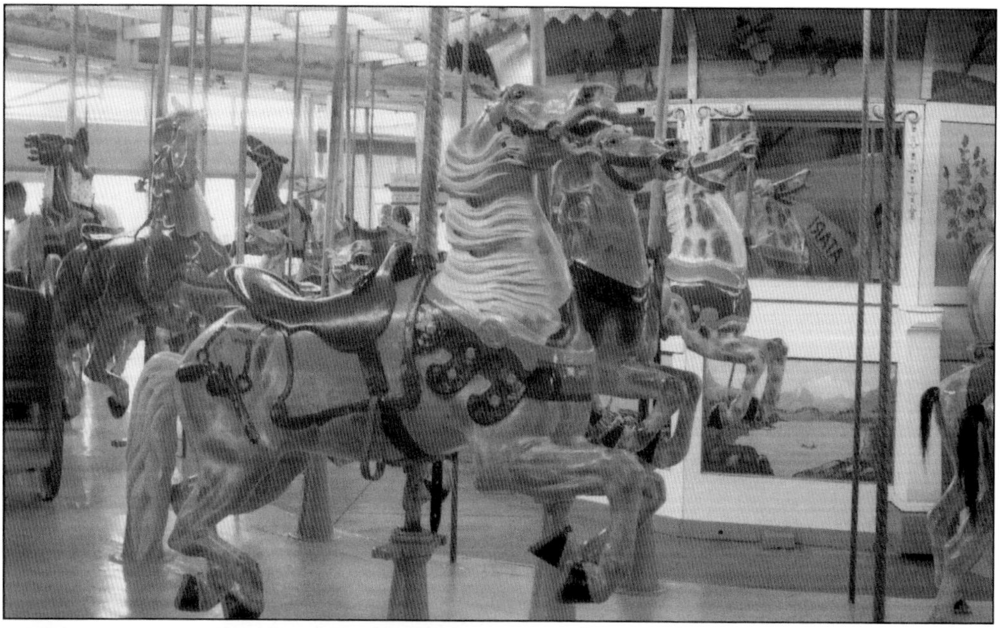

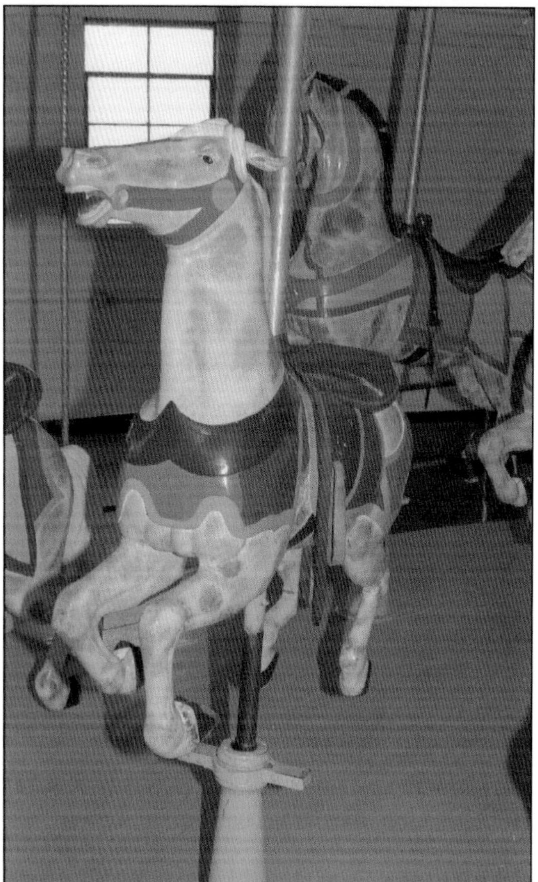

This outside-row jumper was created by Stein & Goldstein around 1910. This horse has its head up and ears slightly back, and its full mane blows forward. While it has a shield, chest strap, and plain saddle, this horse is unique because a Western-style revolver hangs from the saddle. It was sponsored by Cathy, David, Dan, Ali, and Stephen Crist and Liz DiGiovanna. They named it "Lercari Brothers" after Steve, Lou, and Jack Lercari, who ran the park from 1964 until it closed.

Here is a second-row jumper produced by M.C. Illions between 1895 and 1900. The horse has its head up, ears back, and a parted forelock, although his main blows forward. It has straps on its rump and chest and a plain saddle. It was sponsored in memory of loving parents Anita and Joseph Paratore and brother Joseph Paratore Jr. and christened "Anita Joe."

This inner-row jumper, designed by M.C. Illions sometime between 1895 and 1900, has a parted forelock with its head up and its ears back. There are straps on its chest and rump, and it has a plain saddle. It was sponsored by John and Diana Simonetti, who named it "Gentle Bill."

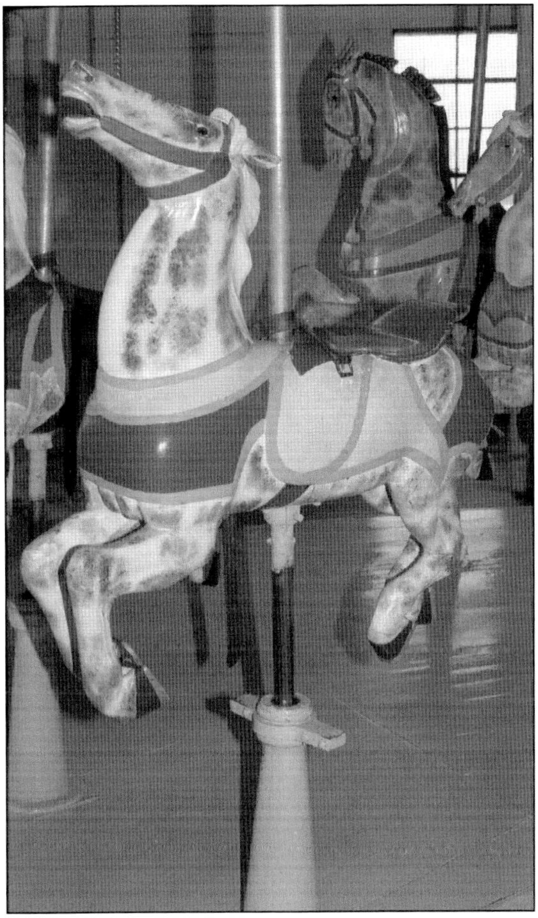

Here is a c. 1910 outside-row jumper by Stein & Goldstein. The horse's head is deeply tucked down with a cropped mane. Its bridle is decorated, and its neck strap has large sleigh bells, tassels, and beads. There is a medallion on its chest and a strap with a string of round disks. It was sponsored by No. 6 School in Lawrence, Long Island. The students dubbed it "The Spirit of Six."

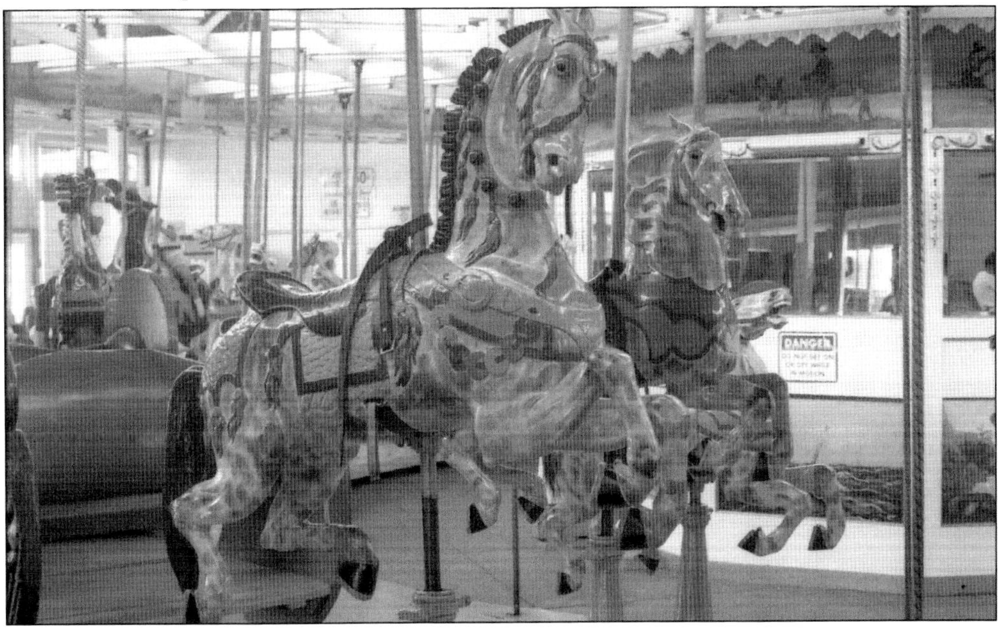

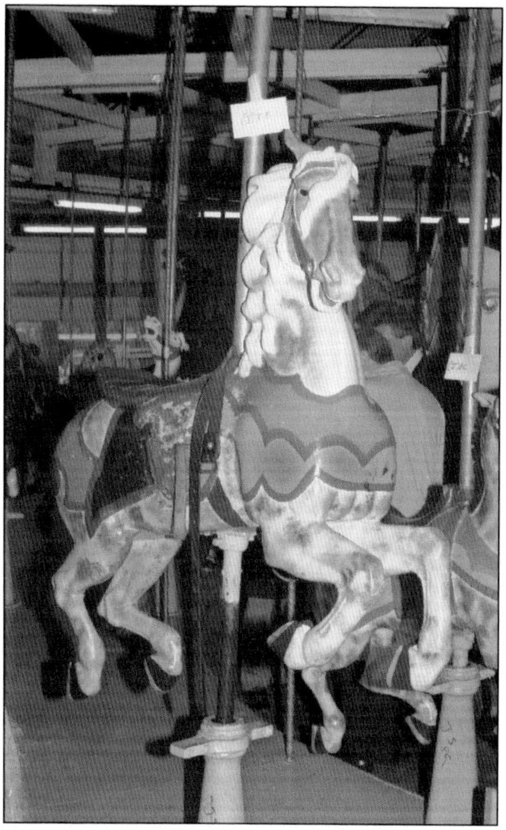

Pictured is a second-row jumper created by M.C. Illions around 1895 to 1900. The mane on this horse billows out and forward with its head tucked. It also has a parted forelock with some of its hair falling across its face. It has chest and rump straps and a plain saddle. It was sponsored by Pesquale and Diane Lore of Baldwin True Value Hardware in Baldwin, Long Island. They named it "Lady Di."

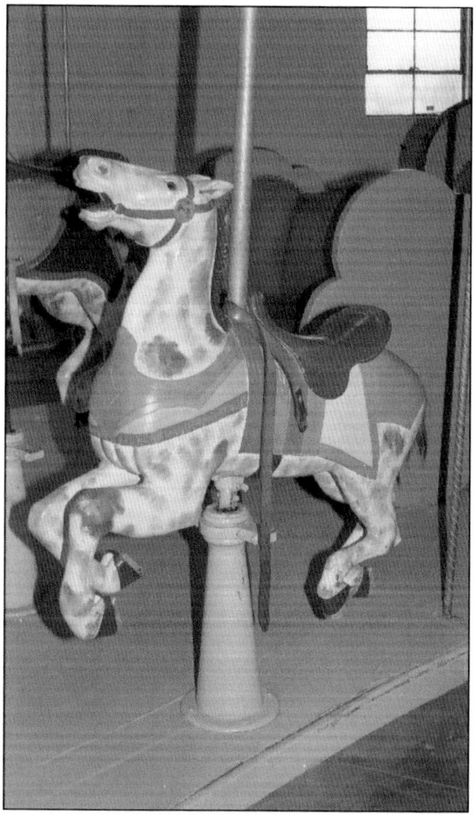

This inner-row jumper was produced by Stein & Goldstein around 1910. The horse has a cropped mane with its head up and ears back. It has a fringed chest and rump drapes and a medallion on its chest. It was sponsored by Marc Wieman and family, who gave their horse the name of "Wonder."

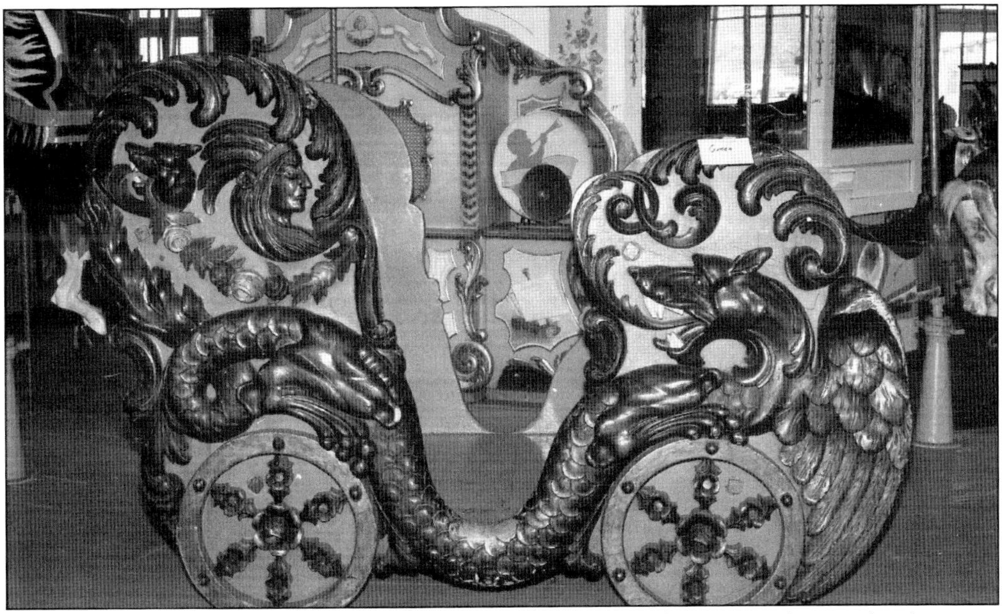

This green chariot was designed in about 1910 by Stein & Goldstein. With a similar design to the carousel's red chariot, it has an intricate carving of a large dragon draped along the lower edge, with wings extending to form the front of the chariot. The tongue of the dragon becomes a garland of Stein & Goldstein trademarked cabbage roses. The chariot was sponsored in loving memory of Jack Lercari, a former owner of Nunley's Amusement Park.

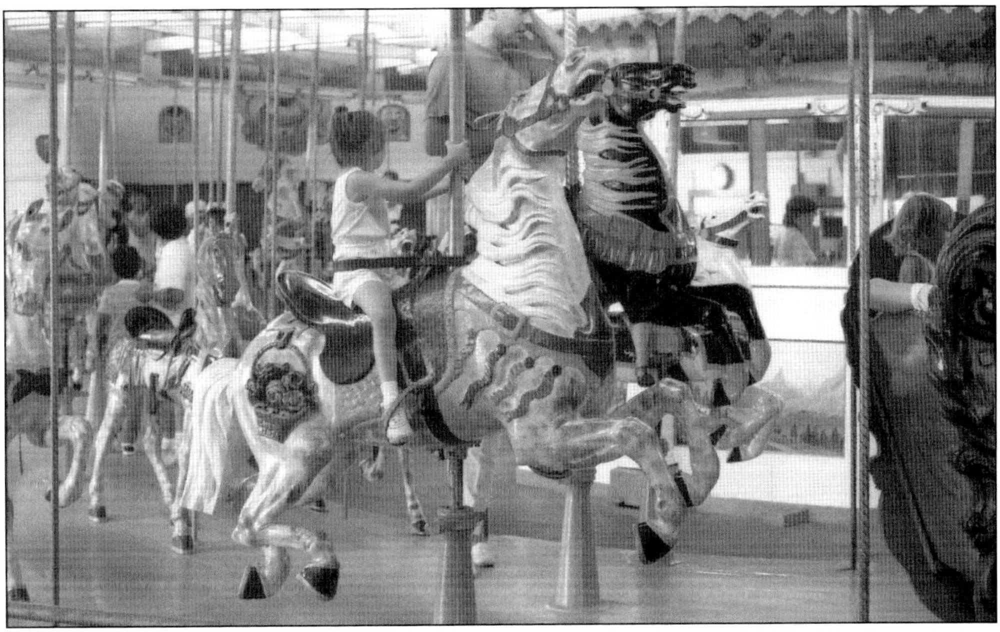

This outside-row jumper by Stein & Goldstein was produced around 1910. The horse is in a fierce pose with its head back and mane forward. The chest strap has trailing ribbons and buckle, and the large saddle holds double blankets. The horse also features a side carving of a basket of flowers. It was sponsored by Lenox Elementary School in Baldwin, Long Island, and the students named it "Lenox."

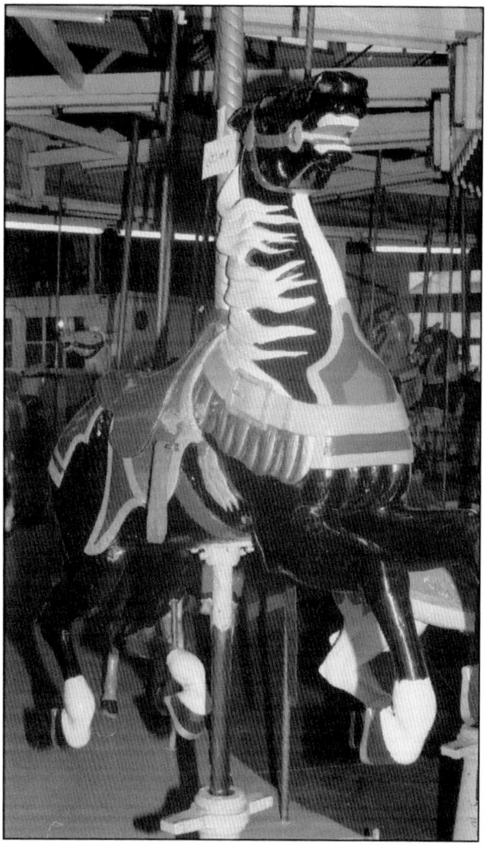

Here is a c. 1910 second-row jumper designed by Stein & Goldstein. The horse has its head up and ears back, as well as a chest strap with a large buckle and long fringe. The blanket it wears is fringed too. It was sponsored by Chestnut Hill Elementary School in Half Hollow Hills, Long Island. The students named it "Wizard."

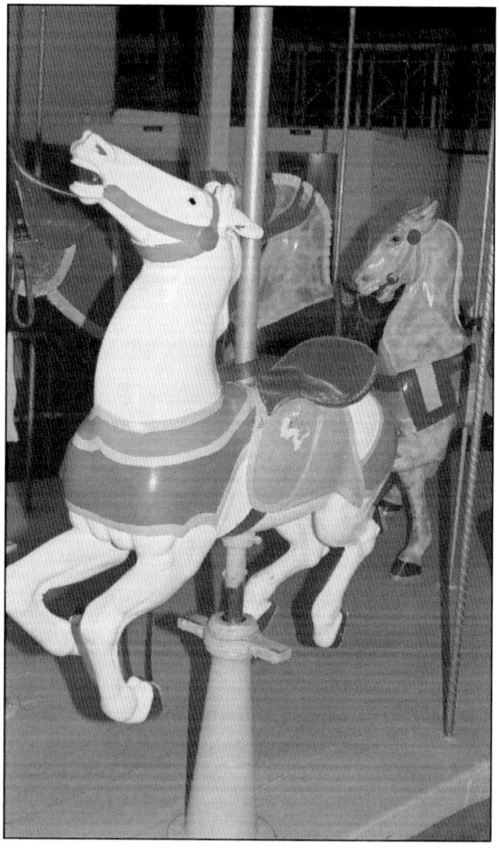

This inner-row jumper was created by M.C. Illions sometime between 1895 and 1900. The horse is in stargazer pose, with parted forelock and mane blowing forward. The blanket and saddle are plain, and there are carved straps across the chest and rump. It was sponsored by Levittown Public Schools in Levittown, Long Island, and was dubbed "William."

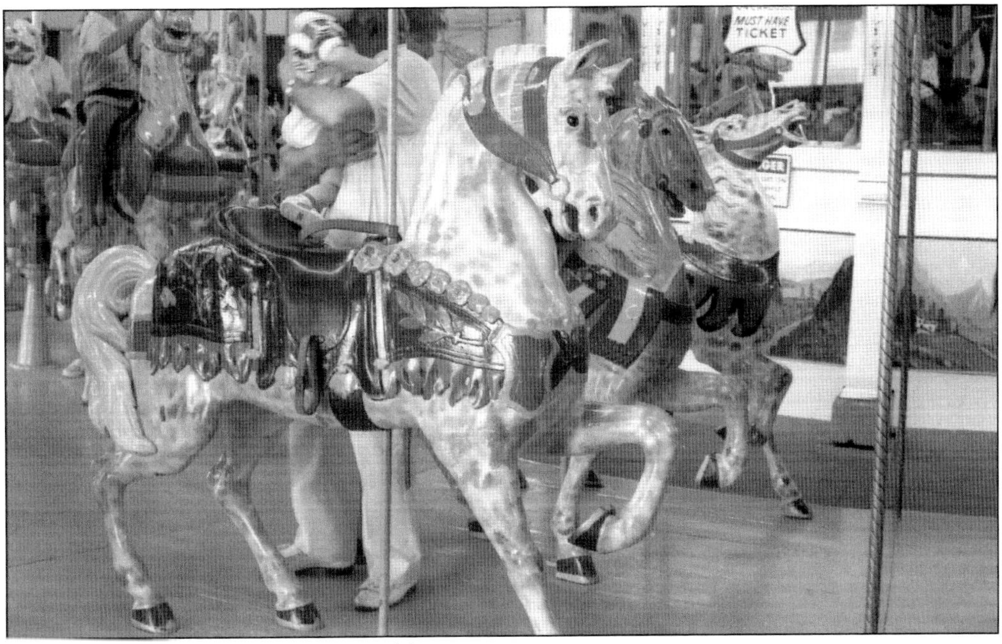

This outside-row jumper was designed by Dentzel sometime around 1910 to 1915. The horse has a fringed bridle and neck strap typical of the Dentzel style. Its head is slightly tucked, and it has a gentle face and cropped mane. Its chest is draped with a shield covered in flowers amid an olive branch and leaves. It was sponsored by Plaza Elementary School in Baldwin, Long Island, and the students named it "Plaza Purebred."

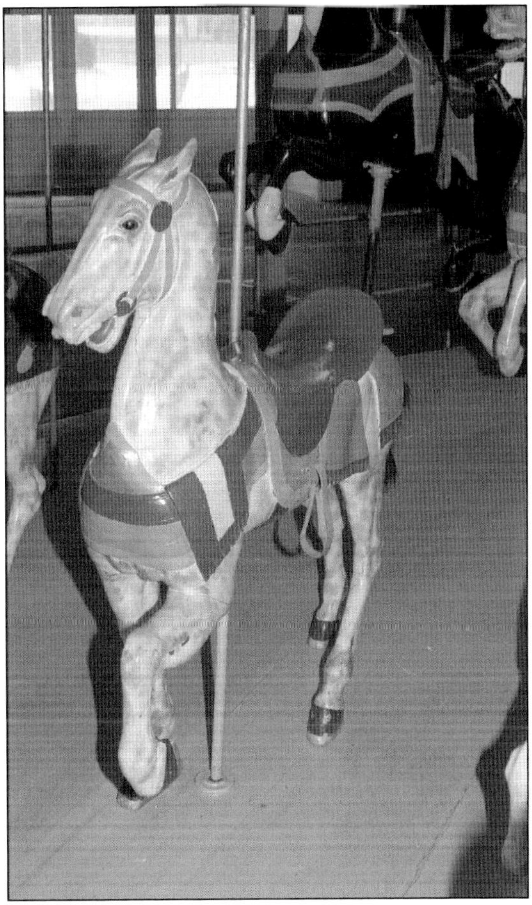

Here is a c. 1910 second-row stander by Stein & Goldstein, produced in about 1910. This horse has an actual horsehair tail, and its head is up with its ears back. It has a fringed chest strap with drapes tucked into it. It was sponsored by the New York Islanders, and the team named their horse "Angel."

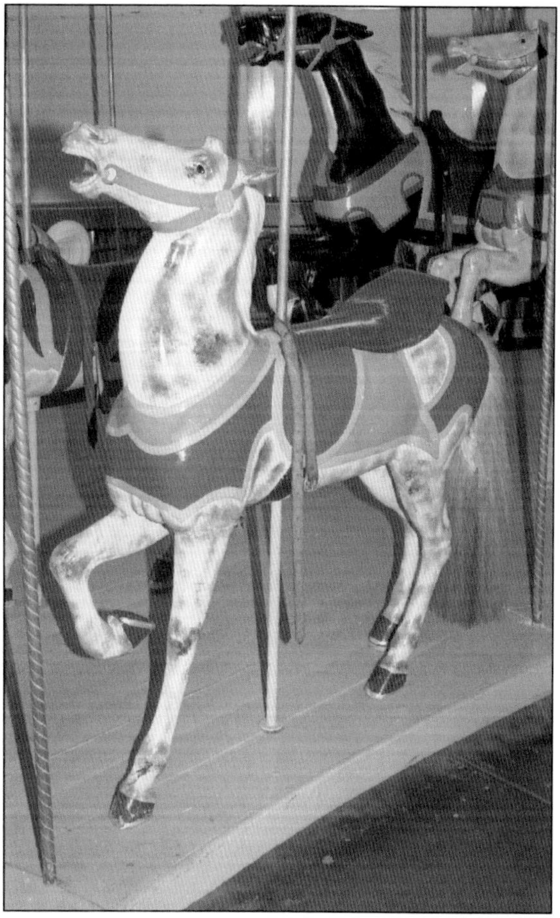

This inner-row stander was designed by M.C. Illions sometime between 1895 and 1900. The head of this horse is in a stargazer pose with its ears back. It has a plain saddle with a double bid cantle, as well as a horsehair tail. It was sponsored by the Schepp family in honor of their father and grandfather. They gave their horse the title of "King Arthur."

Here is a c. 1910 outside-row jumper by Stein & Goldstein. This aggressively posed horse has a draped cloth tucked into its plain strap. Cabbage roses and other flowers fall from the drape at the rump, and it has a large tassel under its saddle. It was sponsored by the Grasso family, who named it "Christina's Charm."

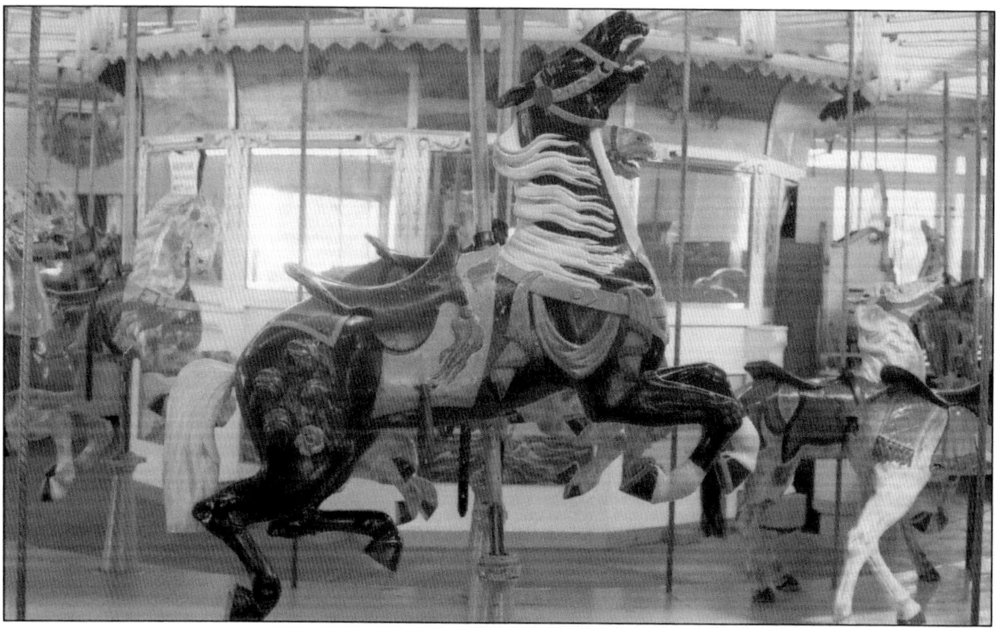

This second-row jumper was designed by Stein & Goldstein around 1910. With its large shield and fringed drapes at the rump, the horse has it head up, ears back, and a horsehair tail. It was sponsored by Marc Wieman and family. They dubbed it "Mary Catherine."

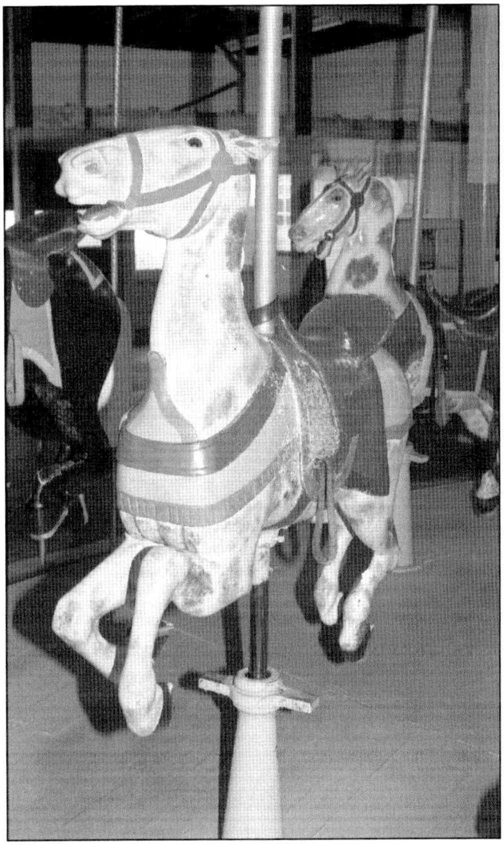

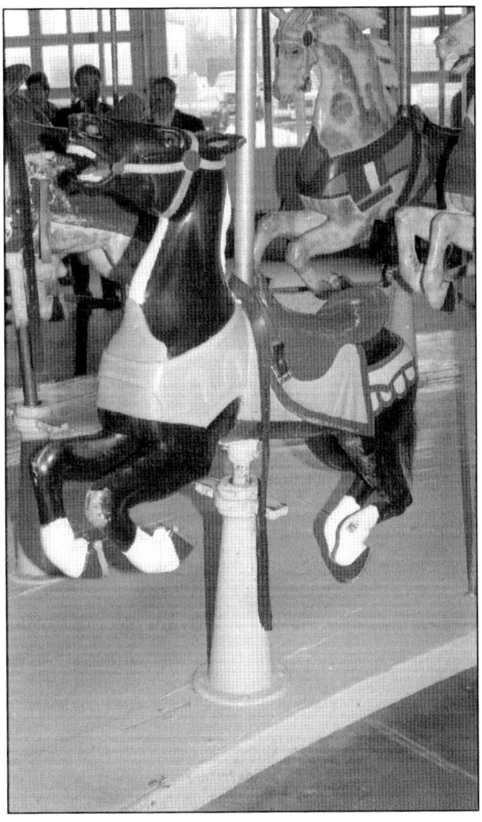

Here is an inner-row jumper by M.C. Illions, produced sometime between 1895 and 1900. The horse has minimal decoration; its head is upwards in stargazer pose, and it has a parted forelock. It was sponsored by Wilson Elementary School in Rockville Centre, Long Island. The students named it "Wilson's Pride."

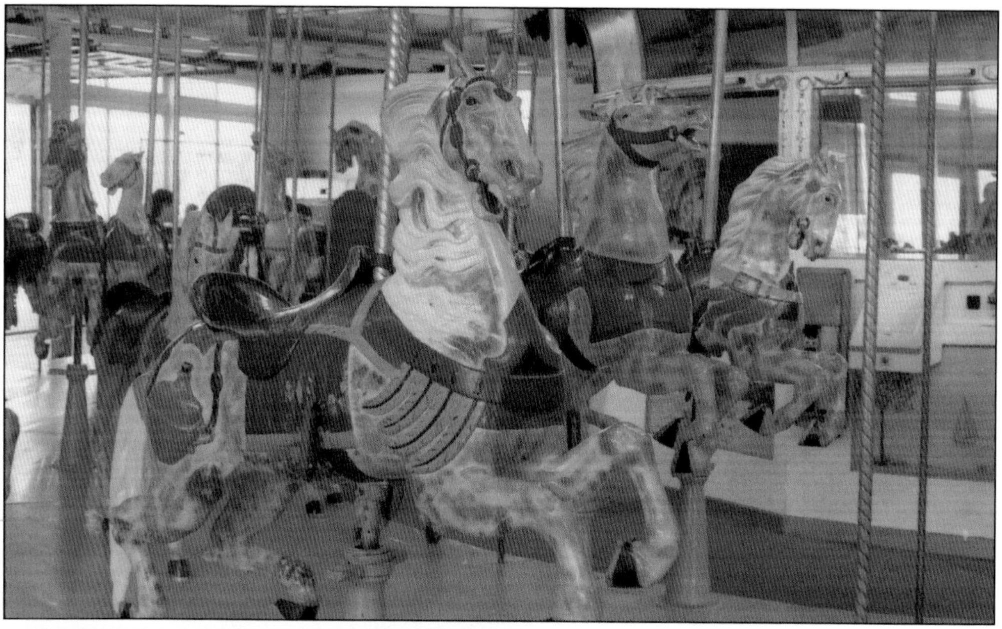

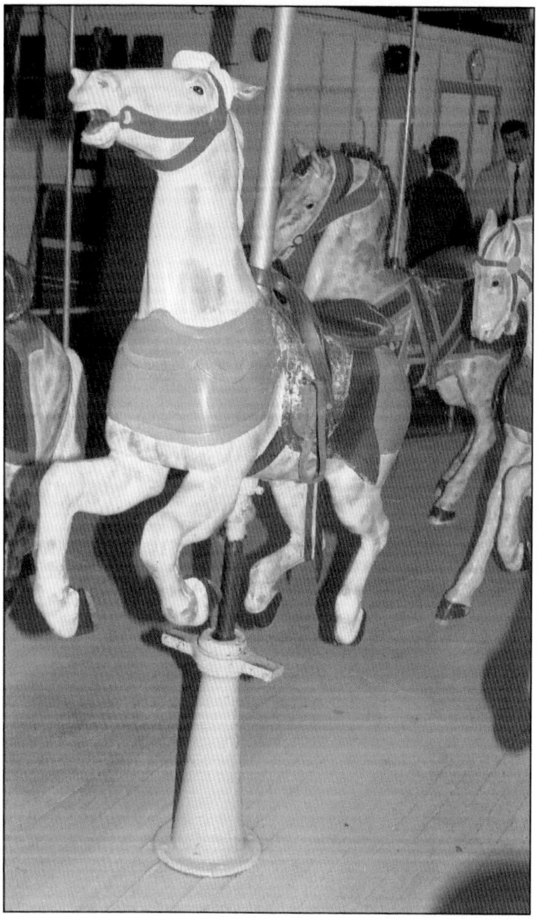

This c. 1910 outside-row jumper was designed by Stein & Goldstein. The horse has a fancy bridle headpiece that is decorated with carved disks. The chest strap has four long feathers, and there is a large chest shield. A water flask with a stopper sits in a basket that hangs from the saddle. It was sponsored by Peggy, Steve, Meghan, Rebecca, and Laura Kirsch, and the family christened it "Wild Cherry."

Here is an inner-row jumper by M.C. Illions, created sometime between 1895 and 1900. Unlike the majority of the carousel's horses, this one's hair blows back and away from the neck. Otherwise, it has a plain saddle, blanket, and straps, and a horsehair tail. It was sponsored in honor of Thomas Robert Schreck's first birthday on July 24, 2007. It was named "Fiona."

This second-row jumper was designed by Stein & Goldstein around 1890 to 1900. With its mane blowing forward, this horse has its head tucked and its ears back. It has wide chest and rump straps, as well as a plain blanket and saddle. It was sponsored for Abigail by her mother and father, who gave it the name of "Trixie's Apple."

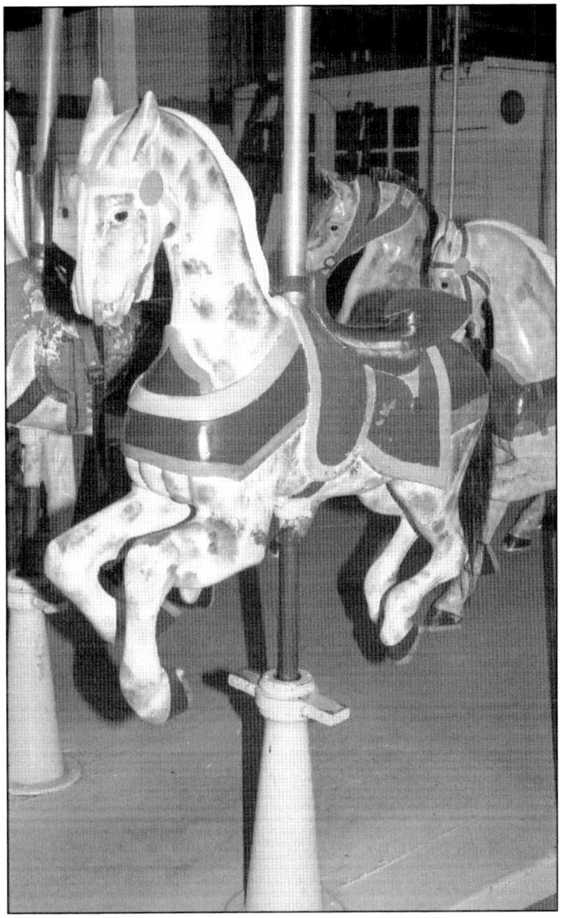

Here is an outside-row stander produced by Dentzel sometime between 1910 and 1915. This horse is described as having a gentle face and features a tucked head, forward ears, and cropped mane. It has carved flowers, leaves, and scrolls along its body, and there is fringe hanging from the strap at the chest. It was sponsored by Nassau County executive Thomas Suozzi.

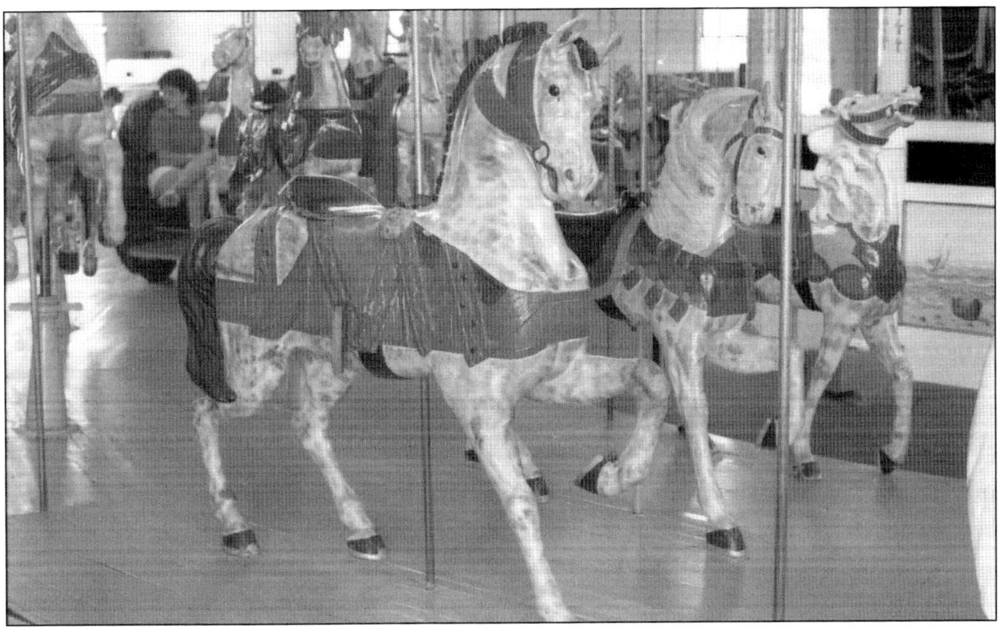

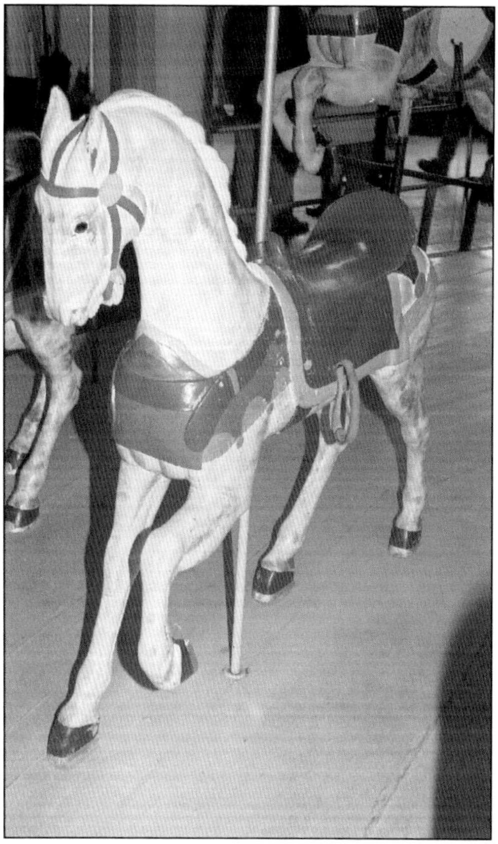

This c. 1910 second-row stander was designed by Stein & Goldstein. The horse has a tucked head and ears back, as well as a large shield at the chest with tassel and fringe carvings. It also has a fringed blanket and horsehair tail. It was sponsored by Sandy and Alan Sadwin in memory of Julie Lynne Zipper and named "Zipper."

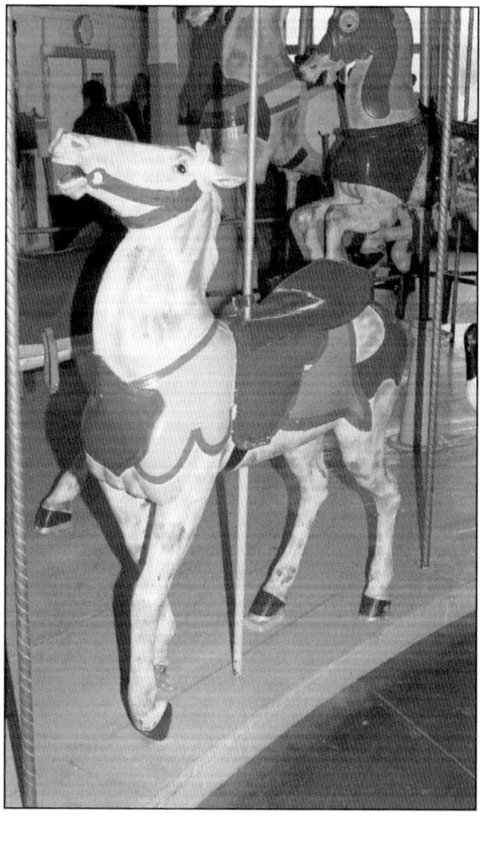

Here is an inner-row stander by M.C. Illions from around 1895 to 1900. This horse is unique because of the unusual positioning of its left front leg, which, instead of being raised, is cocked. The head is in stargazer position with its ears back, and it has a horsehair tail. It was sponsored by Columbus Avenue School in Freeport, Long Island, and legislator D. Dennenberg. The students and legislator named their horse "Super Star."

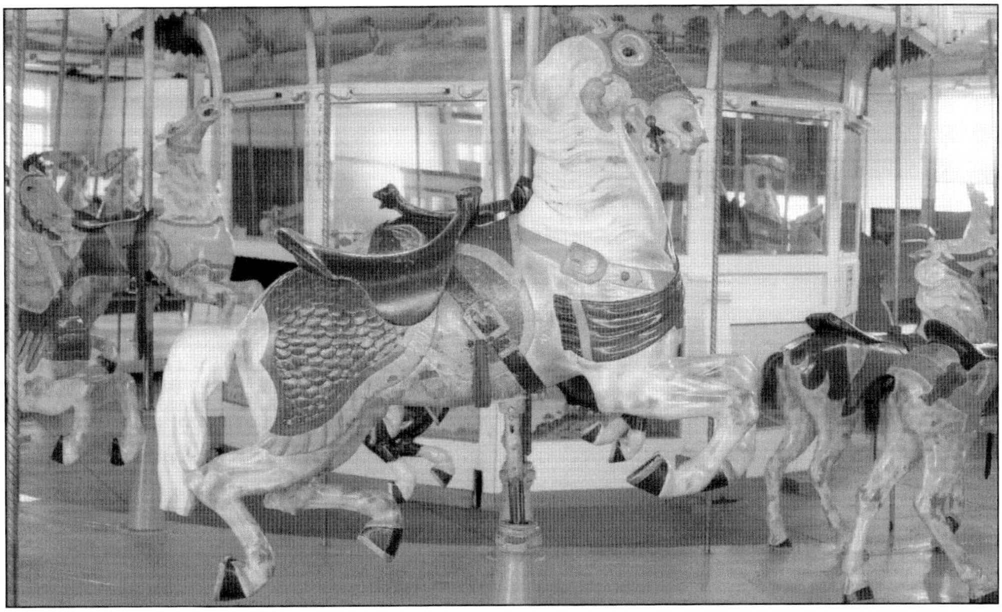

This c. 1910 outside-row armored jumper was created by Stein & Goldstein. The horse is described as being in a dramatic pose with a tucked head and ears back. It has head armor with a fish scale pattern. It was sponsored by Gardners Avenue Elementary School in Levittown, Long Island. The students named it "Mustang Magic."

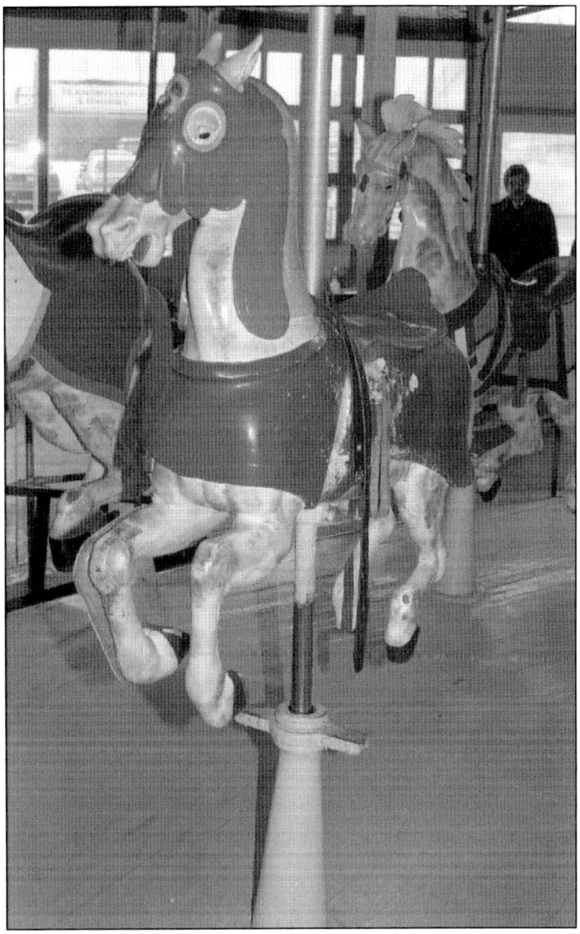

Here is an inner-row armored jumper by M.C. Illions, produced sometime between 1895 and 1900. The horse has full neck and head armor with armor-style body draping. One side features a carving of a knight's head in profile, and the other side depicts an eagle flying while holding a shield. It was sponsored by Davison Avenue Elementary School in Lynbrook, Long Island, and was dubbed "Davison."

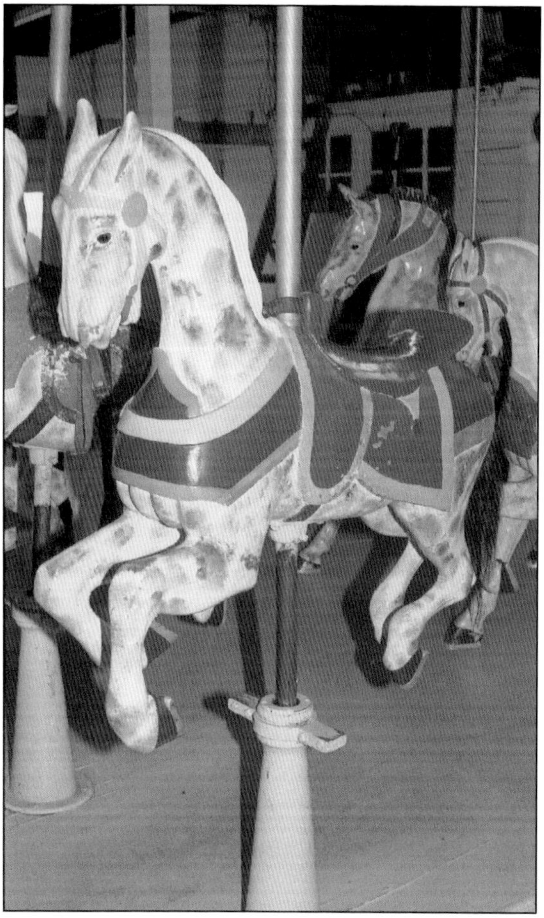

This c. 1910 inner-row jumper was designed by Stein & Goldstein. This plain horse has its head up and ears back. It has a shield, but no decorative elements on its saddle or blankets, and a horsehair tail. It was sponsored by North Side School in East Williston, Long Island. The students gave it the name of "Midnight."

This outside-row jumper was produced by Stein & Goldstein around 1910. Due to its elaborate carvings and dramatic pose, this horse was meant to be the lead horse. Its head is tucked and turned to the side, and it has one ear forward and one ear back. There is a garland of cabbage roses down the neck, as well as one on the rump. It was sponsored by the Progressive School on Long Island and named "Penny."

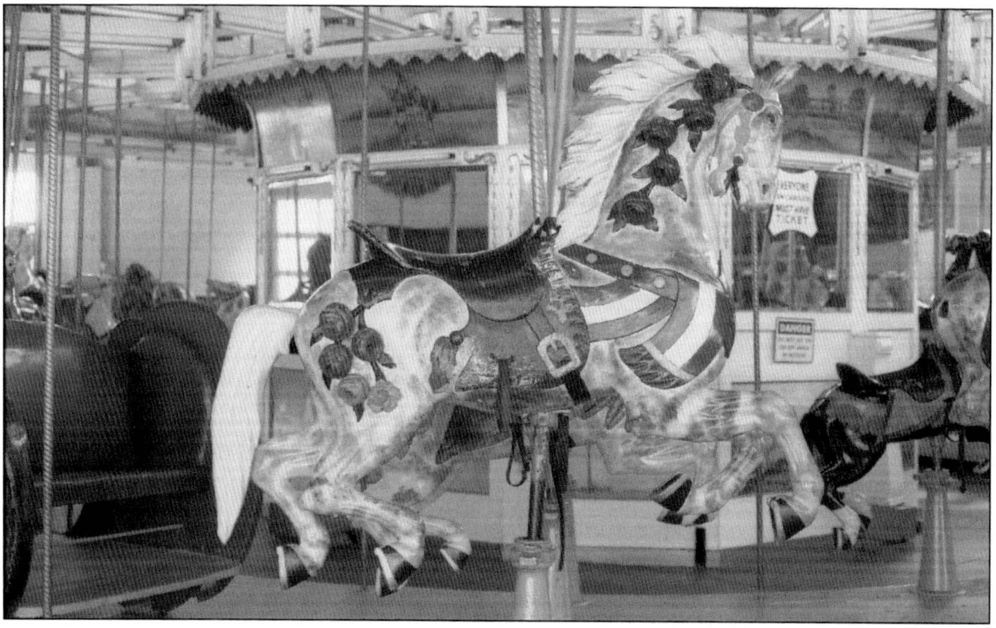

This second-row jumper was designed about 1910 by Stein & Goldstein. This horse has its head up and ears back and features a horsehair tail. Feathers hang from the chest strap. It was sponsored by Edward J. Smits, Nassau County historian, who christened it "Chalk It Up."

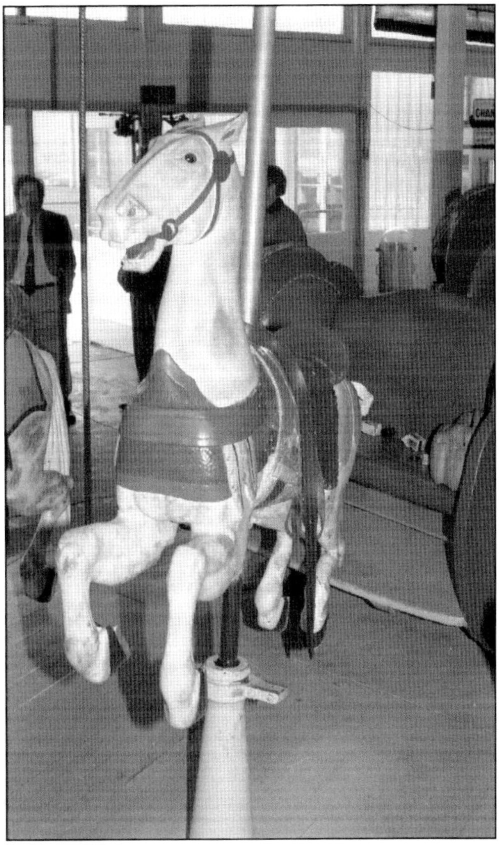

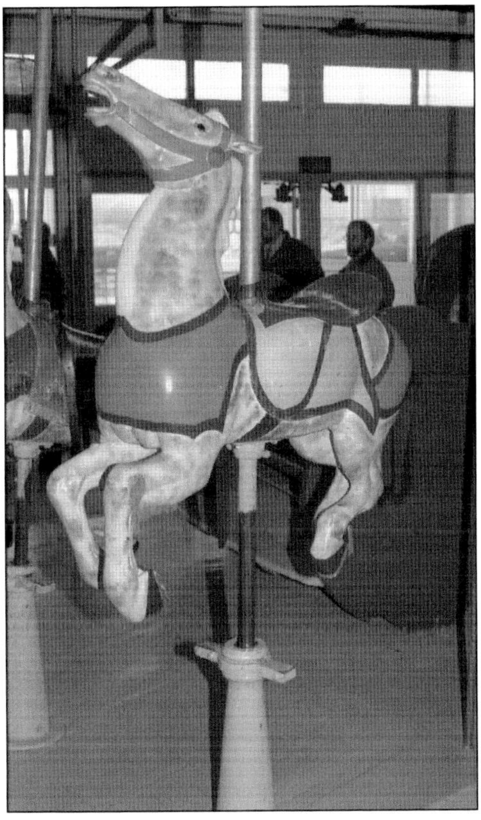

This final horse, an inner-row jumper, was designed by M.C. Illions sometime between 1895 and 1900. It is in stargazer pose with its ears back. It has minimal ornamentation and a wide drape across the chest. It was sponsored by the Kane O'Brien family, who named the horse "Never a Doubt."

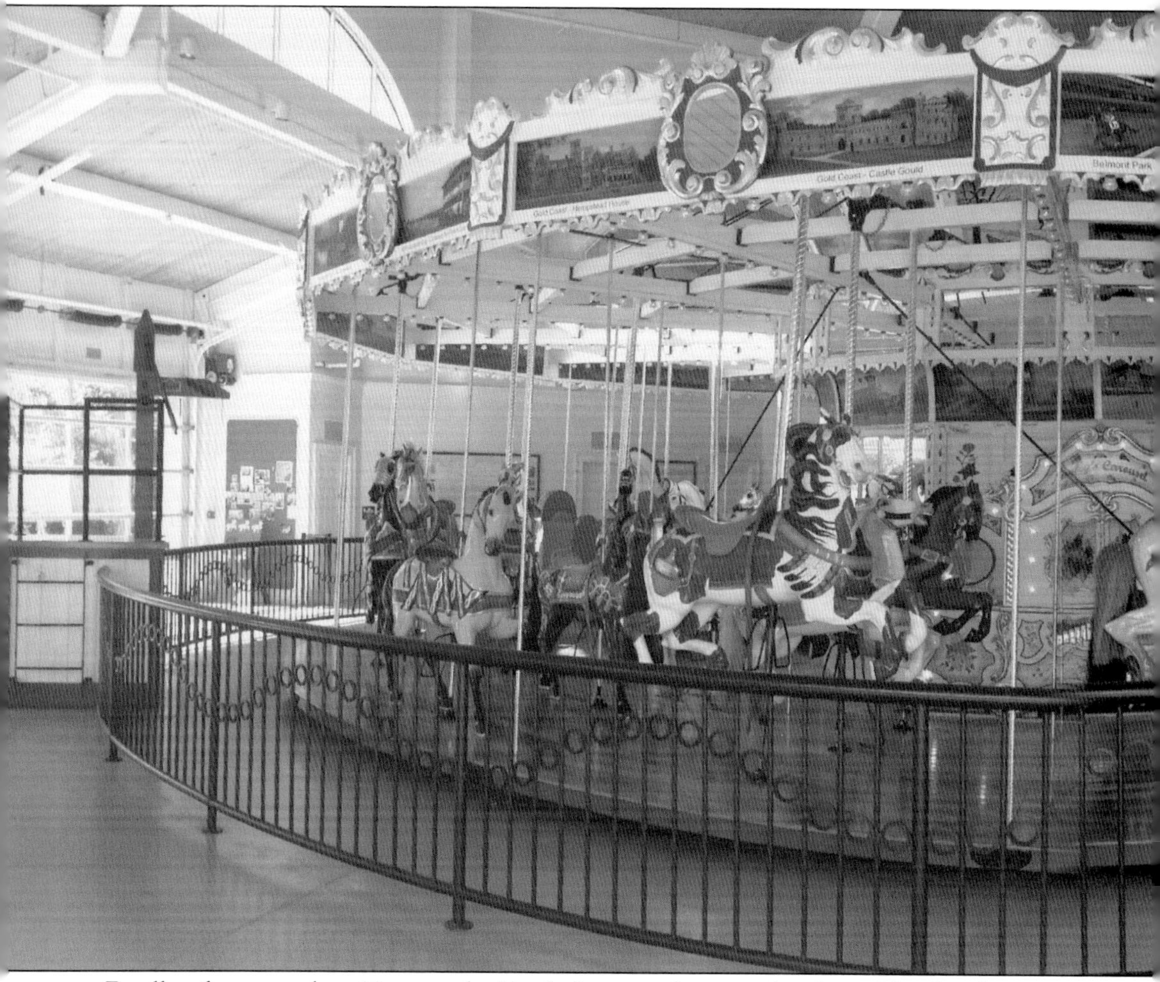

Finally, after more than 10 years, the Nunley's carousel returned to Long Island and to its new home in Museum Row in Garden City. After the closing of the park, threat of auction, local politics, community turmoil, fundraising, and finally, a massive restoration, the carousel was finally ready to open. A new carousel building was designed emulating the original. Cleaned

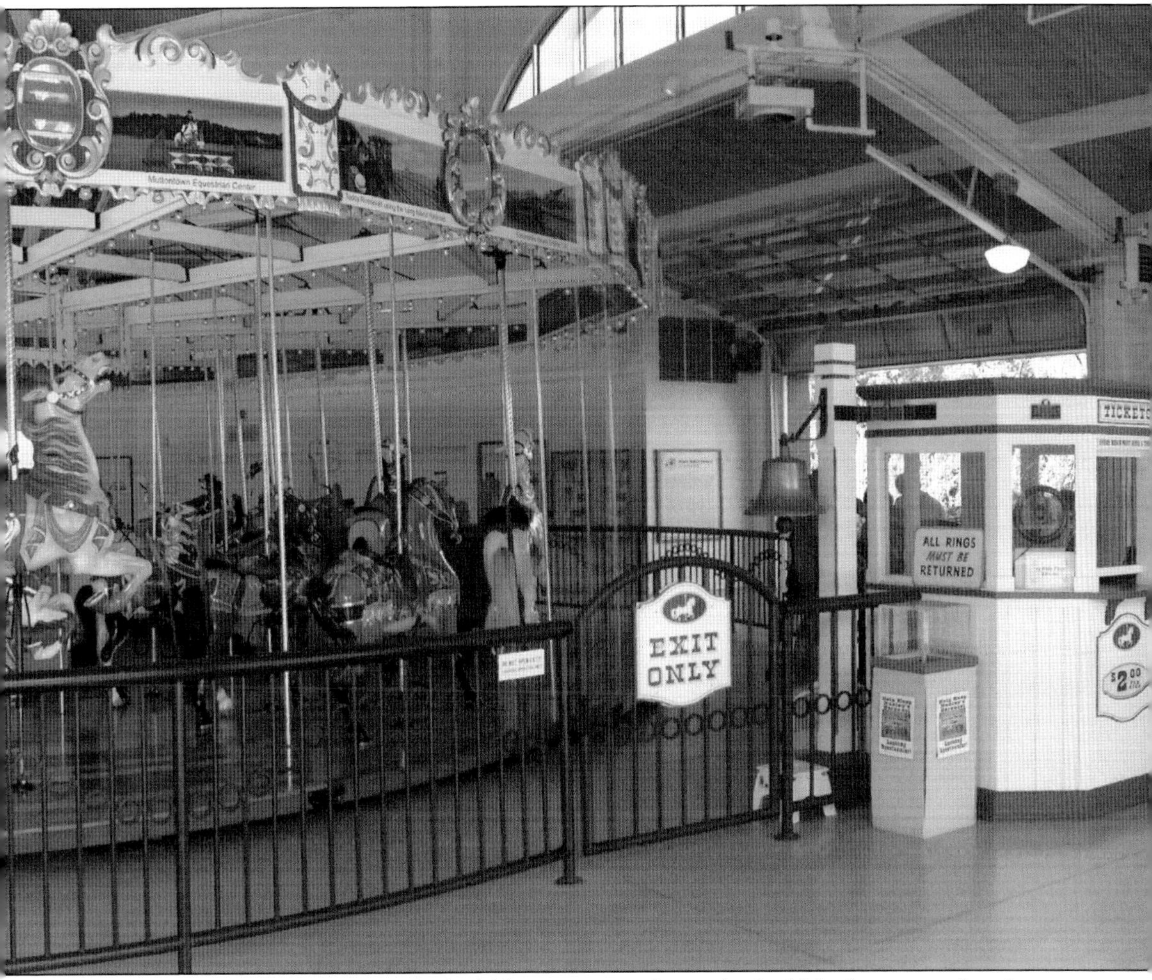

and freshly painted, the carousel looked like new; or rather, it looked like how it used to long ago. The carousel has remained in this location since its grand reopening celebration in 2009. (Author's collection.)

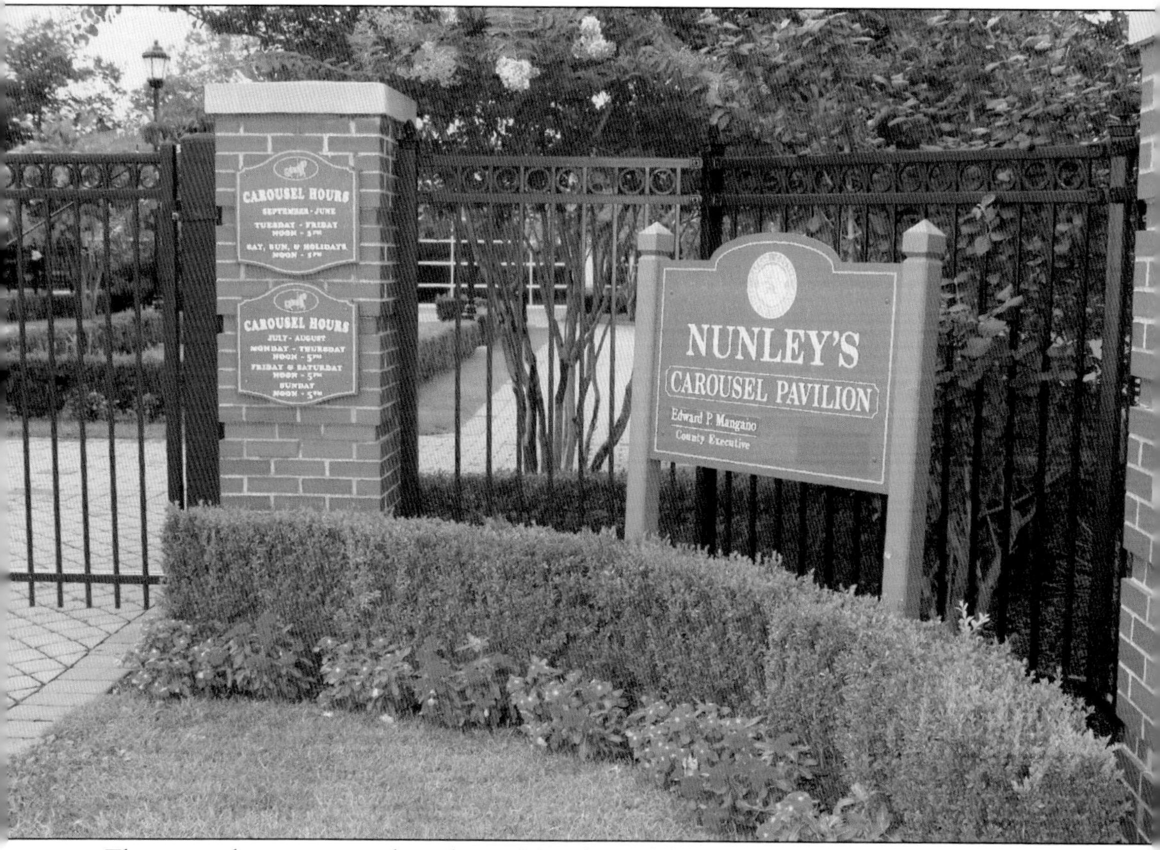

The carousel is now situated in a beautiful park amid the organizations in Museum Row. While many past visitors were sad that it was not reassembled back in Baldwin, this new location is the perfect place to attract a new generation of visitors who are going to the nearby Long Island Children's Museum or the Cradle of Aviation. Fans enjoy that the pavilion has the original ticket booth that was at Nunley's, as well as room for various arcade games, which are brought in for special occasions. The ring arm has also been reinstalled, so a new generation can now chart their growth. The pavilion also has a permanent wall-mounted exhibition that documents the history of the carousel. During the summer months, it is open to the public from 12:00 p.m. to 5:00 p.m., and the rest of the year, it is open from 12:00 p.m. to 3:00 p.m. It now cost $2 per carousel ride per person; gone are the days when it was only 10¢. (Author's collection.)

Four

The Arcade and Other Amusements

The carousel at Nunley's sometimes tends to overshadow other memories of the park, especially with the long journey to its new home in Museum Row; however, there were so many wonderful aspects of the park. The majority of the amusements were rides geared to young children and were the subjects of hundreds of family photo opportunities over the years. But Nunley's wasn't just for little kids by any means. Freeport High School students were daily visitors to the park's restaurant to eat fries, hot dogs, burgers, and pastrami sandwiches for lunch. The miniature golf course was the site for hundreds of dates over the years. The arcade drew long lines of kids with stacks of quarters, itching to try out all the latest games.

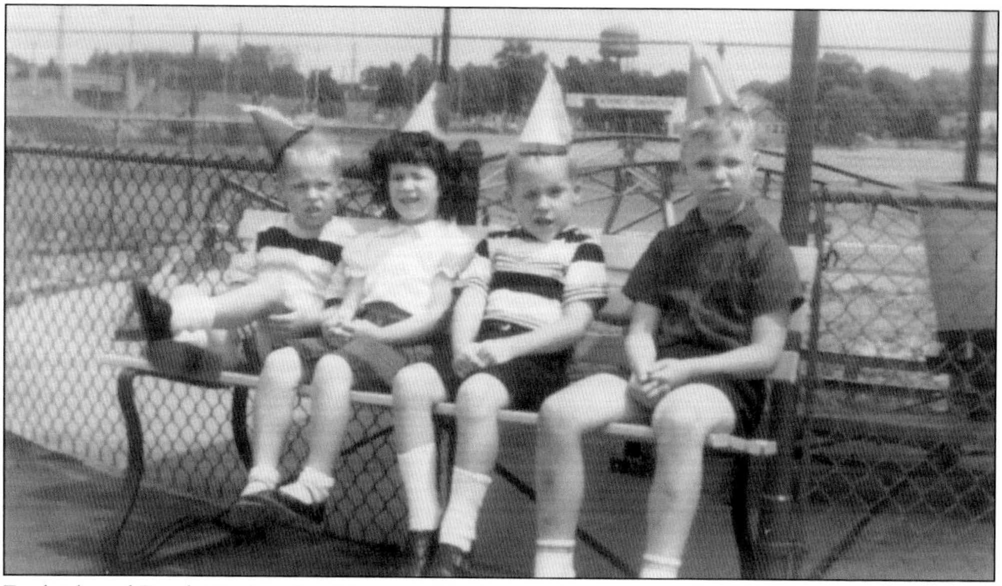

Fredrick and Freida Popken lived in the white house that was attached to the park, so naturally, their grandchildren were regular visitors. Karl Popken, Joanne Corby Wenner, Freddie Popken, and Michael Corby pose on a bench in front of the roller coaster on a sunny day in 1965. They are celebrating Freddie's birthday at their favorite place. (Courtesy of Joanne Wenner.)

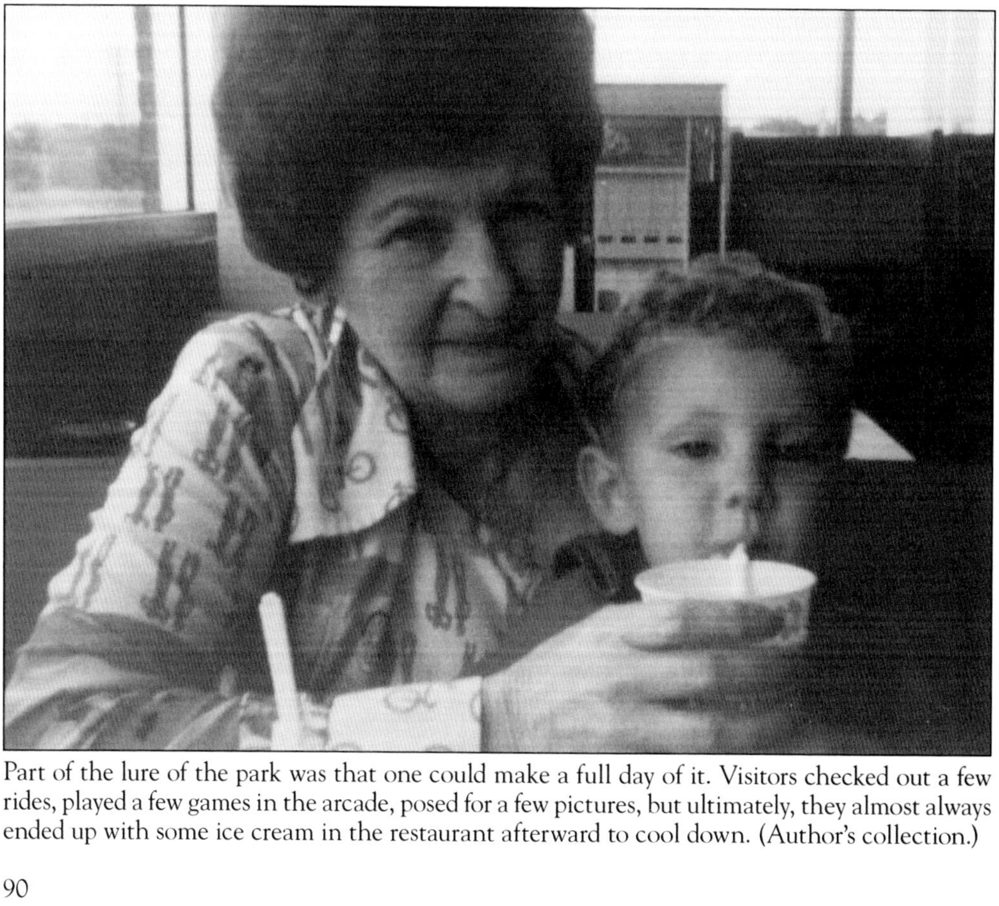

Part of the lure of the park was that one could make a full day of it. Visitors checked out a few rides, played a few games in the arcade, posed for a few pictures, but ultimately, they almost always ended up with some ice cream in the restaurant afterward to cool down. (Author's collection.)

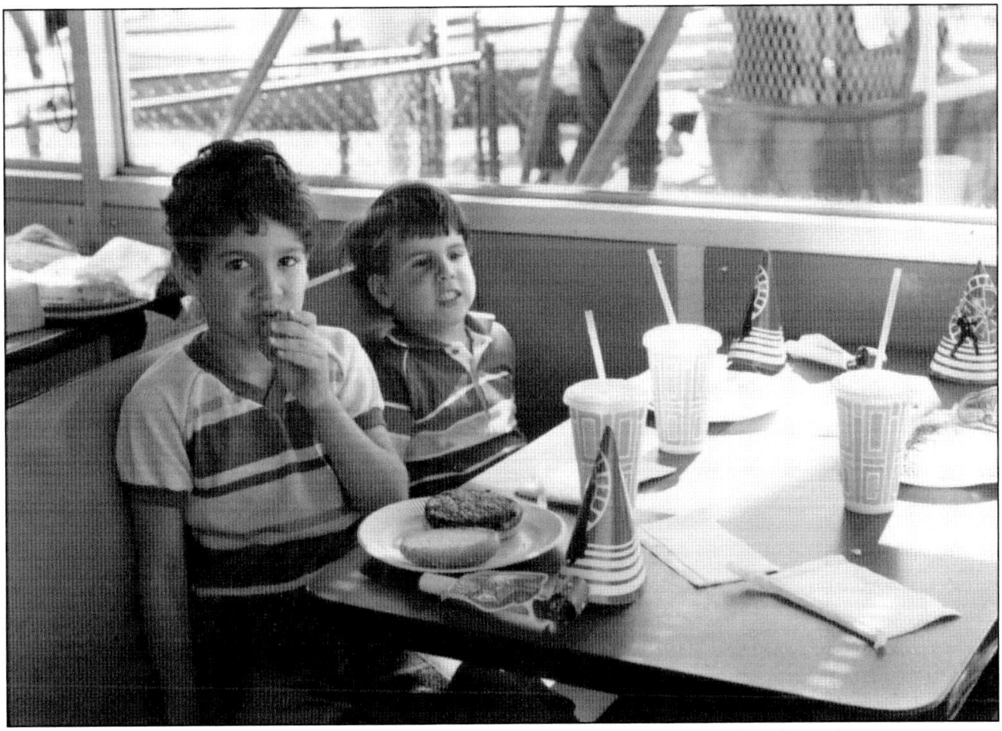

Kids pose for a picture in between bites of pizza and burgers and sips of soda at the restaurant at Nunley's. Visitors remember the smell of the food cooking and the feel of the hard plastic booths. At a birthday party, these children would later be spotted running through the park and on various rides, all the while sporting their party hats. Many claim they attended countless birthday parties at the park. (Both, courtesy of Dennis Ciccone Jr.)

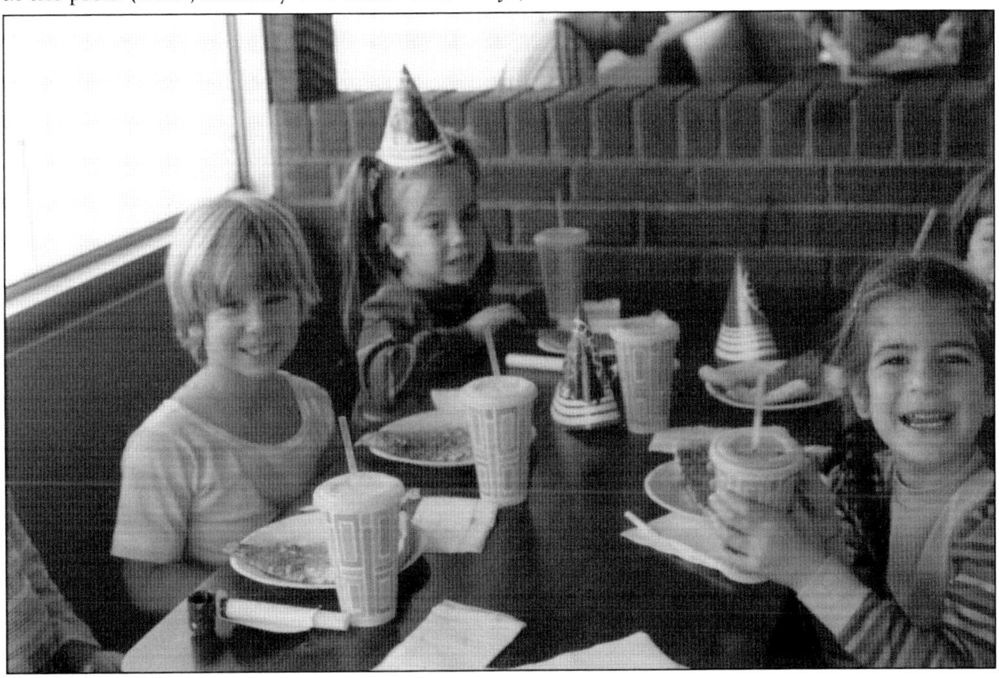

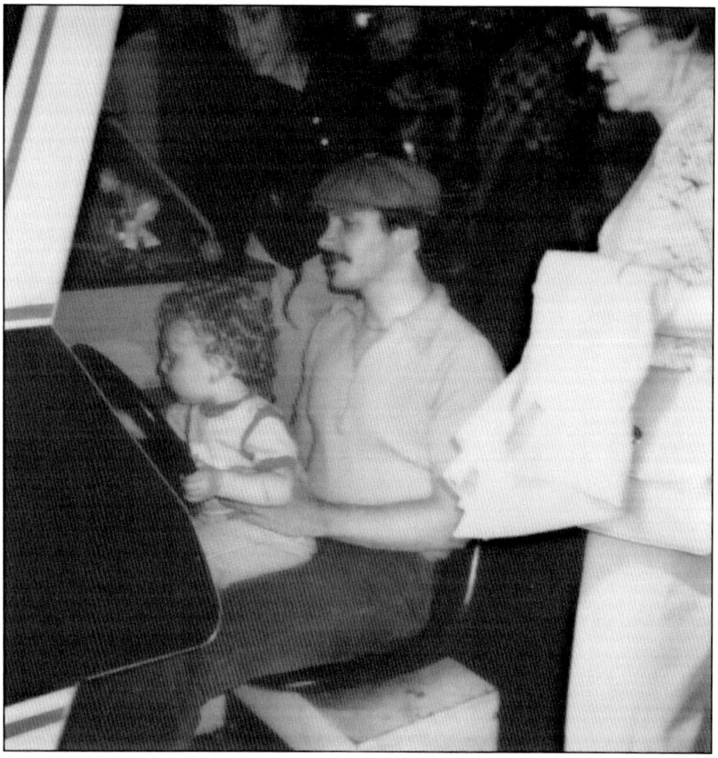

Nunley's arcade was a wondrous place. Nestled beside the carousel, there was a constant hum of the electronic sounds of video games, coins dropping, and frustrated or jubilant yells from players. Visitors recall Space Invaders, Asteroids, and Pac-Man, as well as almost 60 other arcade games from the 1950s through the 1990s. (Author's collection.)

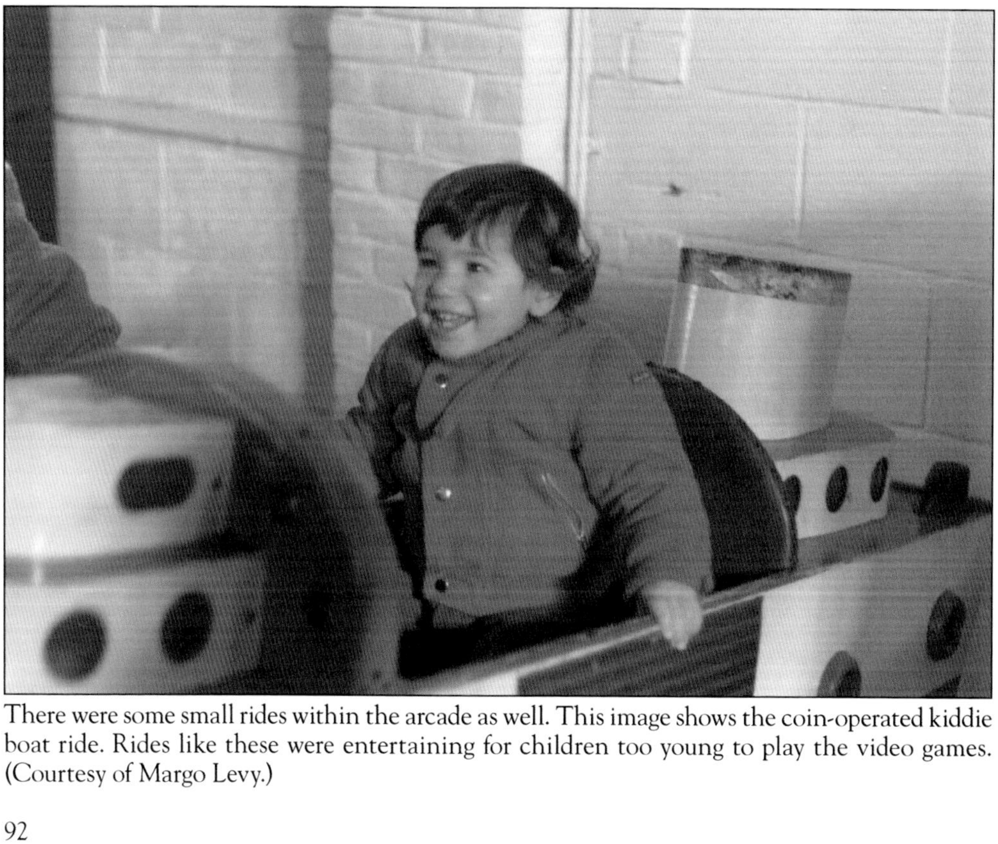

There were some small rides within the arcade as well. This image shows the coin-operated kiddie boat ride. Rides like these were entertaining for children too young to play the video games. (Courtesy of Margo Levy.)

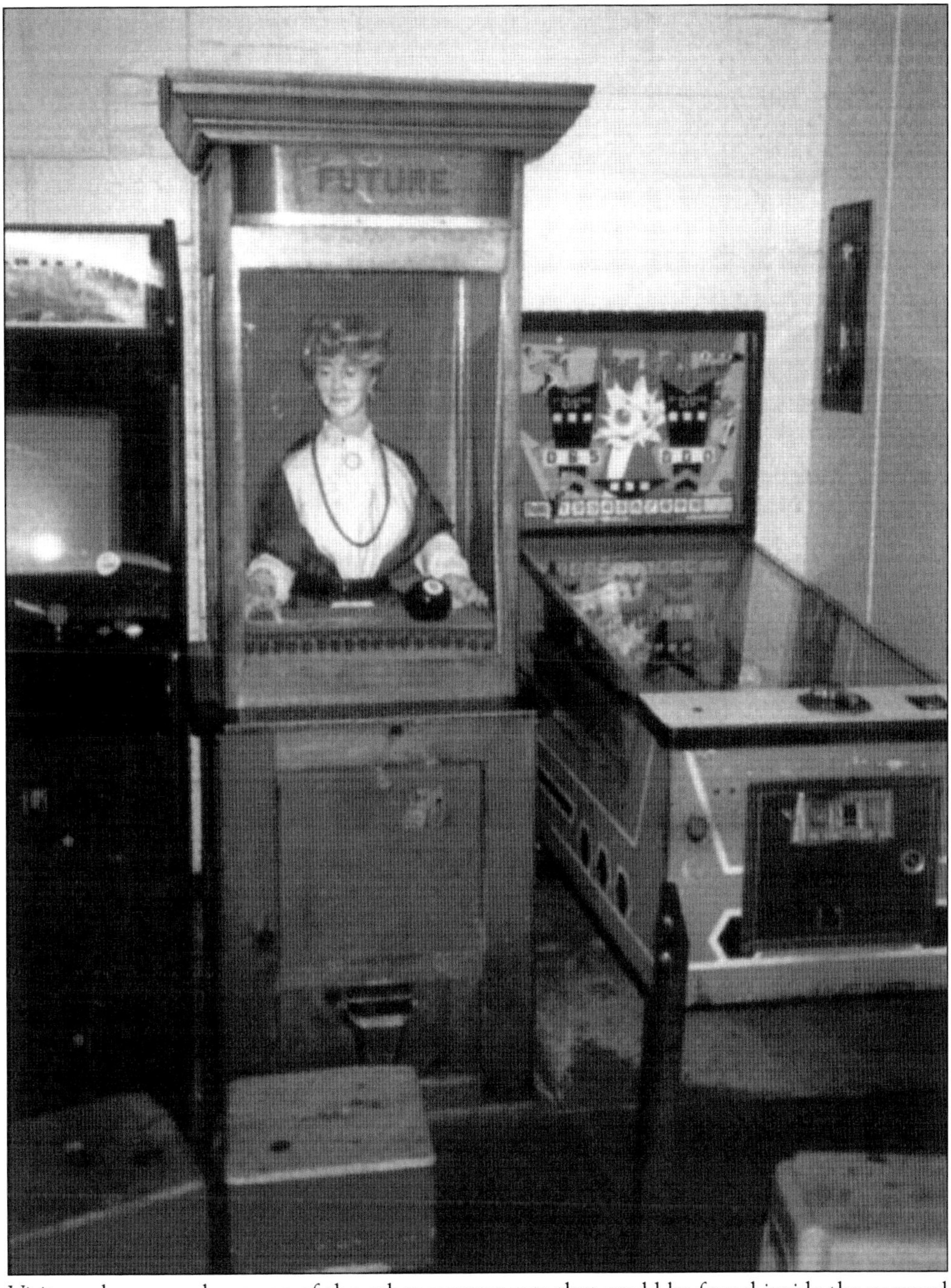

Visitors also remember some of the other amusements that could be found inside the carousel building, including pinball machines, Skee-Ball alleys, strength testers, and other coin-operated games. The Skee-Ball alleys were one of the most popular amusements there, aside from the video games. There was also a rare fortune telling machine. The "Munves Your Future," was in a wooden case with a fortune teller inside. After adding quarters, she presented the user a printout of their fortune. After the 1988 film *Big* came out, in which a similar machine was featured, this particular amusement became even more popular. (Courtesy of Dennis Ciccone Jr.)

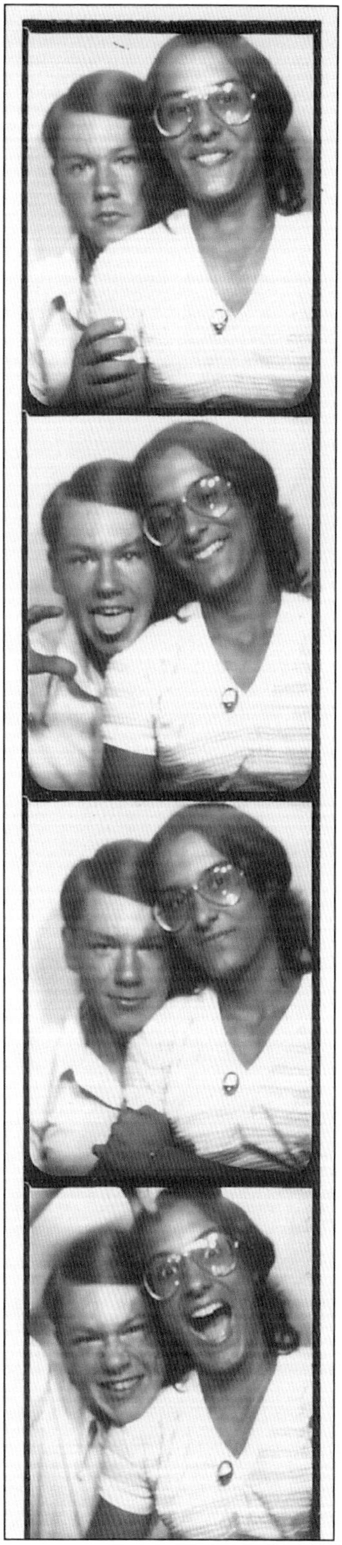

Nancy Ness and Rainer Radecker started dating while attending Freeport High School in the 1970s. They spent many dates at the nearby Nunley's Amusement Park, hanging out and falling in love. This picture was taken at the photo booth on July 7, 1979. They have been married for over 27 years and took their children to the park as well. Recently, they brought their grandchildren to the restored carousel, making it three generations to experience it. (Courtesy of Nancy Radecker.)

The miniature golf course was added to the park in 1961. It was a beloved feature and allowed the park to entertain a maturing audience, as children became young adults. Pictured here is the golf shack. (Courtesy of Elysa Parker.)

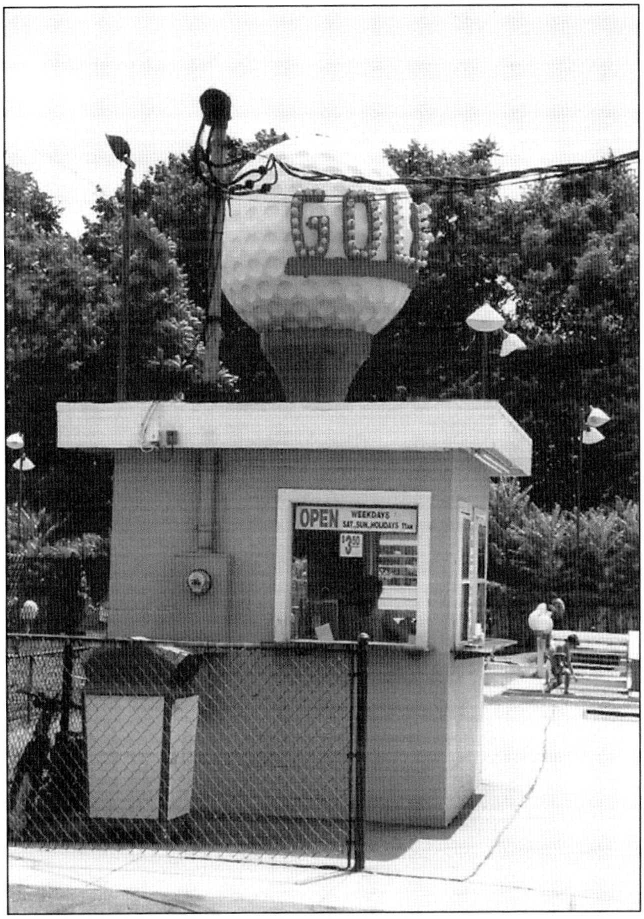

In this wide shot from the parking lot side of Nunley's, some of the golf course, including the giant bunny, can be seen. Although a chain-link fence surrounded the course to contain the balls, many players would still swing with all their strength instead of putting, which got them in trouble with the staff and possibly caused damage to nearby cars and houses. (Courtesy of Gary Monti.)

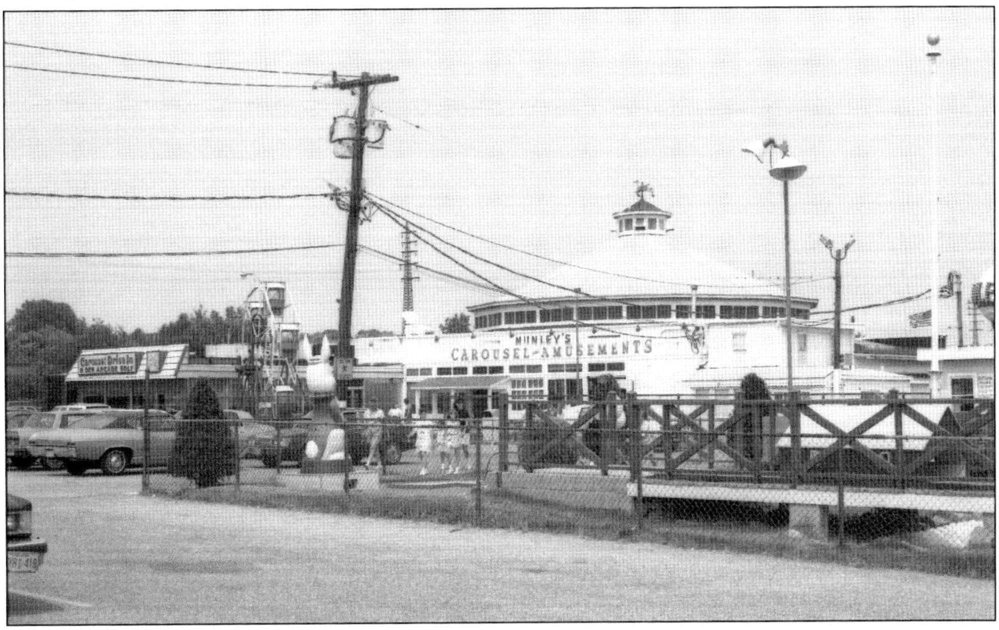

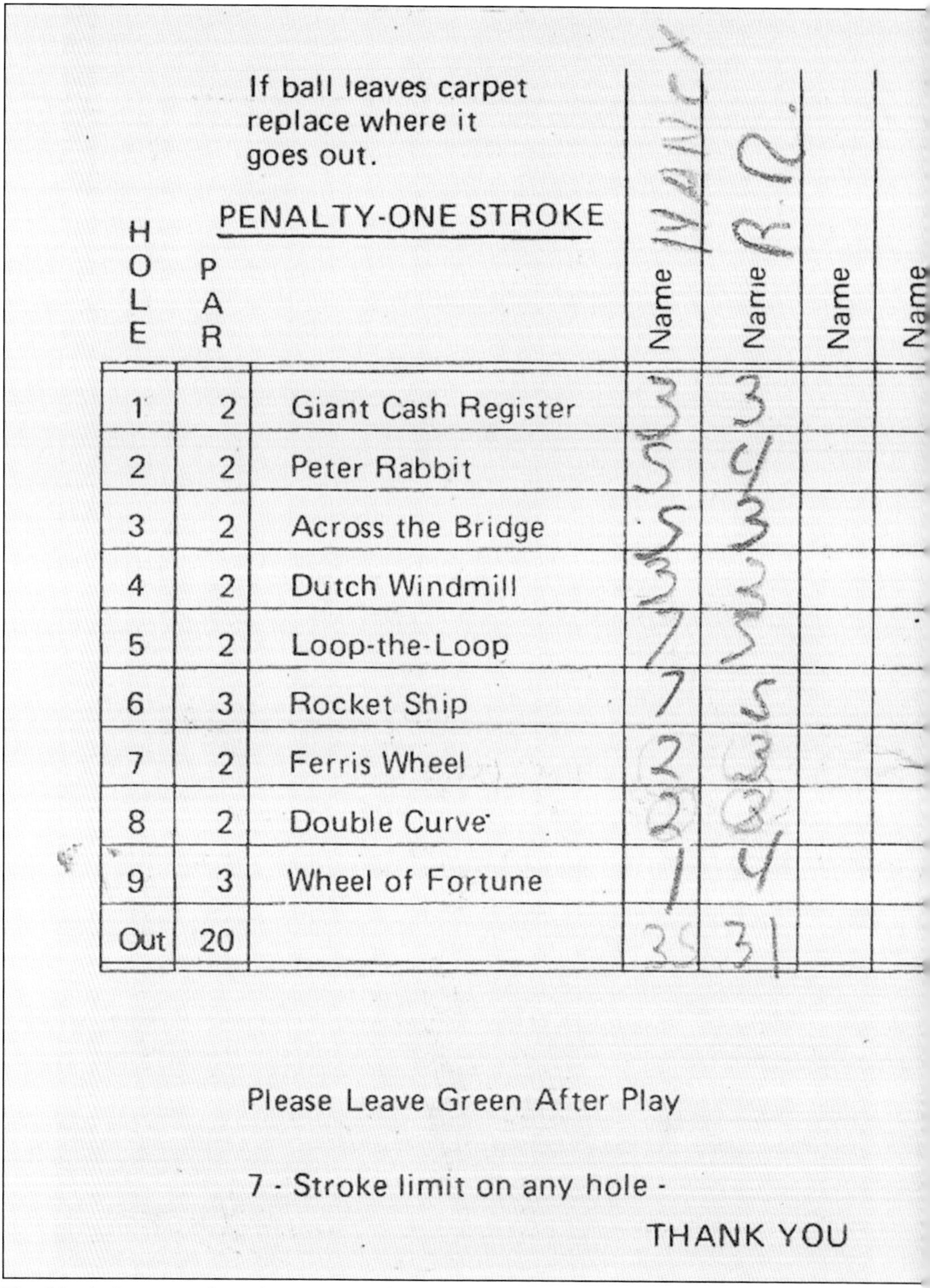

If ball leaves carpet
replace where it
goes out.

PENALTY-ONE STROKE

HOLE	PAR		Name NANCY	Name R.R.	Name	Name
1	2	Giant Cash Register	3	3		
2	2	Peter Rabbit	5	5		
3	2	Across the Bridge	5	3		
4	2	Dutch Windmill	3	3		
5	2	Loop-the-Loop	7	3		
6	3	Rocket Ship	7	5		
7	2	Ferris Wheel	2	3		
8	2	Double Curve	2	[illegible]		
9	3	Wheel of Fortune	1	4		
Out	20		35	31		

Please Leave Green After Play

7 - Stroke limit on any hole -

THANK YOU

This Nunley's scorecard was from a game of miniature golf played by Nancy and Rainer Radecker on July 7, 1979. This rare memento of the park shows the names of each hole of the course. Names

Move ball 6 in.
from any object.

NO PENALTY

PAR		Name	Name	Name	Name
2	Kooky-Kangaroo	4	2		
3	Double Trouble	7	7		
2	Horseshoe Curve	2	4		
2	Lighthouse	2	5		
2	Shooting Stars	4	3		
3	The Hump	4	5		
3	Dbl. Mound Dog Leg	2	3		
2	Olde Mill House	6	4		
3	Frontier Locomotive	3	5		
22		34	38		
20		35	31		
42		69	69		

ay game with interest and you will get a low score.
alk off greens as last putt is made.

OME BACK AGAIN

like "Peter Rabbit," "Horseshoe Curve," and "Double Mound Dog Leg" immediately bring to mind exactly how the course looked so many years ago. (Courtesy of Nancy Radecker.)

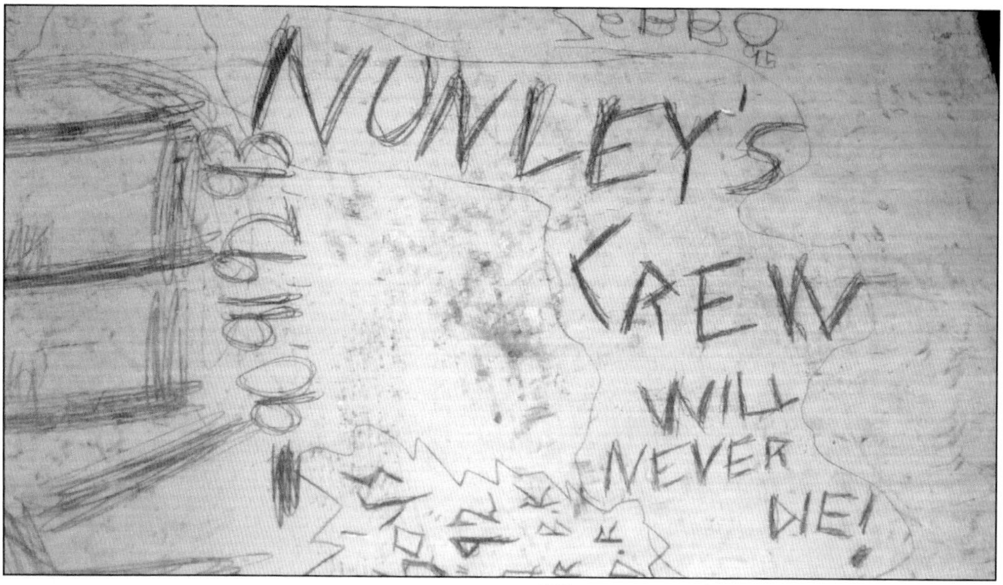

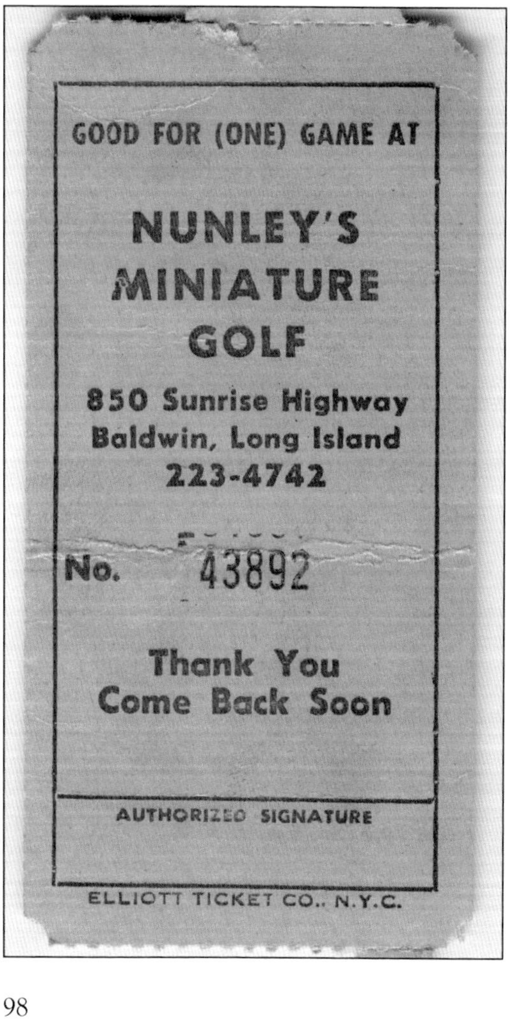

When arriving for mini golf, visitors first had to go to the golf shack to pay and get their clubs, golf balls, mini-pencils, and scorecards. Those who worked at the park may remember the door of the shack, which had years of graffiti from staff members on it. This detail of the door shows how much love the staff had for the park, as well as how much fun they had working there. Pictured at left is a ticket for one game at the course. (Both, courtesy of Dennis Ciccone Jr.)

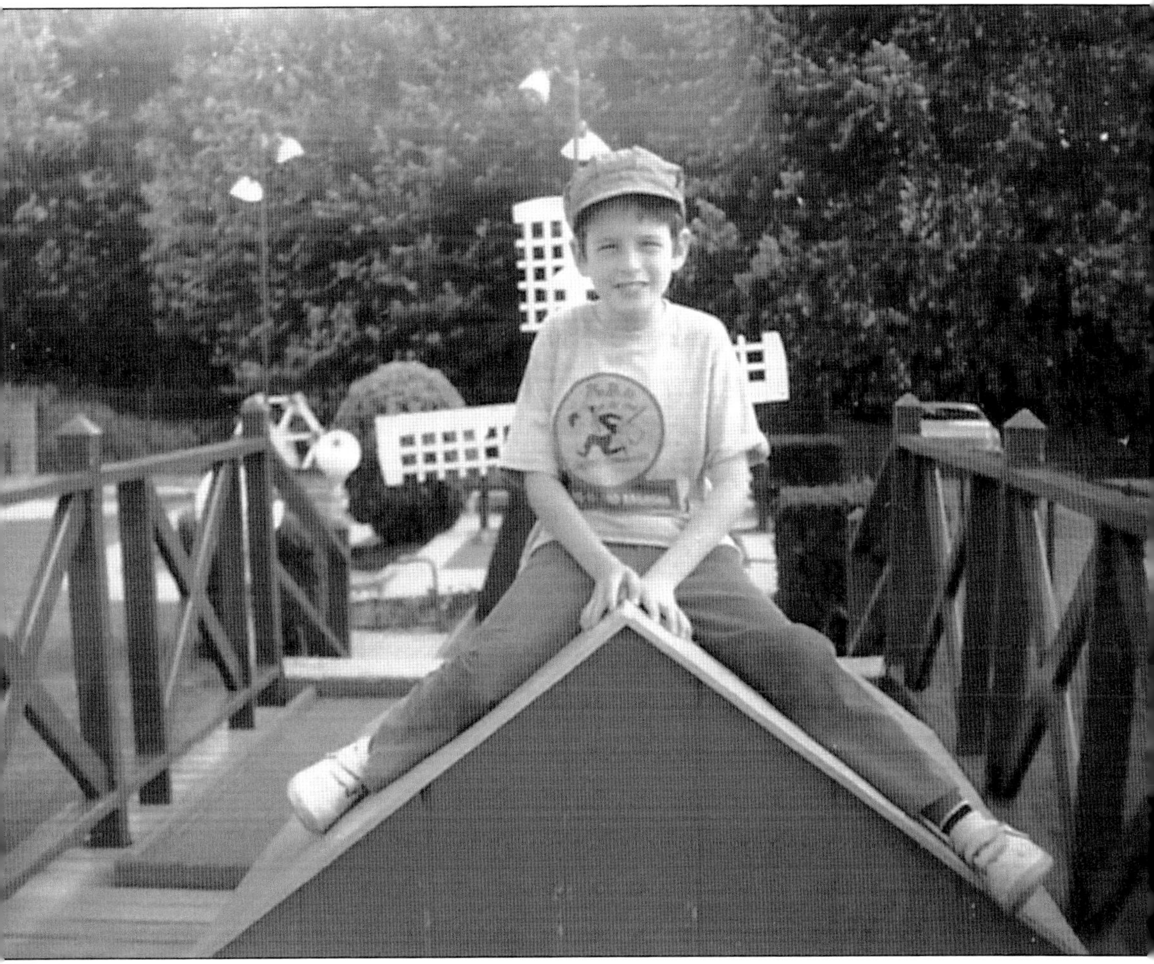

There were 18 holes at the Nunley's golf course. The first one featured a giant cash register. Pictured here is the third hole, "Across the Bridge," followed by the "Dutch Windmill." (Courtesy of Chuck Egbert.)

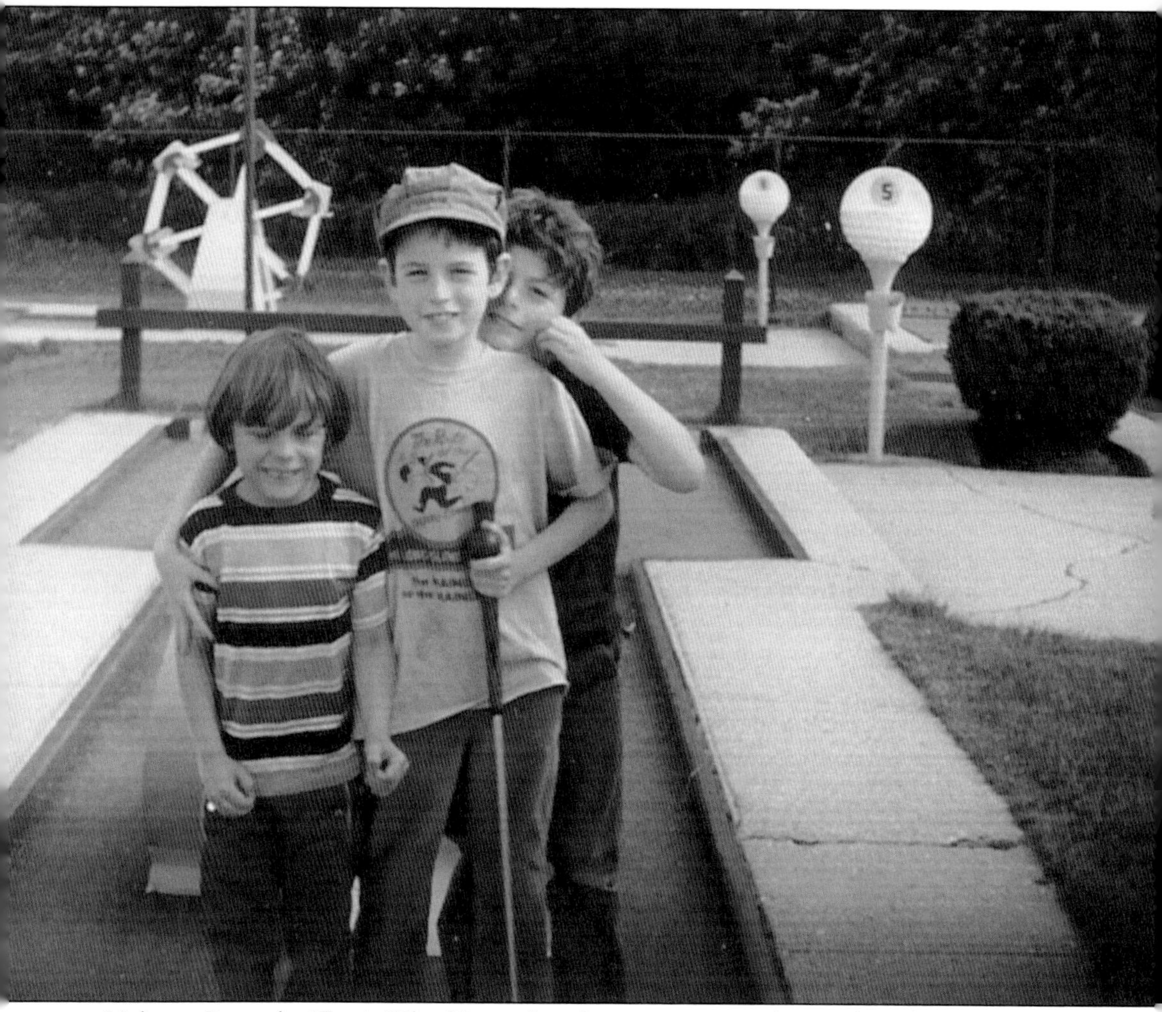

Hole no. 7 was the "Ferris Wheel," a nod to the amusement park next door, but still a difficult hole. From there, it moved to hole no. 8, the "Double Curve," and hole no. 9, "Wheel of Fortune." While this was a small course, it was fun, partially because of the cool buildings and the golf ball–shaped signs at each hole. (Courtesy of Chuck Egbert.)

7 - STROKE LIMIT ON ANY HOLE - 7
RULES

Parties playing together limited to four (4) persons.

Initial stroke on each hole must be played from rubber mats.

Ball may be moved 6 inches from rail or hazard without penalty.

If ball leaves carpet, it must be placed on carpet at place of departure. Penalty one stroke.

The ball is not to be returned to the tee unless it goes out of bounds AT THE TEE.

In case of stymie, ball shall be played or lifted out of the way upon request of other player.

If ball is hit by another ball, the player of hit ball make take new position unless knocked into cup, in which case he MUST take old position and shoot.

Strictly against rules to play anywhere except on carpet.

Please consider others in back of you, keep game moving.

The management reserves the right to refuse admittance to these grounds.

Players then moved through holes 10 through 17: "Kooky-Kangaroo," "Double Trouble," "Horseshoe Curve," "Lighthouse," "Shooting Stars," "The Hump," "Double Mound Dog Leg," and "Olde Mill House." The final hole—no. 18—was the "Frontier Locomotive." (Courtesy of Nancy Radecker.)

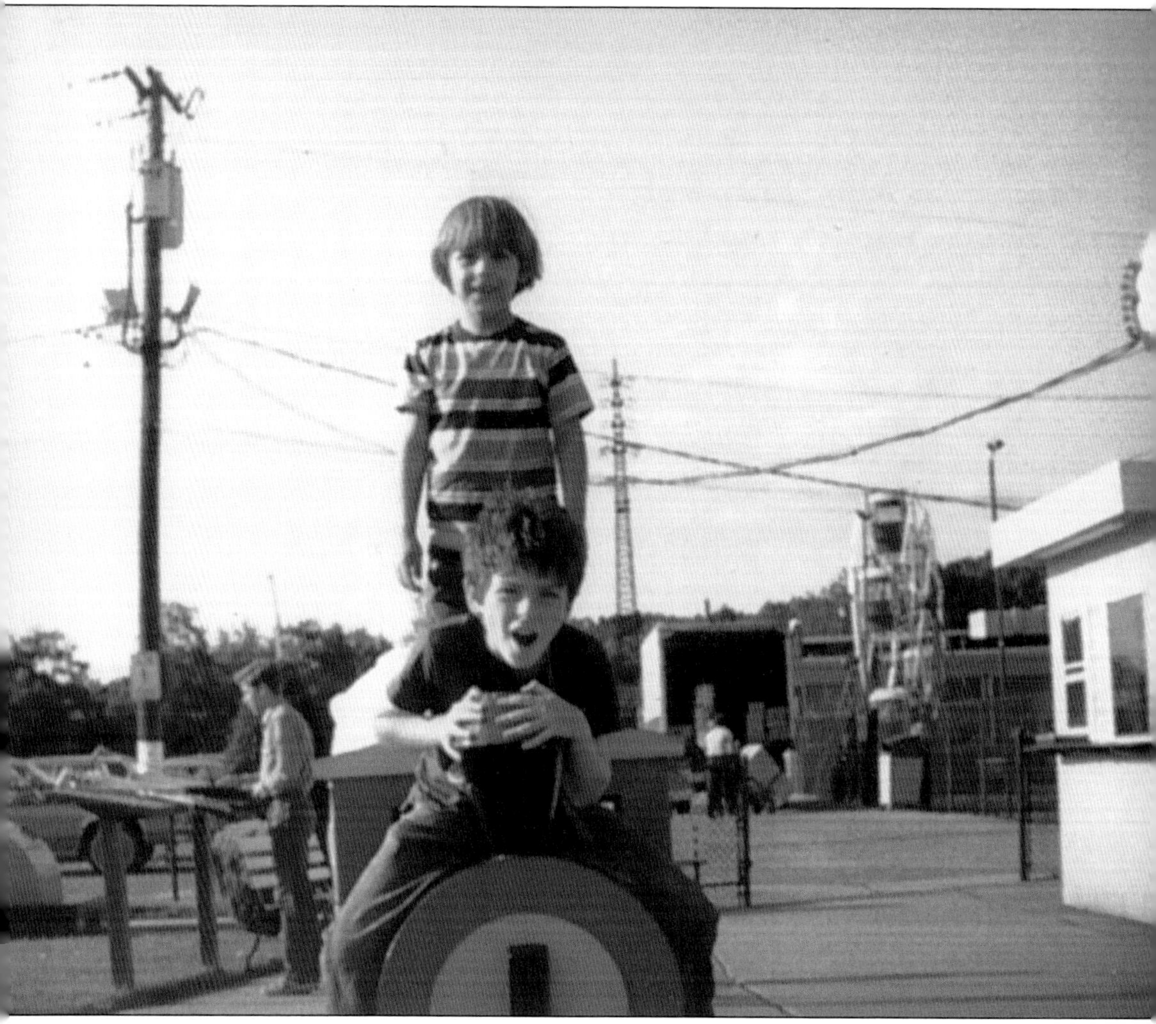

By the time regular visitors to the park were beginning to grow up, they weren't so interested in the kiddie rides. Luckily, the allure of the arcade and miniature golf course was enough to still keep the kids interested in visiting the park. As parents played through the course, they could glance over and see the hot rods and the dune buggies and remember when their children were young enough to want to ride them. When the game ended, the families walked over to the restaurant for pizza and ice cream. They passed the boat ride and the Ferris wheel and again, remembered. But they knew that, at least for now, the kids were still spending time with them, for just a little while longer. (Courtesy of Chuck Egbert.)

Five

End of An Era

It is an amazing feat that Nunley's Amusement Park remained open as long as it did. When the Lercari brothers took over the park in 1964, it was still a lucrative business. But as time passed, and as other small family parks began to close, the park wasn't as profitable with its cheap ticket prices, although it remained a local landmark. When the brothers finally decided to retire and close the park in 1995, the public was crushed. Long Islanders rushed back to the park in its final weeks to say their goodbyes and mourn their lost childhoods. All the rides and the beloved carousel would be sold at public auction—or so they thought. While the rides were sold off one by one, it was the iconic carousel that became the center of a long and heated debate among the public, the county of Nassau, and its owners.

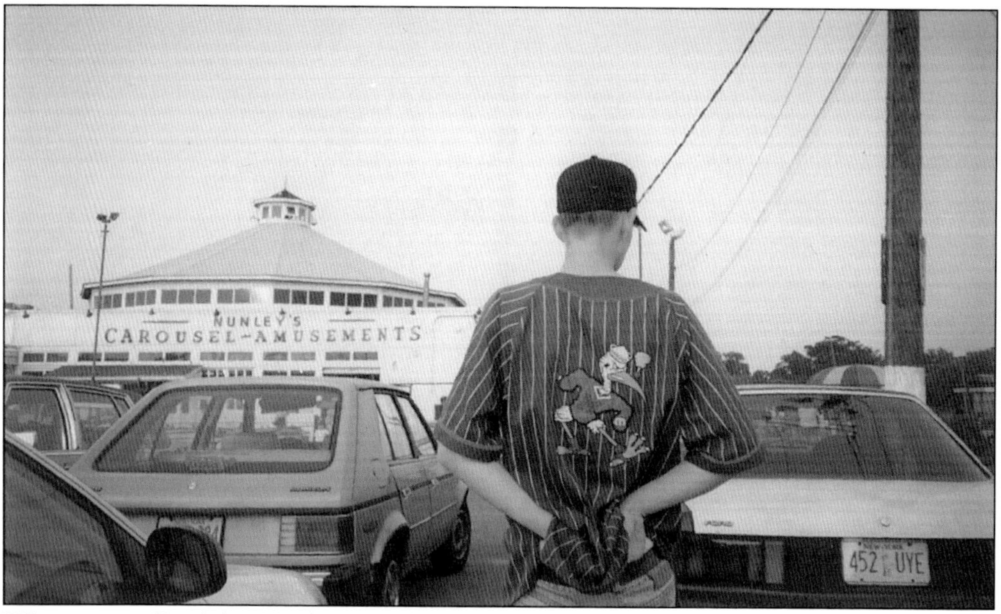

When it was official that Nunley's was closing, the public was deeply saddened. Many went out of their way to head to Baldwin for one last visit. In this picture, Gregg Healey was photographed by his mom on the family's last trip to the park the week it closed in 1995. (Courtesy of Gregg Healey.)

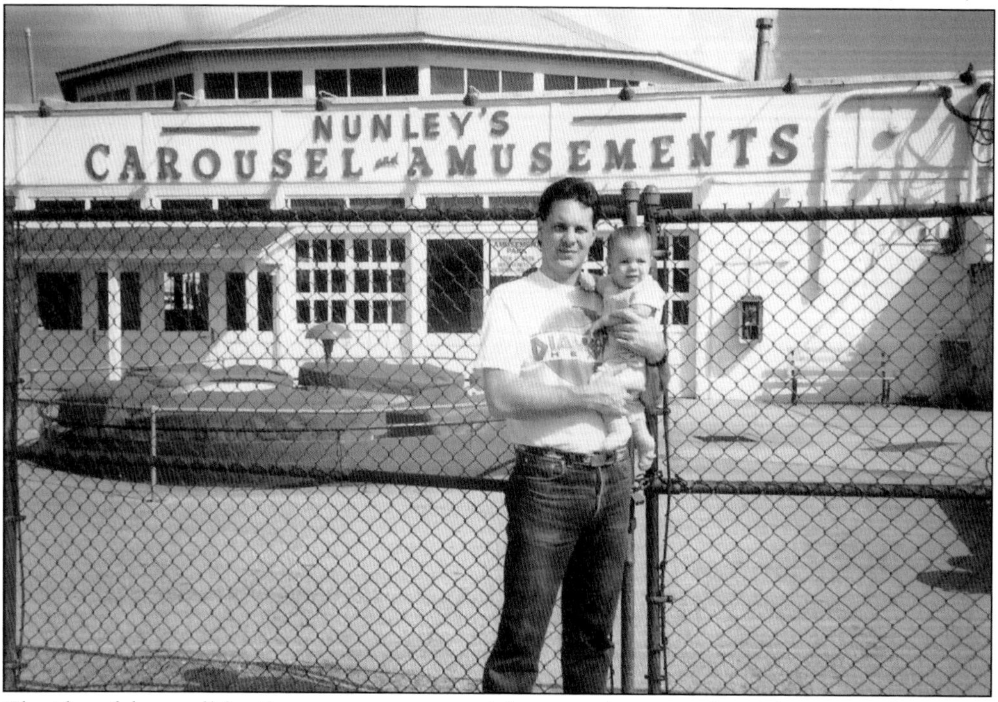

The idea of the small family-run amusement park began to die out in the 1950s as a result of being overtaken by large corporate theme parks. These new parks were larger, with faster and more exciting rides, and could satisfy a wider demographic. Many of these theme parks had small kiddie areas within them, so the entire family could enjoy various amusements. Here Ron SanFilippo poses with his son Jonathan in front of the locked gates. (Courtesy of Ron SanFilippo.)

The three Lercari brothers—Lou, Steve, and John—acquired partial ownership of the park in 1964 from Lou's wife's aunt, Miriam Nunley. The brothers dedicated their lives to the park, and were beloved by the visitors and staff. Visitors sometimes referred to Lou Lercari as "Mr. Nunley." Pictured here are Lou and Edna Nunley on their wedding day outside the Immaculate Conception Church on Staten Island. (Courtesy of Steve Lercari.)

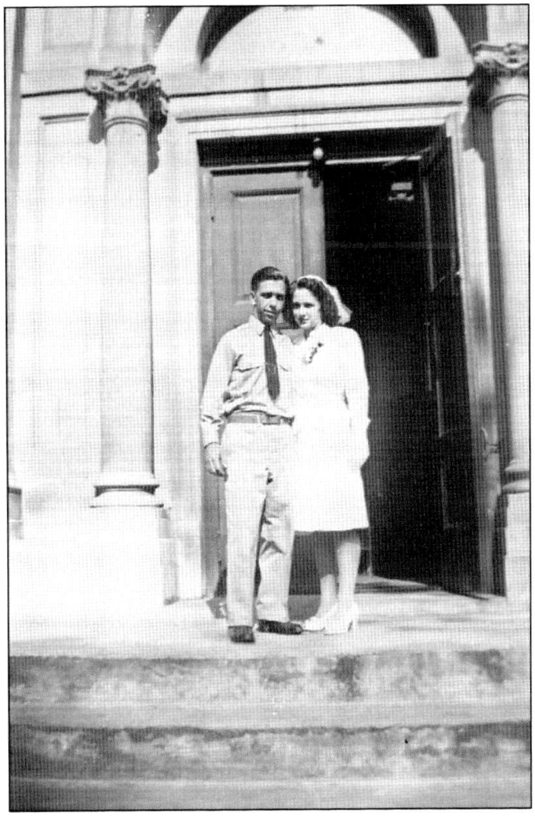

This photograph, taken in 1988 of a closed and empty Nunley's, foreshadows what was to come in a few short years. Soon enough, the public had to get used to the feeling of being shut out from the park. (Courtesy of Gary Monti.)

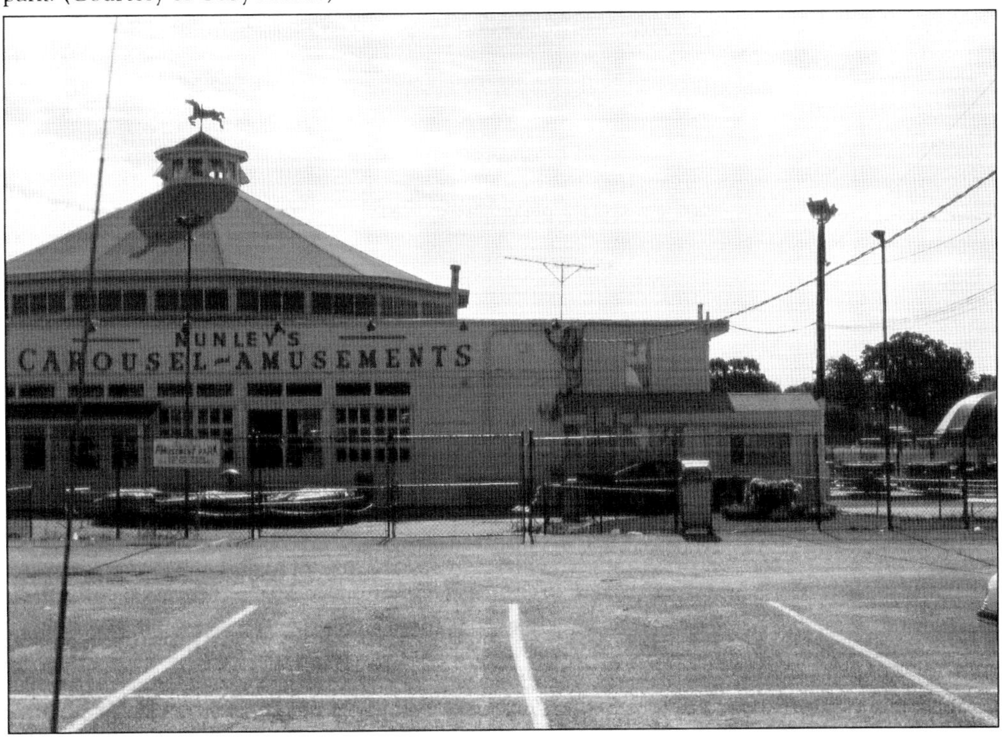

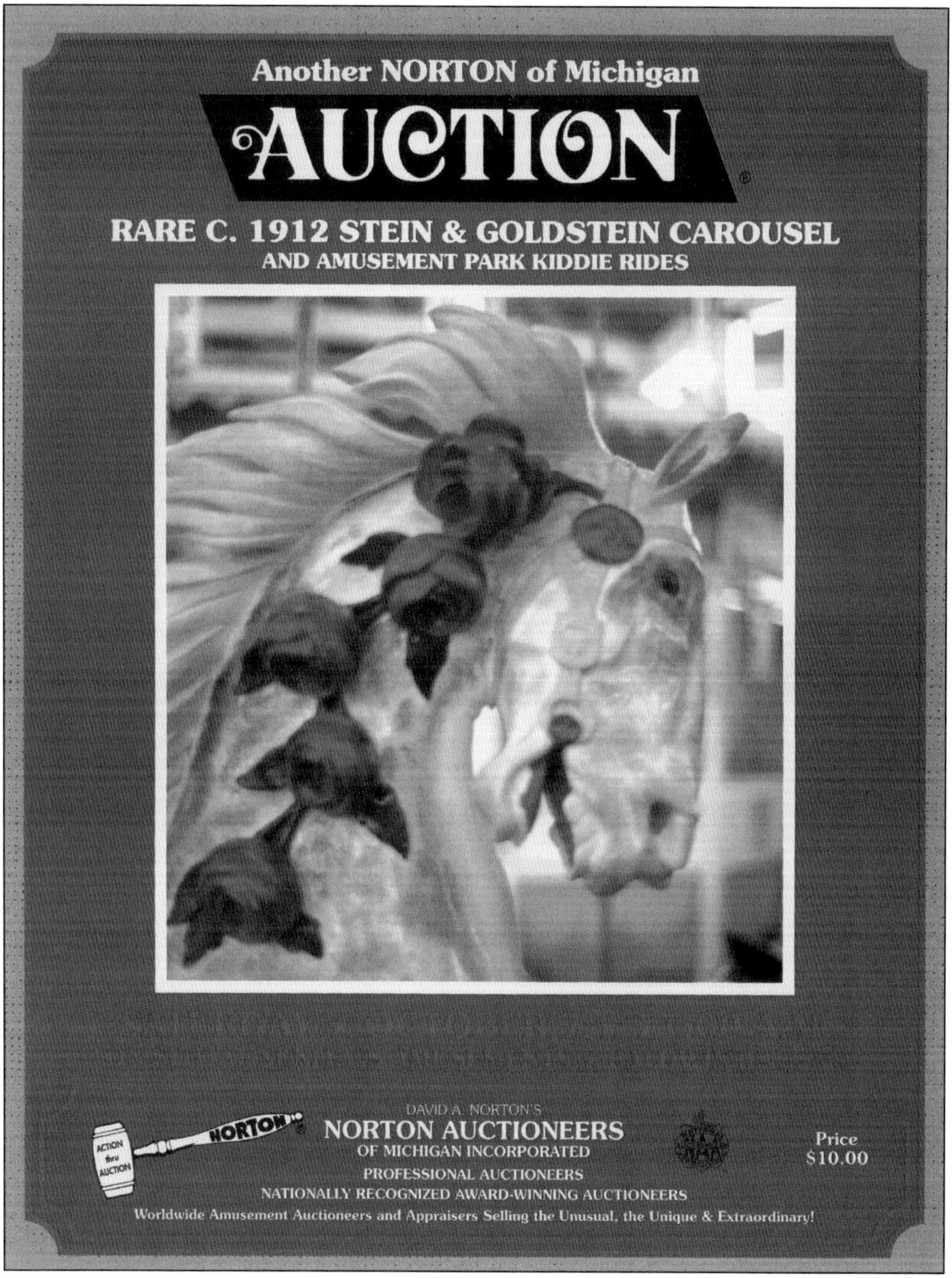

As much as everyone loved the park, the public took it for granted and believed it would always be there. The park had been open for over 50 years and was a landmark in the community; no one could imagine the end of Nunley's. In 1995, when it was announced the park would close, the public was shocked, but it was too late. Inexpensive ticket prices and low visitor numbers, as well as aging owners, had taken their toll. It was time to retire. The carousel and rides would go to public auction. Nunley's was closing, and not just for the winter. (Courtesy of Dennis Ciccone Jr.)

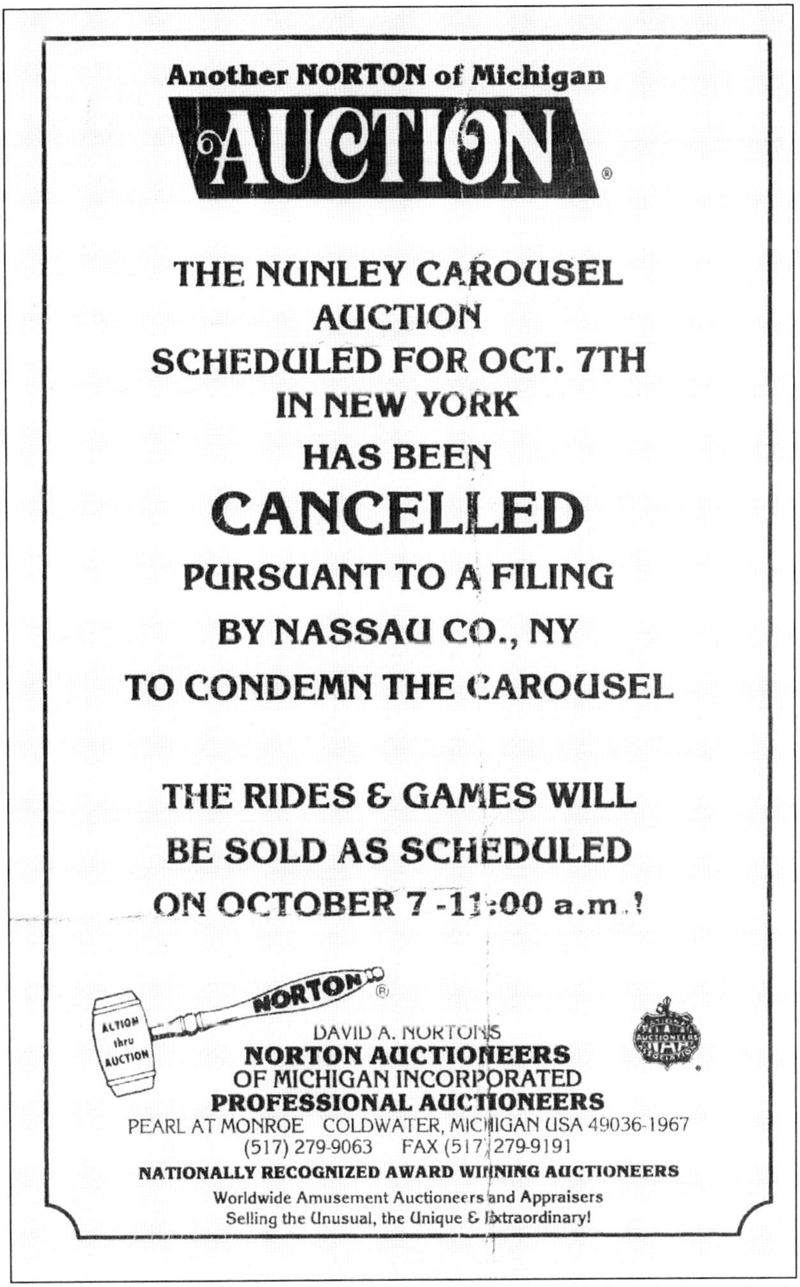

Another NORTON of Michigan

AUCTION®

THE NUNLEY CAROUSEL
AUCTION
SCHEDULED FOR OCT. 7TH
IN NEW YORK
HAS BEEN

CANCELLED

PURSUANT TO A FILING
BY NASSAU CO., NY
TO CONDEMN THE CAROUSEL

THE RIDES & GAMES WILL
BE SOLD AS SCHEDULED
ON OCTOBER 7 -11:00 a.m.!

ACTION thru AUCTION

NORTON®

DAVID A. NORTON'S
NORTON AUCTIONEERS
OF MICHIGAN INCORPORATED
PROFESSIONAL AUCTIONEERS
PEARL AT MONROE COLDWATER, MICHIGAN USA 49036-1967
(517) 279-9063 FAX (517) 279-9191
NATIONALLY RECOGNIZED AWARD WINNING AUCTIONEERS
Worldwide Amusement Auctioneers and Appraisers
Selling the Unusual, the Unique & Extraordinary!

Baldwin residents and fans of the park were heartbroken for their beloved carousel to leave town. In an unexpected twist, the county of Nassau stepped in and canceled the auction, declaring that they would purchase the carousel as a whole so it could remain in the community. Local newspapers wrote countless articles week after week about the fate of the carousel and its possible future location. At first, it was planned to remain in its original location, but as a feature of a new King Kullen supermarket that was interested in the property. Then, other Baldwin locations were introduced, like the park surrounding Silver Lake and the intersection of Sunrise Highway and Grand Avenue. Others stepped in with possible locations, including musician Billy Joel, who tried to get the carousel moved to his hometown of Oyster Bay. (Courtesy of Dennis Ciccone Jr.)

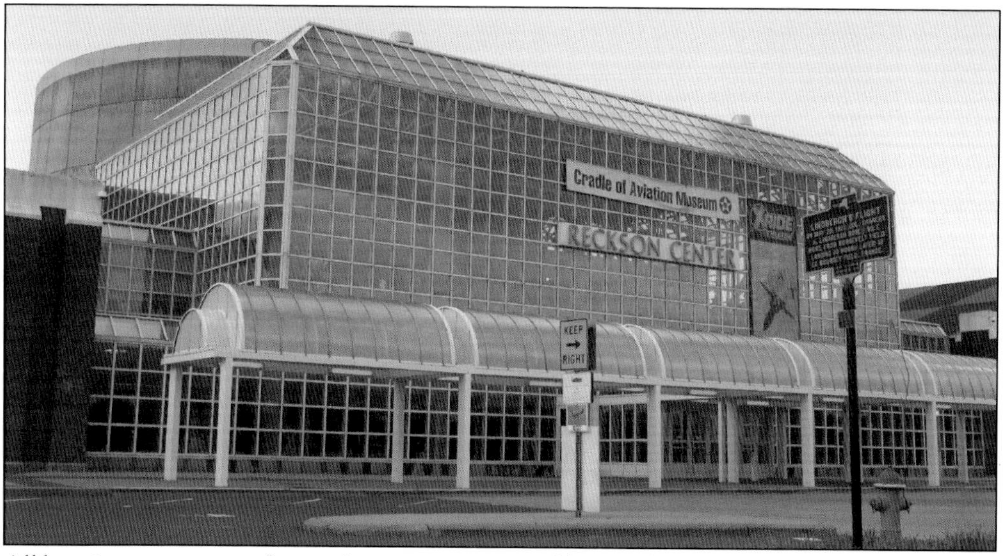

All locations were met with mixed reviews; no one could agree about where the carousel should go. Numerous community organizations were established to save the beloved ride. When a spot was finally found, between the Cradle of Aviation Museum and the Long Island Children's Museum, it was just the beginning. A significant amount of public funds had been needed to purchase the carousel, and now more was needed to restore it and create its new home. (Author's collection.)

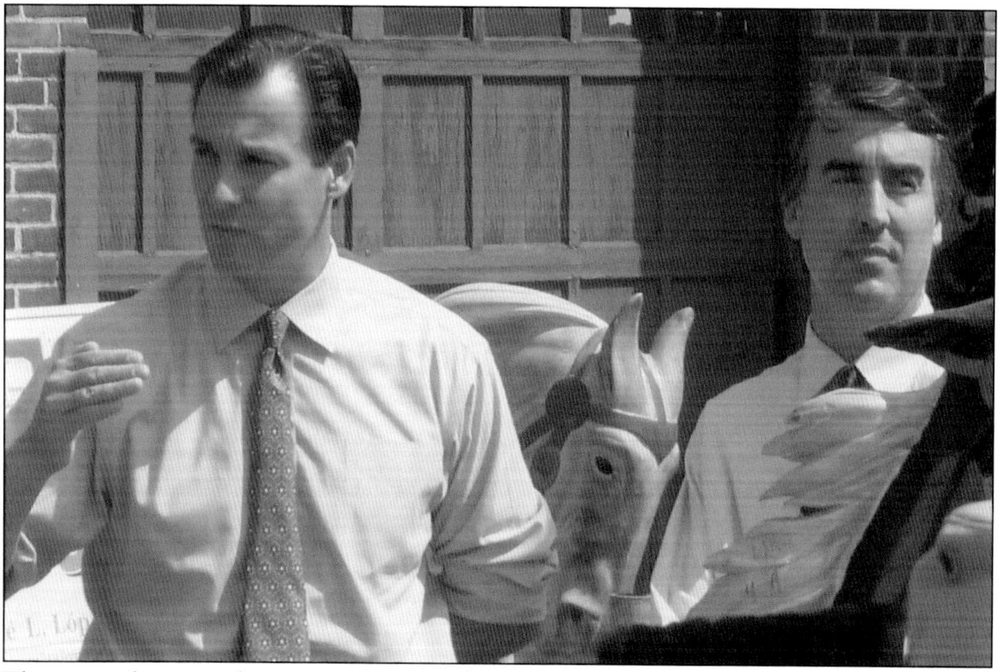

The carousel remained in storage for more than 10 years. In 2007, nine-year-old local resident Rachel Obergh created the program "Pennies for Ponies." It encouraged local schools to raise the needed funds for the restoration. The program raised more than $81,000, the majority of which was raised by schools. Each sponsor got to name a horse. Here, Nassau County executive Thomas Suozzi and Nassau County legislator Joseph Scannell are pictured speaking to the press. (Courtesy of Dennis Ciccone Jr.)

Six

The Nunley's Legacy

Nunley's Amusement Park is gone, but it will exist forever in the hearts and memories of those who have been there. The Nunley and Lercari families devoted their lives to the community and gave so many Long Islanders an amazing opportunity to celebrate childhood. Nunley's still lives on in many ways today, more than 15 years after its closing. Numerous online forums celebrating the park have popped up, in which fans share stories, photographs, and memorabilia they have held on to over the years. It allows people the opportunity to reminisce on their childhoods with old friends and, in some cases, reconnect with their hometown, even if they have moved far away. After all these years, Nunley's still manages to inspire and delight, and luckily, there are still opportunities to share pieces of Nunley's with future generations.

Villanelle on the Demise of Nunley's Amusement Park

My favorite is the merry-go-round–
the white horse with red roses in its mane.
Children and machines make a merry sound.

I greet repeated faces I have found
and hum on the calliope's refrain.
My favorite is the merry-go-round

where the horses really lift up in safe bounds,
the only pitch, the roof's. Shaded from rain,
children and machines make a merry sound.

Our son no longer fears leaving the ground,
and his skeeball scores amaze us, measured gain.
But my favorite is the merry-go-round
for watching parents' pleasure doubled round--
our childhood remembered, our children's for now remain.
Children and machines make us merry.

Sound one sad note when they tear this place down;
our youth and theirs will not be quite the same.
My favorite was the merry-go-round.
Children and machines made a merry sound.

As so many Long Island parents can relate to, Ellen Pickus of Baldwin loved bringing her son to Nunley's over the years. After Nunley's closed, Pickus was deeply saddened. She eventually wrote this poem about her memories of the park. (Courtesy of Ellen Pickus.)

Nunley's touched the hearts of those who experienced the park in so many ways. Lynda Bertinetti visited the park multiple times in the 1950s with her father. When they rode the carousel, he would always grab the rings for her since she was too small to reach. When he passed away years later, Lynda, who saved a few of the rings, placed one in his casket as an eternal memory of the happy times they shared. (Courtesy of Dennis Ciccone Jr.)

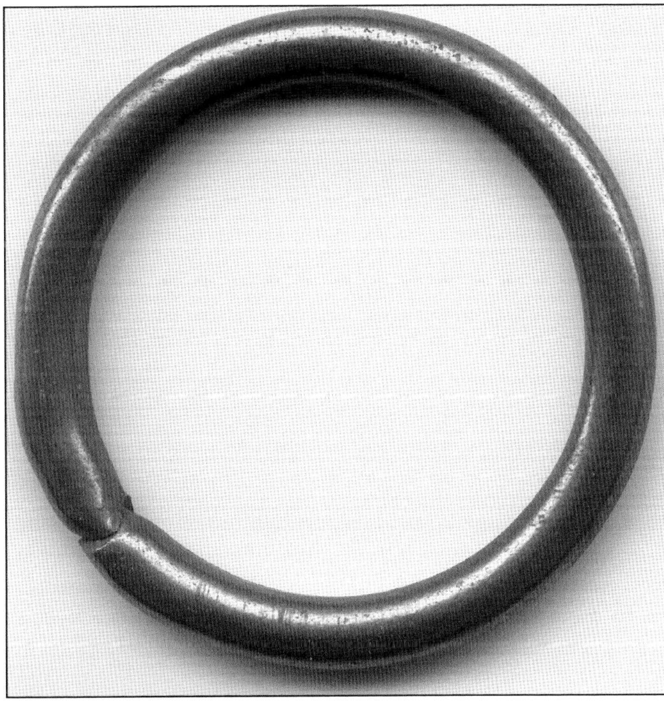

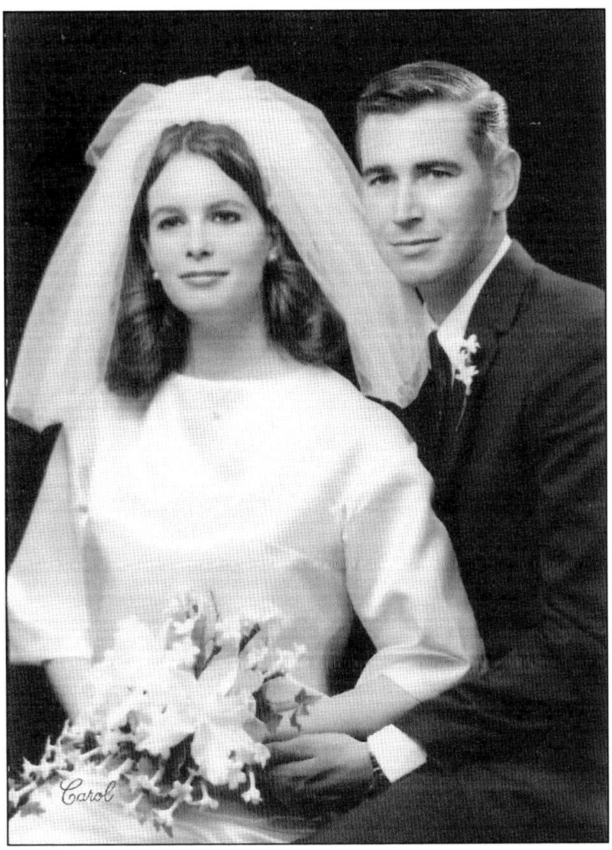

Thomas Slade grew up in Oceanside, and in December 1959, he went to Nunley's with some friends to find cute girls. He held up a sign with his phone number right next to the ring arm of the carousel, and indeed, a cute girl grabbed it. They started going steady the next week and were married in June 1966. They had five children and took them to Nunley's over the years. When reflecting on the park, Slade said, "My whole life has been beautiful, thanks to Nunley's and the wife I met there so many happy years ago." (Courtesy of Thomas E. Slade.)

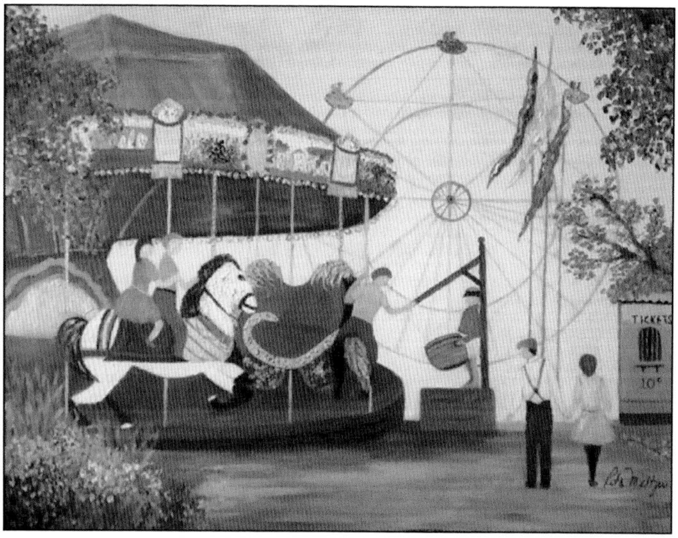

This painting, inspired by Nunley's Amusement Park, was created by Rita Meltzer for her granddaughter Victoria. Victoria loved visiting the park and went almost every Sunday for dinner with her grandfather. While the layout of the actual park was quite different from how it is depicted here, the nostalgic feel is a reminder of the long journey the Nunley's carousel made through different parks across Long Island. (Courtesy of Victoria Meltzer.)

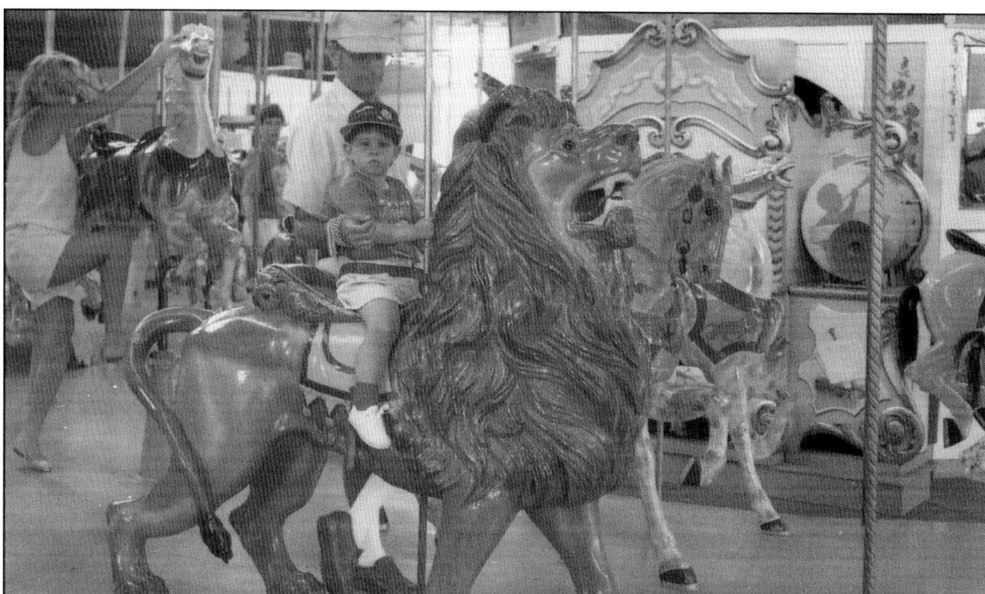

Simon Walter Placek III used to visit Nunley's with his parents. One evening, they stopped at the restaurant for a quick bite and realized that the carousel was gone. "The carousel that I used to ride all the time, the one that I measured my growth by my ability to eventually lean over enough to grab onto the rings that they used to dangle for the customers to try to snatch as the ride was going around, was gone," mourns Placek. "The room was bare and eerily silent, as all the arcades were also gone. I was sad at the time, as I realized that it is just another part of growing up, things change." (Courtesy of Gary Monti.)

Musician Deanna Kirk grew up in Freeport, attended Freeport High School, and was a regular visitor to the park. On her album *Where Are You Now*, released in 1997, is a song entitled "Carousel," inspired by going to the park with her grandmother. (Courtesy of Deanna Kirk.)

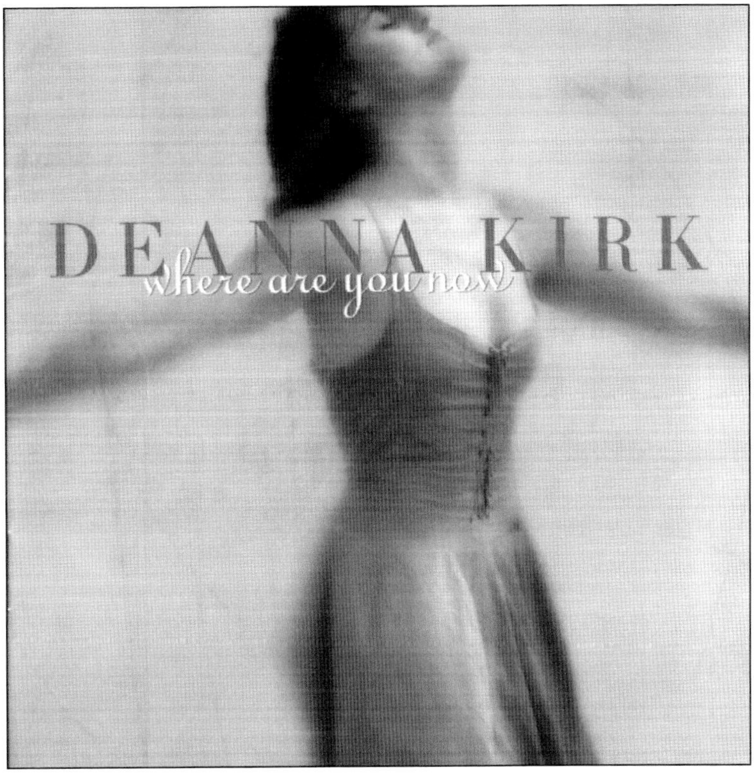

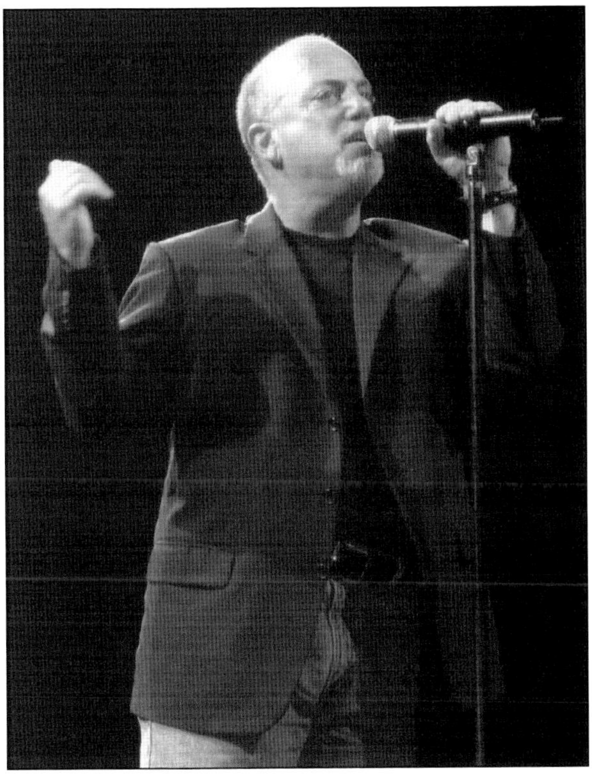

Nunley's most famous visitor was legendary rocker Billy Joel. Joel was raised in Hickville, Long Island. His first solo album, released in 1971, was entitled *Cold Spring Harbor*, after the Long Island town. When the carousel's restoration plans were announced in the media, Joel agreed to allow his "Waltz No. 1 for piano (Nunley's Carousel), Op. 2" to be played on the restored carousel organ. (Public domain.)

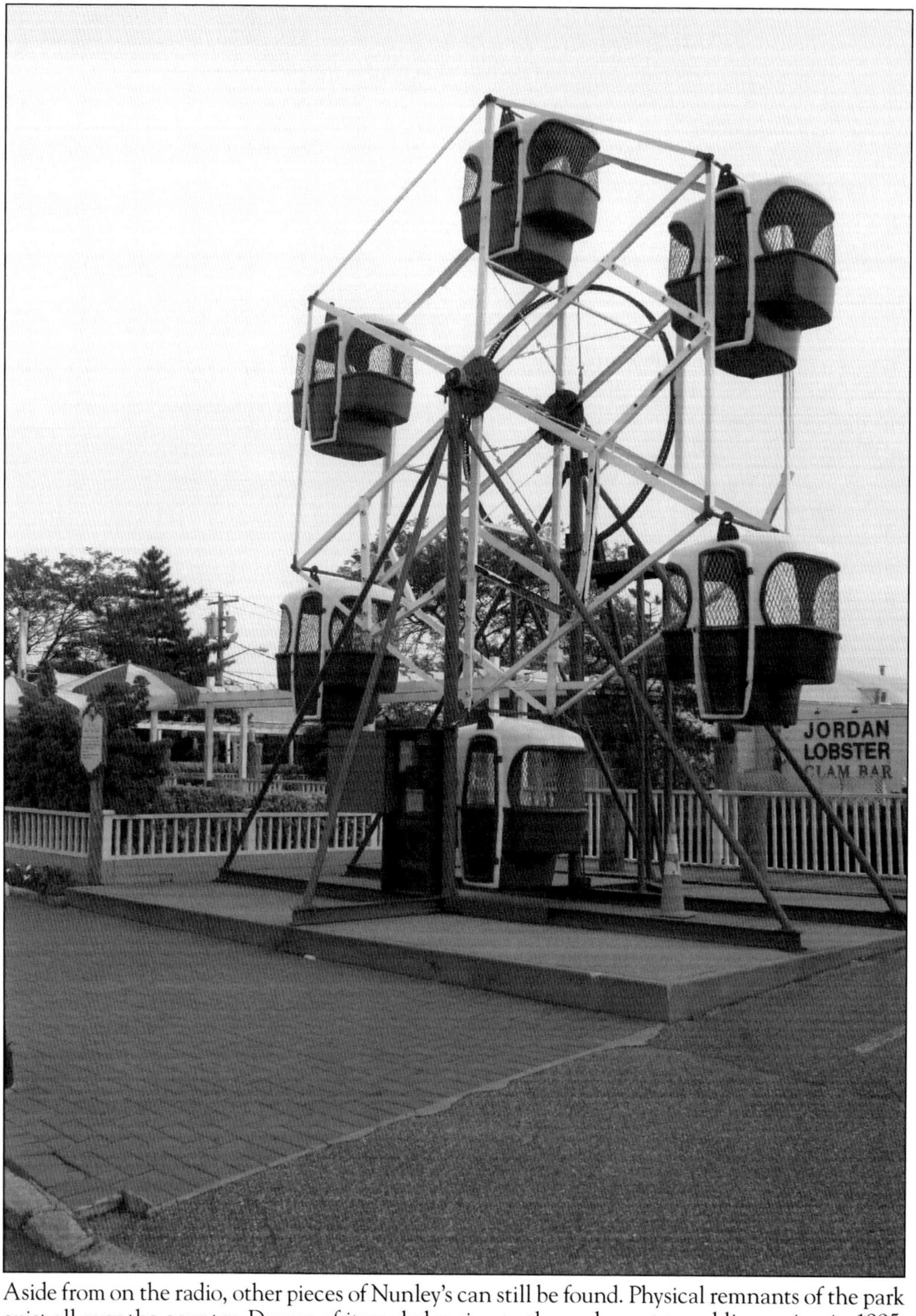

Aside from on the radio, other pieces of Nunley's can still be found. Physical remnants of the park exist all over the country. Dozens of items belonging to the park went to public auction in 1995. Fans of the park were able to purchase Skee-Ball lanes, hot rods, benches, and even arcade games. In Barnum Island, a hamlet between Oceanside and Long Beach, the Ferris wheel that was at the park stands today. Privately owned, it sits facing out towards the water. (Author's collection.)

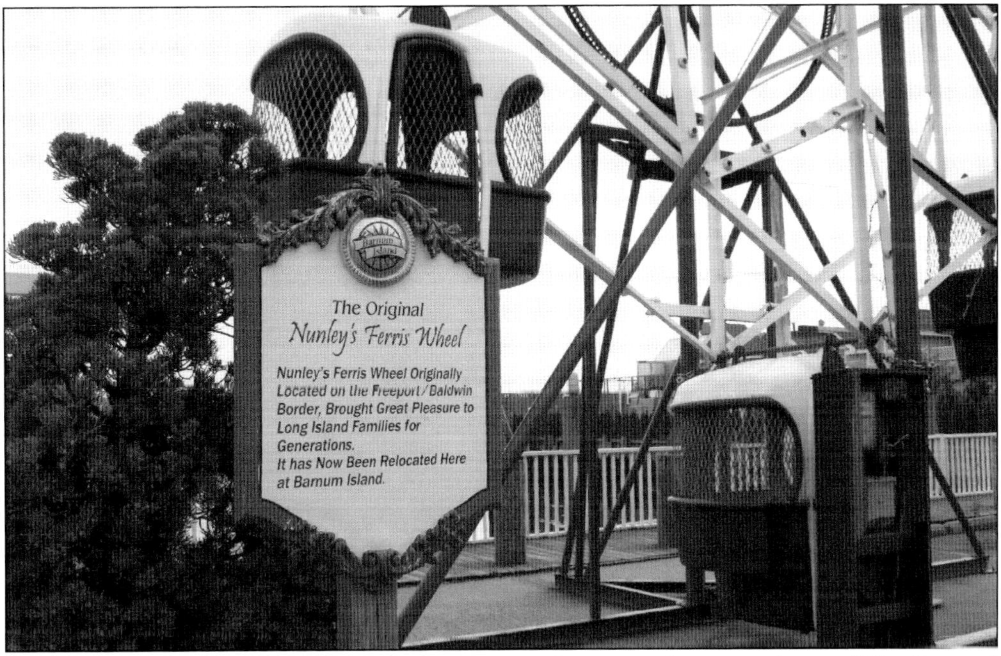

Next to the ride is a sign briefly explaining its significance and previous home: "The Original Nunley's Ferris Wheel: Nunley's Ferris Wheel Originally Located on the Freeport/Baldwin Border, Brought Great Pleasure to Long Island Families for Generations. It has Now Been Relocated Here at Barnum Island." It seems fitting that the ride ended up near the ocean, as the first amusement parks in Coney Island thrived because of their proximity to the beach and fresh air. Now, passersby can look with curiosity at the children's amusement on the side of the road, while others will understand and remember fondly. (Both, author's collection.)

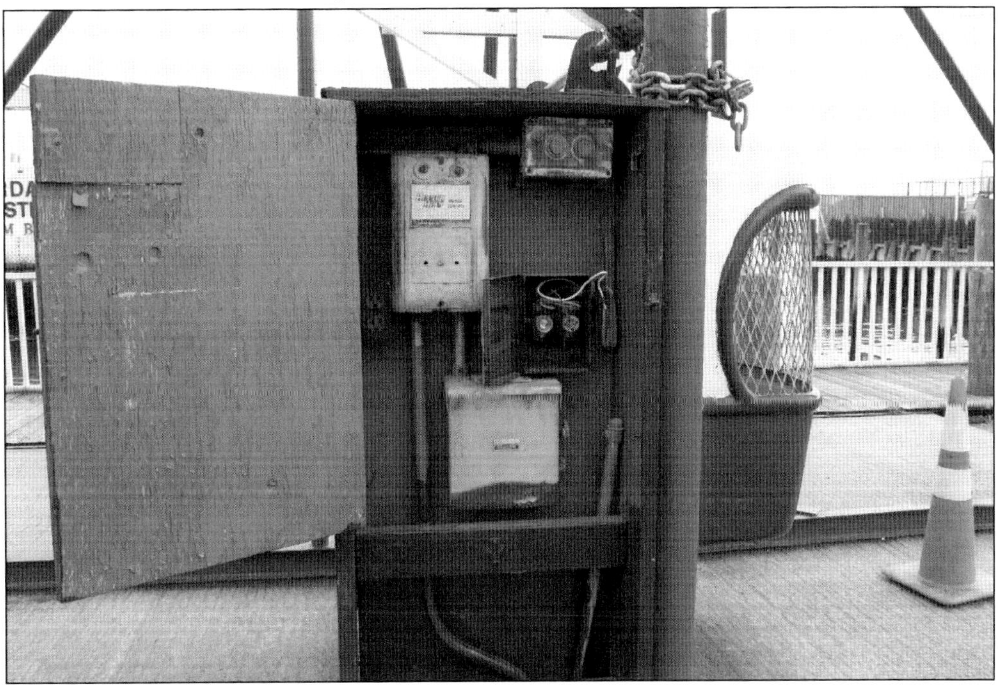

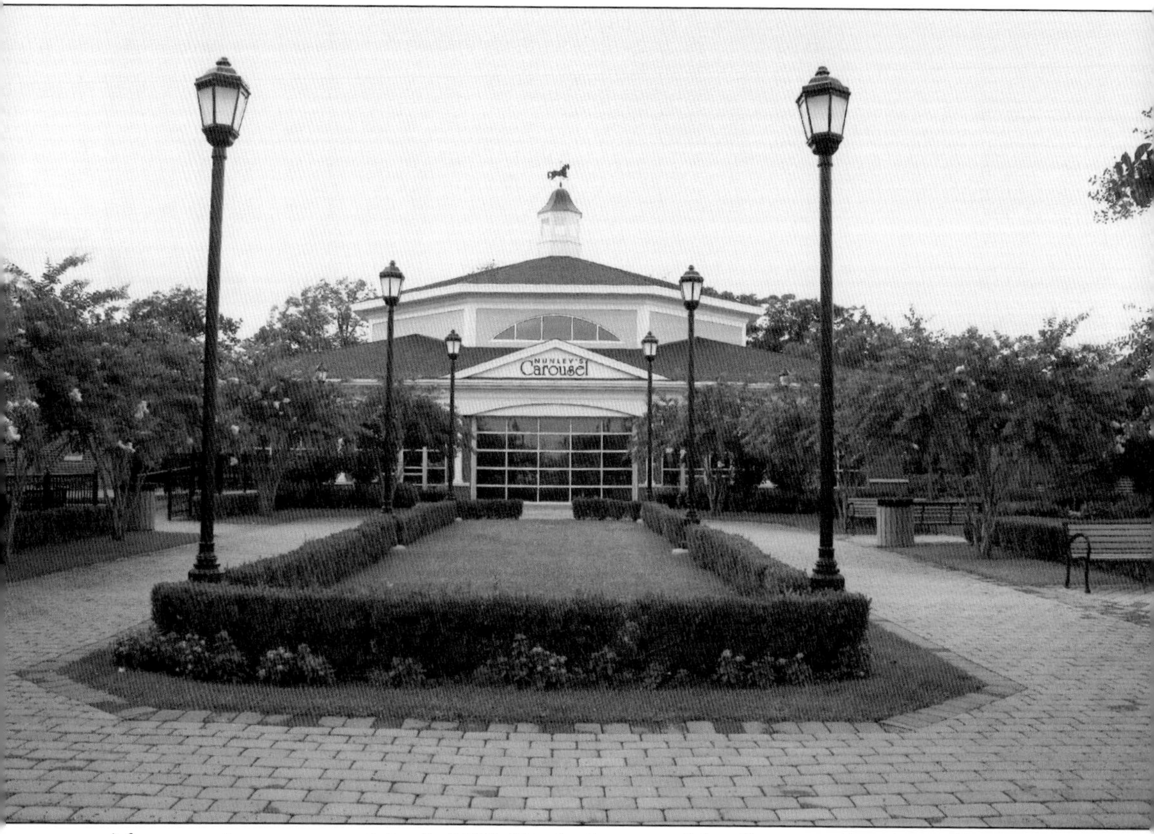

After years in storage, on May 2, 2009, Nunley's carousel finally opened to the public at its new home. Nestled between two popular cultural sites—the Cradle of Aviation and the Long Island Children's Museum—Museum Row has now become the ideal family destination. The carousel was a perfect fit for this area and its rich history. Before Charles Lindbergh began his transatlantic flight, he visited Coney Island and rode a carousel to sooth his nerves. Supposedly, he also rode the Cyclone and was recorded as saying that the experience was more frightening than flight. (Author's collection.)

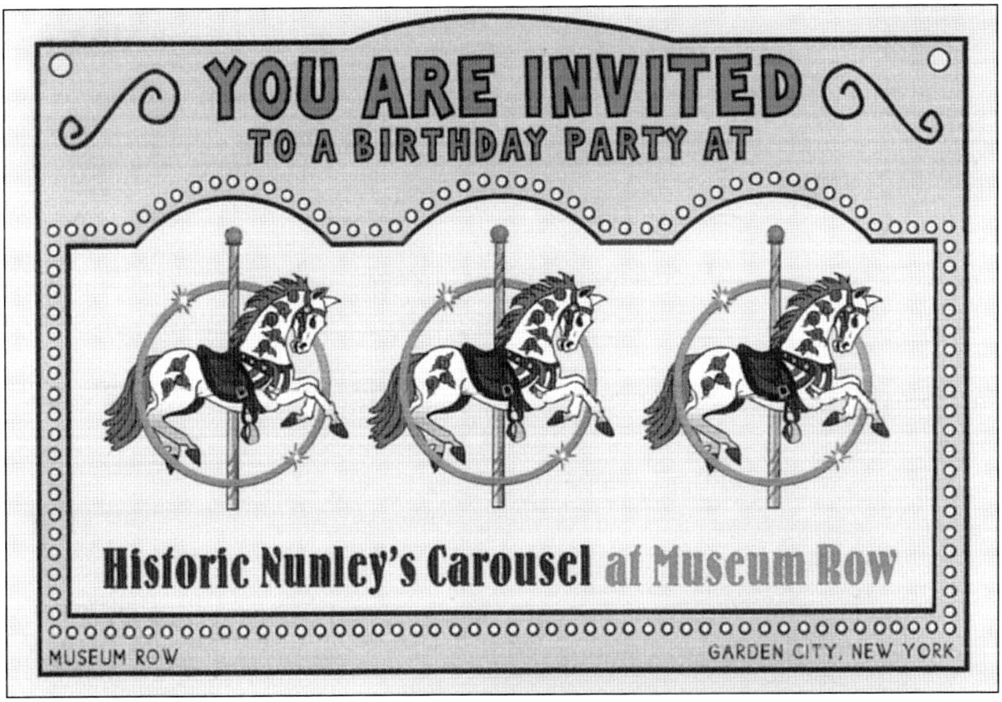

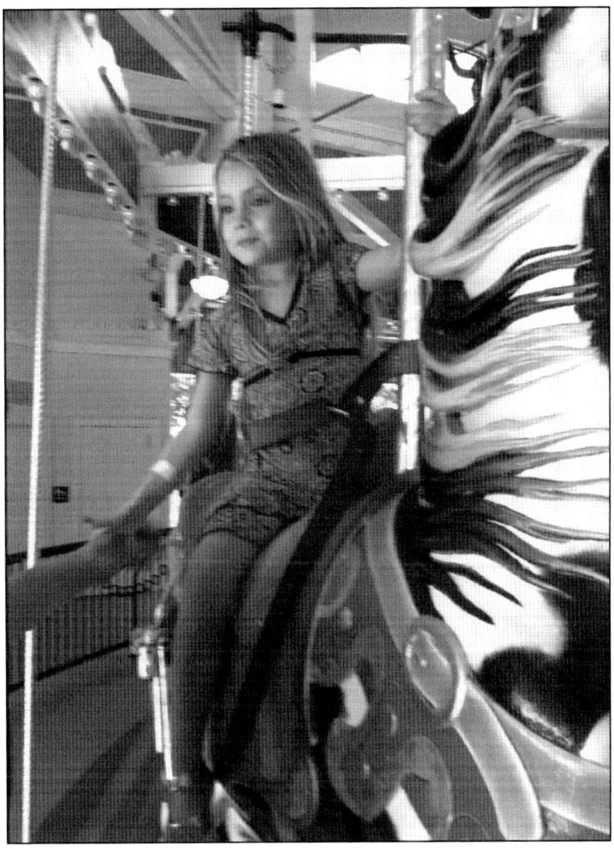

There are not nearly as many opportunities for kids to experience traditional carousels today. Luckily, parents can now bring their children to the restored carousels that they themselves once rode. To further honor their childhoods, parents can host their children's birthday parties at Nunley's carousel. With pizza, soda, and unlimited carousel rides, these parties are reminiscent of the hundreds of birthdays celebrated at Nunley's over the years. Above is the invitation to a carousel birthday party offered by the Cradle of Aviation Museum, which maintains the ride. At right, Quinn Ries celebrates her fourth birthday in 2011 with a party at the carousel. At her "Carousel Princess Party," guests also made their own crowns and heard the story of the "Princess and the Carousel." (Above, courtesy of Cradle of Aviation; right, courtesy of Lisa Ries.)

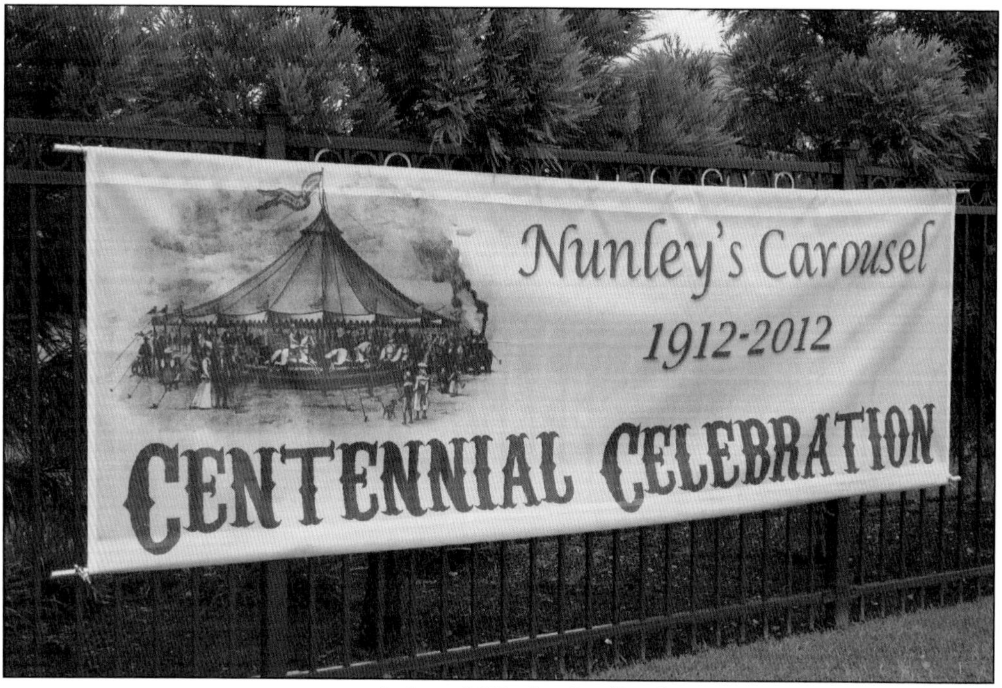

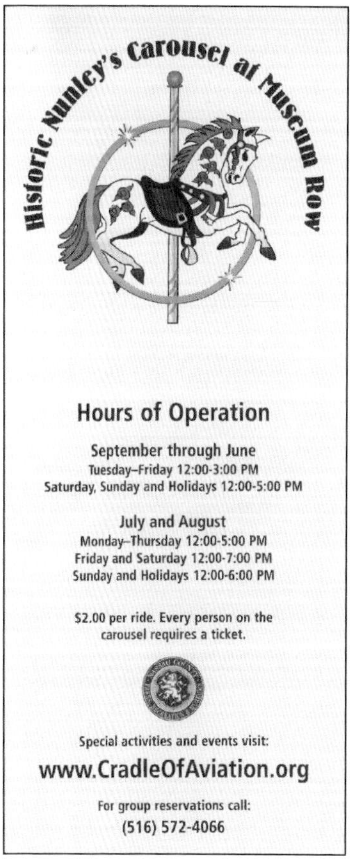

In June 2012, the Cradle of Aviation hosted a special centennial celebration in honor of the carousel's 100th anniversary. The weekend-long festival included games and food like those found in 1912 along the Coney Island boardwalk—the carousel's first home. Festivities also included music by a barbershop quartet and an appearance by a Theodore Roosevelt impersonator, as Roosevelt ran for reelection in 1912. Pictured here is the banner announcing the festival and the anniversary. Also seen is a new brochure produced by the Cradle of Aviation and Nassau County with information, history, and rules for the carousel. (Both, author's collection.)

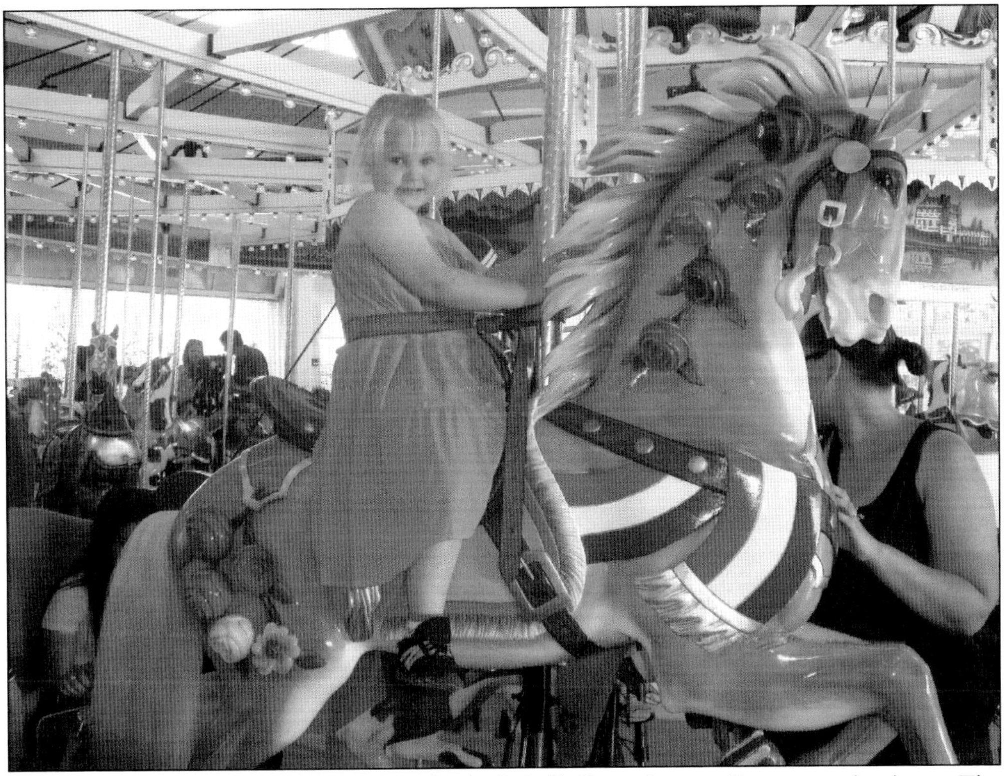

Here, fourth-generation Nunley's carousel rider Isabelle Denecke proudly poses on her horse. The family was at Museum Row during the centennial celebration of the carousel in June 2012. At this event, her grandmother Nancy got to play an old shooting game like the one that was at the arcade at Nunley's. (Both, courtesy of Nancy Radecker.)

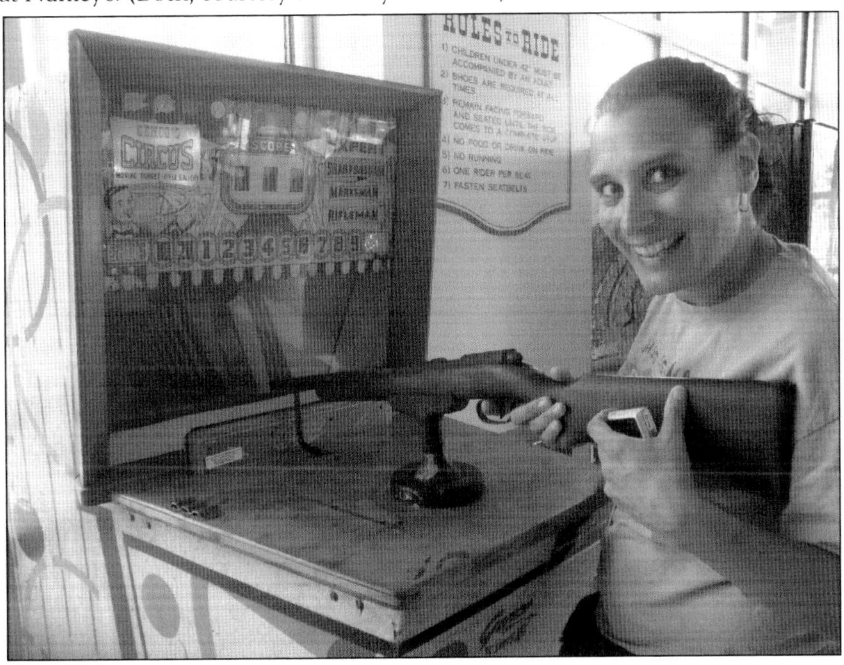

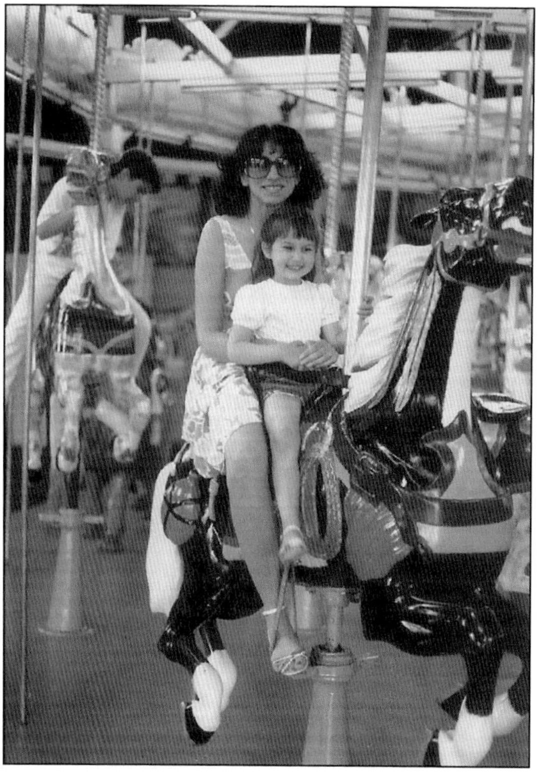

With the carousel back in operation, Long Islanders have flocked to Museum Row each year for another ride and a flashback. Here, Joan Scharf of Oceanside and daughter Erica ride the carousel at Nunley's in 1987 (left) and then take a spin on the restored carousel, 25 years later. Many families revisited the carousel, and in many cases, they bring their children and grandchildren; however, there are still many who have yet to discover that the carousel is back in operation, especially those who no longer live locally. (Both, courtesy of Erica Scharf.)

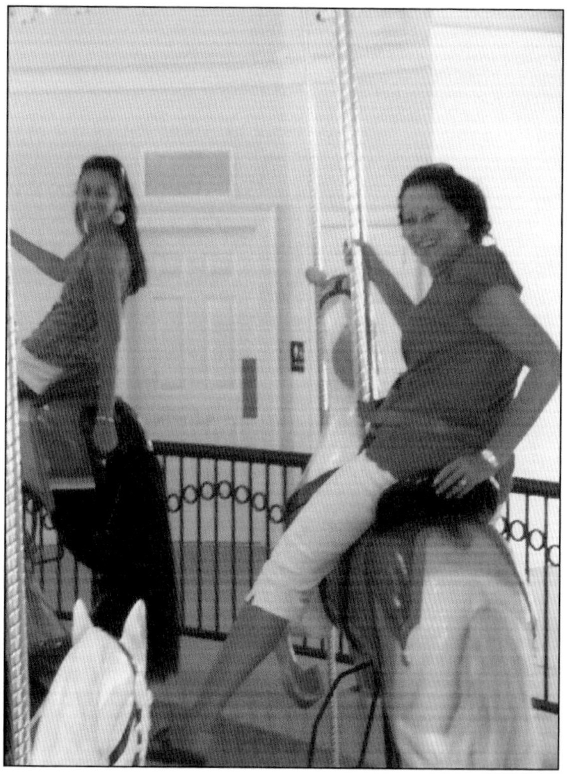

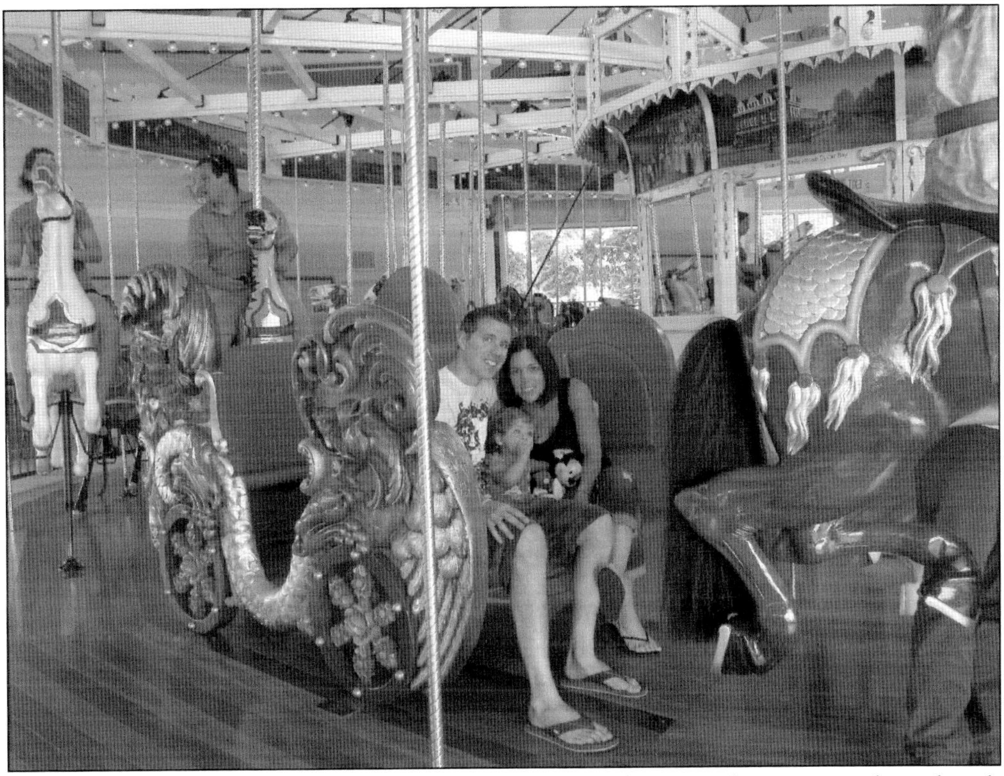

Michelle and Greg Bergmann both grew up in Oceanside and were regular visitors to the park with their families. They have since moved to Florida but were able to bring their daughter with them to experience the carousel they loved when they were young. (Courtesy of Bergmann family.)

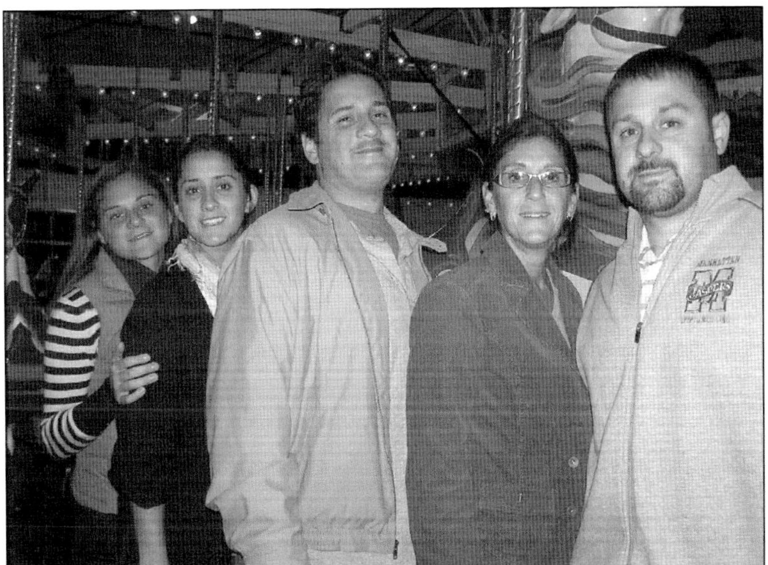

Vicky Geary Cornicello grew up in Baldwin and was a frequent visitor to the park as a child; she later visited the park with her own children. Still a Long Island resident, she celebrated her birthday in October 2010 at the restored carousel with family and friends. (Courtesy of Vicky Geary Cornicello.)

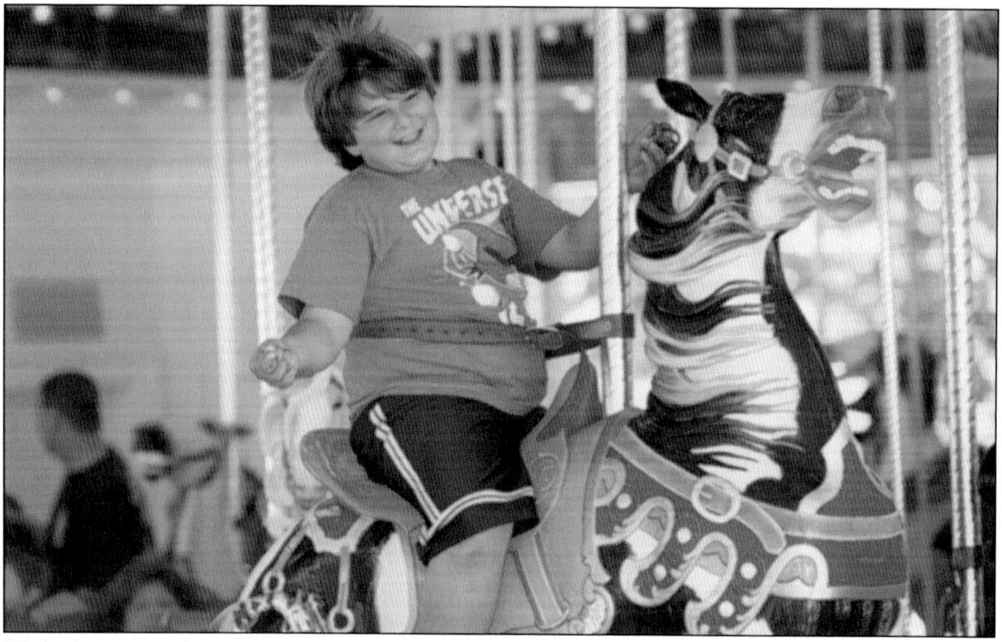

With the carousel open again, a new generation gets to experience the traditional carousel rides and, luckily, reach for the rings again. Here, third-generation rider Logan Foley-Riddle proudly displays the rings he managed to snatch. On his last ride, he amazingly captured 21 rings. (Courtesy of Charles Foley.)

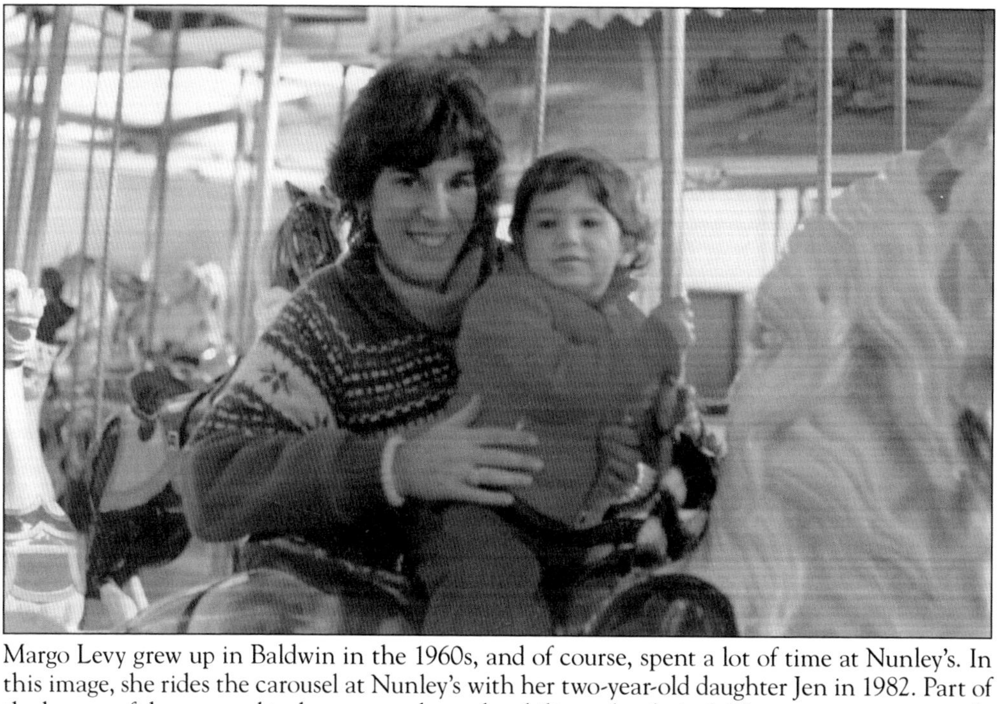

Margo Levy grew up in Baldwin in the 1960s, and of course, spent a lot of time at Nunley's. In this image, she rides the carousel at Nunley's with her two-year-old daughter Jen in 1982. Part of the beauty of the carousel is that parents have the ability to let their children experience a simple element of life in the exact same way, even though the world is constantly changing. (Courtesy of Margo Levy.)

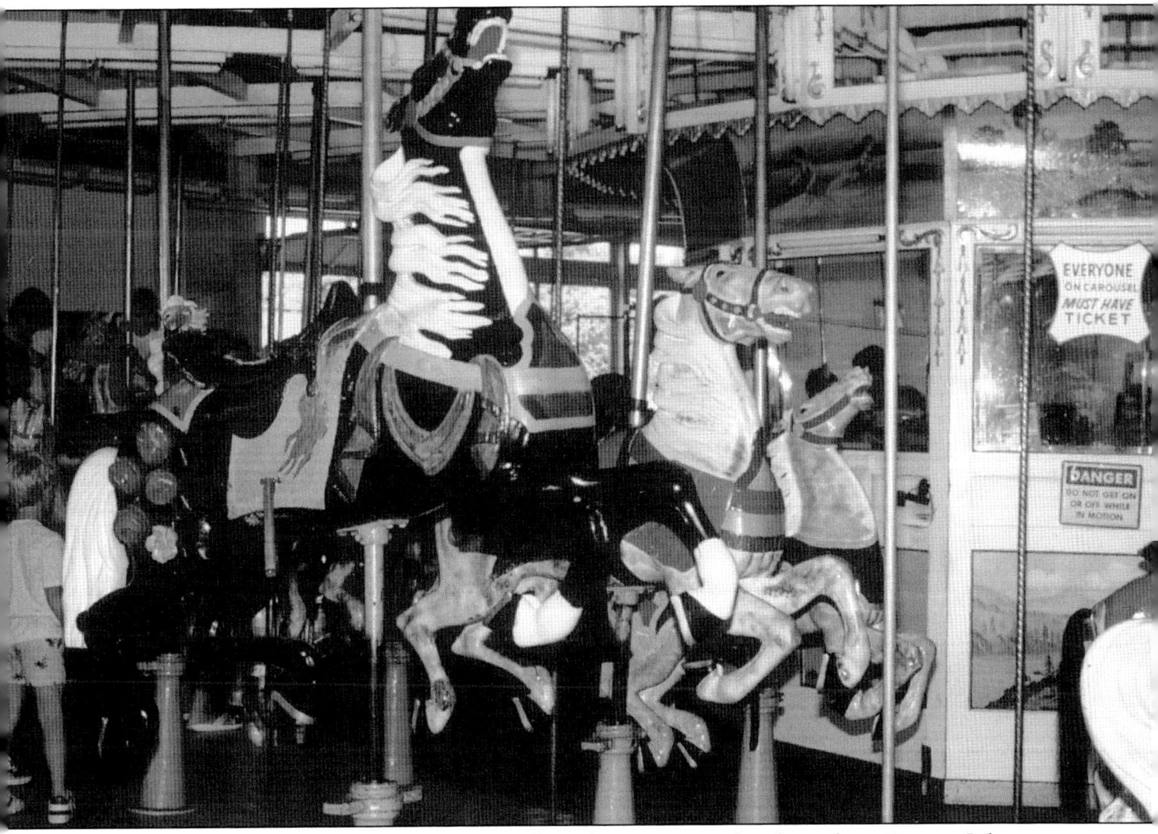

There is something magical about a carousel, and it's not just for the riders. Grayce Johnson Gardner-Castellano remembers how her aunt Sophie Frohnhoeffer, a Baldwin resident since 1926, adored Nunley's and its famous carousel. Frohnhoeffer suffered from polio as a child and walked with a limp, even as an adult, but she loved taking her nieces and nephews to the carousel. According to Gardner-Castellano, "She loved the organ and the waltzes it played, and I can still see her sitting by the ticket booth, smiling and clapping each time one of us caught the brass ring. Though she has long ago passed away, I know there has to be a Nunley's in heaven where she is riding on that black horse with the roses and catching her own brass ring." (Courtesy of Gary Monti)

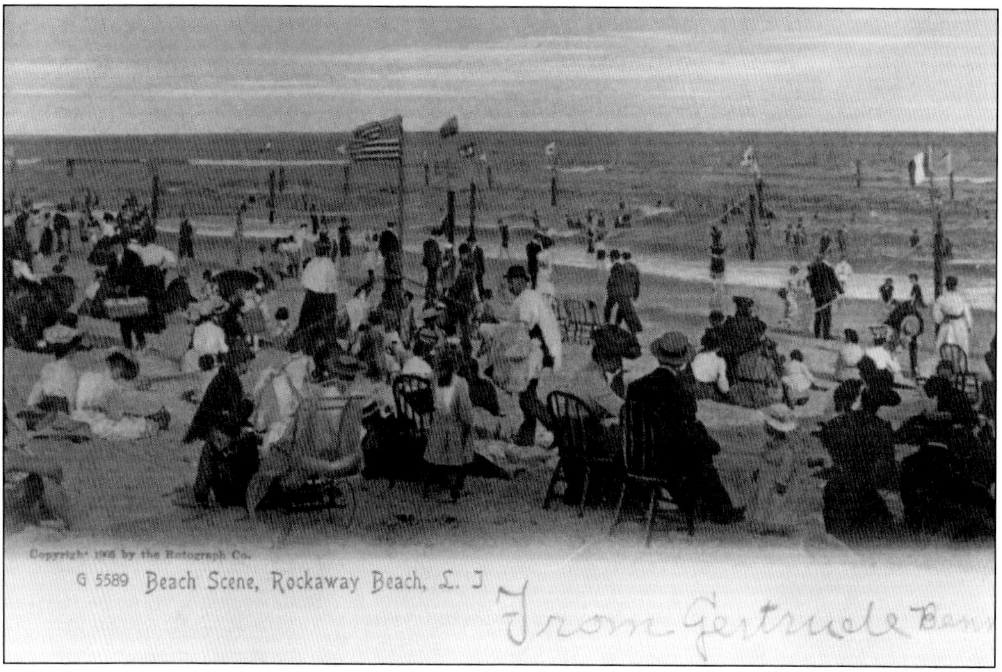

From seaside beach resorts, to monumental amusement areas, to family-run kiddie parks, the story of how Nunley's came to be is a long and interesting tale. The public will always yearn for leisure, and children will always look to play. Nunley's owners offered visitors a resource for fun and pleasure that was right in their community. There are so few family-run amusement parks that still exist, so Long Islanders are lucky to have had Nunley's for as long as we did. (Above, courtesy of Queens Borough Public Library, Long Island Division, Emil R. Lucev Collection; below, courtesy of Jennifer Heinser.)

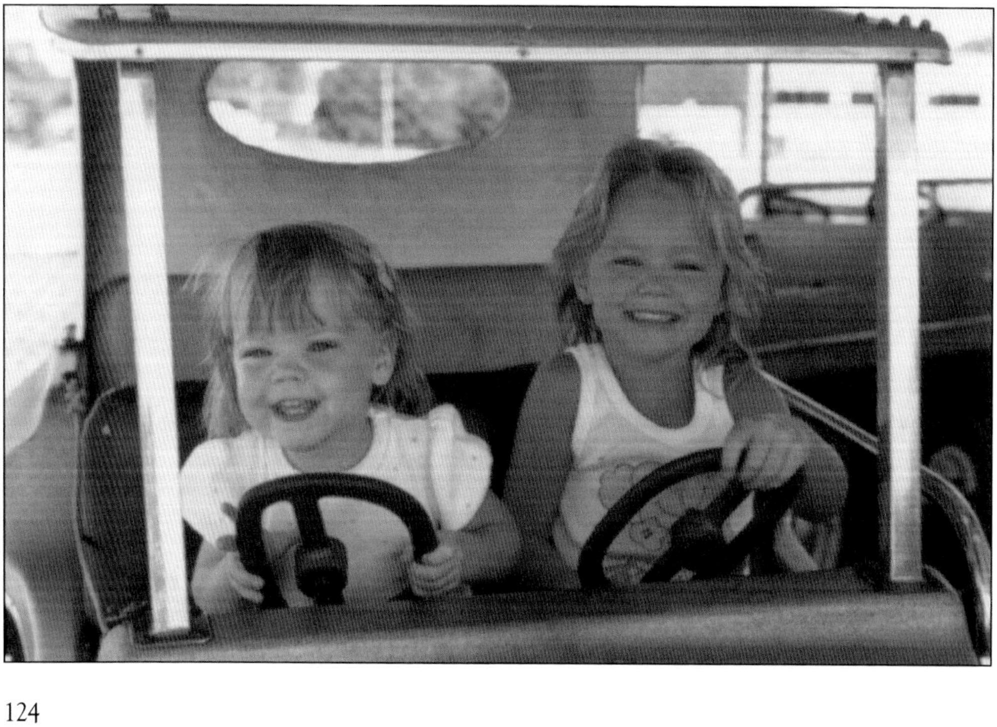

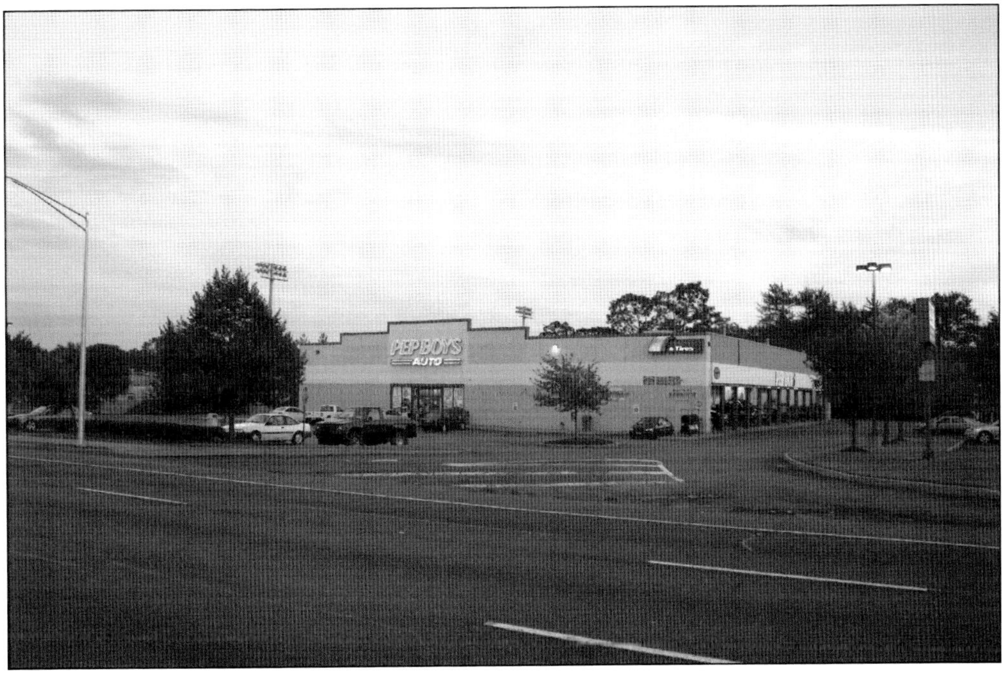

Today, the site where Nunley's once stood is home to a Pep Boys automotive store. Looking at the shop from the street, it is difficult to imagine that anything else could have been there. When one see the bleachers by the Freeport High School football field, it's hard to imagine that a roller coaster was once on the other side of the fence. Was there really a miniature golf course, rides, and games? The answer is yes. Nunley's will always live on through photographs, memories, and maybe even a brass ring. (Above, author's collection; below, courtesy of Chuck Ebert.)

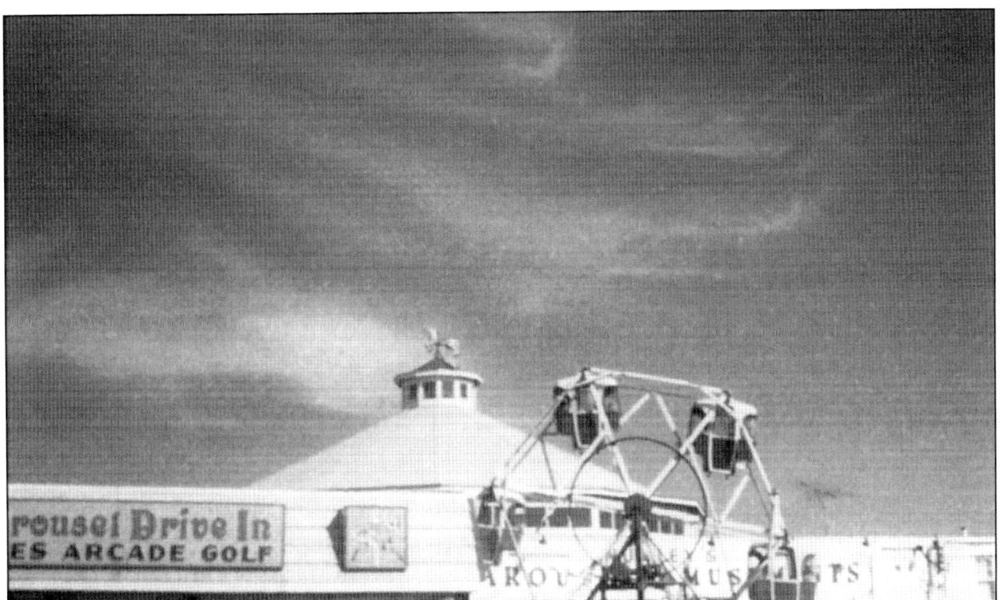

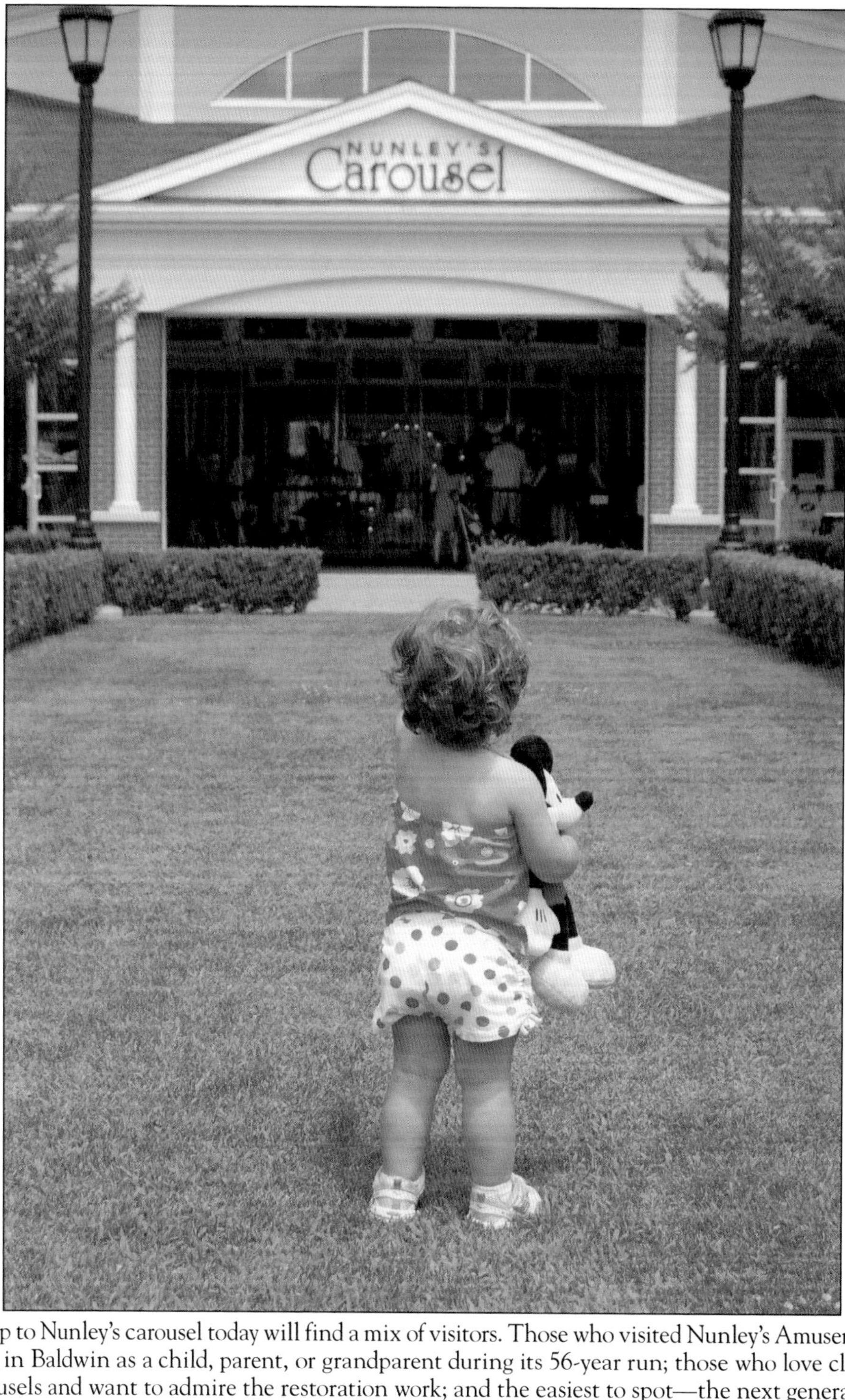

A trip to Nunley's carousel today will find a mix of visitors. Those who visited Nunley's Amusement Park in Baldwin as a child, parent, or grandparent during its 56-year run; those who love classic carousels and want to admire the restoration work; and the easiest to spot—the next generation of riders who are eager to make their own memories in what to them is a brand new and wondrous place. (Courtesy of Bergmann family.)

Bibliography

Donohue, Donald. *Nunley's Carousel Appraisal*. Maryland: Americana Antiques, 1996.

Futrell, Jim. *Amusement Parks of New York*. Mechanicsburg, PA: Stackpole Books, 2006

Hirsh, Rose Ann. Images of America: *Western New York Amusement Parks*. Charleston, SC: Arcadia Publishing, 2011.

Immerso, Michael. *Coney Island: The People's Playground*. New Brunswick, NJ: Rutgers University Press, 2002.

Krieg, Cynthia J. and Regina G. Feeney. Images of America: *Freeport*. Charleston, SC: Arcadia Publishing, 2012.

Lucev Sr., Emil R.Images of America: *The Rockaways*. Charleston, SC: Arcadia Publishing, 2007.

Discover Thousands of Local History Books Featuring Millions of Vintage Images

Consistent with our mission to preserve history on a local level, this book was printed in South Carolina on American-made paper and manufactured entirely in the United States. Products carrying the accredited Forest Stewardship Council (FSC) label are printed on 100 percent FSC-certified paper.

MADE IN THE USA